Home Landscaping

CRE▲TIVE
HOMEOWNER®

Home Landscaping
Southeast Region

Roger Holmes & Rita Buchanan

CREATIVE HOMEOWNER®, Upper Saddle River, New Jersey

Produced by WordWorks.

Editors: Roger Holmes and Rita Buchanan
Assistant editors: Monica Norby and Sarah Disbrow
Copyeditor: Nancy J. Stabile
Design and layout: Deborah Fillion
Illustrators: Steve Buchanan (Portfolio of Designs);
    Michelle Angle Farrar, Lee Hov, Robert La Pointe,
    Rick Daskam, and Teresa Nicole Green (Guide to
    Installation)
Indexer: Barbara E. Cohen
Cover design: Michelle Halko
Cover photograph: Dan Dempster/
    Dembinsky Photo Assoc. Inc.

Printed in the United States of America

Current Printing (last digit)
10 9 8

Library of Congress Catalog Card Number: 97–075270
ISBN: 1–58011–003–7

CREATIVE HOMEOWNER®
A Division of Federal Marketing Corp.
24 Park Way
Upper Saddle River, NJ 07458
Web site: **www.creativehomeowner.com**

Safety First

Though all the designs and methods in this book have been reviewed for safety, it is not possible to overstate the importance of using the safest construction methods possible. What follows are reminders—some do's and don'ts for landscaping. They are not substitutes for your own common sense.

▲ *Always* use caution, care, and good judgment when following the procedures described in this book.

▲ *Always* be sure that the electrical setup is safe; be sure that no circuit is overloaded and that all power tools and electrical outlets are properly grounded. Do not use power tools in wet locations.

▲ *Always* read container labels on paints, solvents, and other products; provide ventilation and observe other warnings.

▲ *Always* read the tool manufacturer's instructions for using a tool, especially the warnings.

▲ *Always* wear eye protection when using power tools or striking metal on metal or concrete.

▲ *Always* know the limitations of your tools. Do not try to force them to do what they were not designed to do.

▲ *Always* remove the key from any drill chuck before starting the drill.

▲ *Always* make sure that any power-tool adjustment is locked before proceeding.

▲ *Always* wear the appropriate rubber or work gloves when handling chemicals or doing heavy construction.

▲ *Always* wear a disposable face mask or a special filtering respirator when creating sawdust or working with toxic gardening substances.

▲ *Always* keep your hands away from the business ends of blades, cutters, and bits.

▲ *Always* check your local building codes when planning new construction. The codes protect public safety.

▲ *Never* work with power tools when you are tired or under the influence of alcohol or drugs.

▲ *Never* cut very small pieces of wood or pipe. Whenever possible, cut small pieces off larger pieces.

▲ *Never* change a blade or a bit unless the power cord is unplugged.

▲ *Never* work with power tools while wearing loose clothing, hanging hair, open cuffs, or jewelry.

▲ *Never* use a power tool on a workpiece that is not firmly supported or clamped.

▲ *Never* carry sharp or pointed tools, such as utility knives, awls, or chisels, in your pocket. If you carry such tools, use a special-purpose tool belt.

The Landscape Designers

Kim Hawks is founder and owner of Niche Gardens, based in Chapel Hill, N.C., a national retail mail-order nursery specializing in nursery-propagated North American native plants, particularly those of the southeastern United States. Holder of a degree in horticulture from North Carolina State University, Ms. Hawks has written for *Fine Gardening, The Herb Companion,* and other magazines, as well as publishing her own award-winning nursery newsletter. She lectures widely on native plants, gardening and garden design. Her designs appear on pp. 32–35, 36–39, 44–47, and 68–71.

Glenn Morris has designed southern landscapes for many years. Trained as a landscape architect at North Carolina State University, he specializes in homeowner-directed problem solving and has received an award for design excellence from the American Society of Landscape Architects. Mr. Morris has also written extensively about gardening and design. He was landscape editor for *Southern Living* magazine and is author of three books in the Southern Living Garden Guide series (*Trees, Shrubs,* and *Low Maintenance Landscapes*). He was a contributor to *Taylor's Master Guide to Gardening* as well as several other titles in the Taylor's Guide series. After living and working for many years in the South, he now lives in Pennsylvania. His designs appear on pp. 20–23, 40–43, 56–59, 60–63, 76–79, 80–83, and 88–91.

Dan Sears is principal in the Sears Design Group of Raleigh, N.C., a firm specializing in residential land planning and landscape design. In 25 years as a landscape architect, he has won 21 regional and national design awards and has had more than 40 projects published in various magazines and journals. Mr. Sears has been a member of the North Carolina Board of Landscape Architects and has lectured at the North Carolina State University School of Design and the University of Maryland School of Architecture. His designs appear on pp. 24–27, 28–31, 48–51, 64–67, 92–95, 100–103, and 108–111.

Jimmy and Becky Stewart are professional gardeners in Atlanta, Ga., where they design and install residential gardens. As designers, they strive to create year-round interest in their gardens. As avid plant enthusiasts, they are constantly experimenting with new and different plants to see which do best in the Atlanta area. Their designs have been featured in many publications, including *Fine Gardening, Better Homes & Gardens,* and *Southern Living.* Their designs appear on pp. 72–75, 84–87, 96–99, and 104–107.

Contents

PORTFOLIO OF DESIGNS

GUIDE TO INSTALLATION

PLANT PROFILES

About This Book

Of all the home improvement projects homeowners tackle, few offer greater rewards than landscaping. Paths, patios, fences, arbors, and, most of all, plantings can enhance home life in countless ways, large and small, functional and pleasurable, every day of the year. At the main entrance, an attractive brick walkway flanked by eye-catching shrubs and perennials provides a cheerful send-off in the morning and welcomes you home from work in the evening. A carefully placed grouping of small trees, shrubs, and fence panels creates privacy on the patio or screens a nearby eyesore from view. An island bed showcases your favorite plants while dividing the backyard into areas for several different activities.

Unlike some home improvements, the rewards of landscaping can lie as much in the activity as in the result. Planting and caring for lovely shrubs, perennials, and other plants can afford years of enjoyment. And for those who like to build things, outdoor construction projects can be a special treat.

While the installation and maintenance of plants and outdoor structures are within the means and abilities of most people, few of us are as comfortable determining exactly which plants or structures to use and how best to combine them. It's one thing to decide to dress up the front entrance or patio, another to come up with a design for doing so.

That's where this book comes in. Here, in the Portfolio of Designs, you'll find designs for nearly two dozen common home landscaping situations, created by landscape professionals who live and work in the Southeast region. Drawing on years of experience, they balance functional requirements and aesthetic possibilities, choosing the right plant or structure for

the task, confident of its proven performance in similar situations.

Complementing the Portfolio of Designs is the Guide to Installation, the book's second section, which will help you install and maintain the plants and structures called for in the designs. The third section, Plant Profiles, gives information on all the plants used in the book. The discussions that follow take a closer look at each section; we've also printed representative pages of the sections on pp. 9 and 10 and pointed out their features.

Portfolio of Designs

This section is the heart of the book, providing examples of landscaping situations and solutions that are at once inspiring and accessible. Some are simple, others more complex, but each one can be installed in a few weekends by homeowners with no special training or experience.

For each situation, we present two designs, the second a variation of the first. As the sample pages on the facing page show, the first design is displayed on a two-page spread. A perspective illustration (called a "rendering") shows what the design will look like several years after installation, when the perennials and many of the shrubs have reached mature size. The rendering also shows the planting as it will appear at a particular time of year. (For more on how plantings change over the course of a year, see "Seasons in Your Landscape," pp. 12–15.) A site plan shows the positions of the plants and structures on a scaled grid. Text introduces the situation and the design and describes the plants and projects used.

The second design, presented on the second two-page spread, addresses the same situation as the first but differs in one or more important aspects. It might show a

planting suited for a shady rather than a sunny site, or it might incorporate different structures or kinds of plants (adding annuals to a perennial border, for example). As for the first design, we present a rendering, site plan, and written information, but in briefer form. The second spread also includes photographs of a selection of the plants featured in the two designs. The photos showcase noteworthy qualities—lovely flowers, handsome foliage, or striking form—that these plants contribute to the designs.

Installed exactly as shown here, these designs will provide years of enjoyment. But individual needs and properties will differ, and we encourage you to alter the designs to suit your site and desires. Many types of alterations are easy to make. You can add or remove plants and adjust the sizes of paths, patios, and fences to suit larger or smaller sites. You can rearrange groupings and substitute favorite plants to suit your taste. Or you can integrate the design with your existing landscaping. If you are uncertain about how to solve specific problems or about the effects of changes you'd like to make, consult with staff at a local nursery or with a landscape designer in your area.

Guide to Installation

In this section you'll find detailed instructions and illustrations covering all the techniques you'll need to install any design from start to finish. Here we explain how to think your way through a landscaping project and anticipate the various steps. Then you'll learn how to do each part of the job: readying the site; laying out the design; choosing materials; building paths, trellises, or other structures; preparing the soil for planting; buying the recommended plants and putting them in place; and car-

Portfolio of Designs

First Design Option
An overview of the situation and the design.

Concept Box
Summarizes an important aspect of the design; tells whether the site is sunny or shady and what season is depicted in the rendering.

Site Plan
Positions all plants and structures on a scaled grid.

Plant Portraits
Photos of a selection of the plants used in both designs.

Second Design Option
Addressing the same situation as the first design, this variation may differ in design concept, site conditions, or plant selection.

Plants & Projects
Noteworthy qualities of the plants and structures and their contributions to the design.

Rendering
Shows how the design will look when plants are well established.

Rendering
Depicts the design when plants are well established.

Site Plan
Plants and structures on a scaled grid.

Concept Box
Site, season, and design summary.

Guide to Installation

Clearing the Site

The site you've chosen for a landscaping project may or may not have any man-made objects (fences, old pavement, trash, etc.) to be removed, but it will almost certainly be covered with plants.

Before you start cutting plants down, try to find someone—a friend or neighbor who enjoys gardening—to identify them for you. As you walk around together, make a sketch that shows which plants are where, and attach labels to the plants, too. Determine if there are any desirable plants worth saving—mature shade trees that you should work around, shapely shrubs that aren't too big to dig up and relocate or give away, worthwhile perennials and ground covers that you could divide and replant, healthy sod that you could lay elsewhere. Likewise, decide which plants have to go—diseased or crooked trees, straggly or overgrown shrubs, weedy brush, invasive ground covers, tattered lawn.

You can clear small areas yourself, bundling the brush for pickup and tossing soft-stemmed plants on the compost pile, but if you have lots of woody brush or any trees to remove, you might want to hire someone else to do the job. A crew armed with power tools can turn a thicket into a pile of wood chips in just a few hours. Have them pull out the roots and grind the stumps, too. Save the chips; they're good for surfacing paths or you can use them as mulch.

Smothering weeds

❶ Smothering kills weeds by depriving them of light. Cut the tops off close to the ground.

❷ Cover with thick newspaper or cardboard.

❸ Top with several inches of mulch. Wait a few months to be sure weeds are dead; then let rotted newspaper and mulch into the soil.

Working around a tree

If there are any large, healthy trees on your site, be careful as you work around them. It's okay to prune off some of a tree's limbs, as shown on the facing page, but respect its trunk and its leaves. Try never to cut or wound the bark on the trunk (don't nail against a tree), as that exposes the tree to disease organisms. Don't pile soil or mulch against the trunk, since that keeps the bark wet and can make it rot.

Killing perennial weeds

Some common weeds that sprout back from perennial roots or runners are bindweed, blackberry and other briers, Johnson grass, kudzu, nutsedge, and poison ivy. Garden plants that can become weedy include ajuga, akebia, bamboo, bishop's weed, bouncing Bet, comfrey, English ivy, Japanese climbing fern, Japanese honeysuckle, loosestrife, and mint. Once they get established, perennial weeds are hard to eliminate. You can't just cut off the tops, because they keep sprouting back. You need to dig the weeds out, smother them with mulch, or kill them with an herbicide, and it's better to do this before rather than after you plant a bed.

Digging. In many cases, you can do a pretty good job of removing a perennial weed if you dig carefully where the stems enter the ground, find the roots, and follow them as far as possible through the soil, pulling out every bit of root that you find. Some plant roots go deeper than you can dig, and most plants will sprout back from the small bits that you miss, but these leftover sprouts are easy to pull.

Smothering. This technique is easier than digging, particularly for eradicating large infestations, but much slower. First mow or cut the tops of the weeds as close to the ground as possible ❶. Then cover the area with sections from the newspaper, overlapped like shingles ❷, or flattened-out cardboard boxes. Top with a layer of mulch, such as straw, grass clippings, tree leaves, wood chips, or other organic material spread several inches deep ❸.

Smothering works by excluding light, which stops photosynthesis. If any shoots reach up through the covering and produce green leaves, pull them out immediately. Wait a few months, until you're sure the weeds are dead, before you dig into the smothered area and plant there.

Spraying. Herbicides are easy, fast, and effective weed killers when chosen and applied with care. Look for those that break down quickly into more benign substances, and make sure the weed you're trying to kill is listed on the product label. Apply all herbicides exactly as directed by the manufacturer. After spraying, you usually have to wait from one to four weeks for the weed to die completely, and some weeds need to be sprayed a second or third time before they give up. Some weeds just "melt away" when they die, but if there are tough or woody stems and roots, you'll need to dig them up and discard them.

Replacing turf

If the area where you're planning to add a landscape feature is currently part of the lawn, you have a fairly easy task ahead—easier than clearing brush or killing weeds,

116 Guide to Installation

Moving turf

❶ With a sharp shovel, cut healthy turf into squares or strips of manageable size.

❷ Slice a few inches deep under each square, lift it, and place as soon as possible in a new spot.

anyway. How to proceed depends on the condition of the turf and on what you want to put in its place. If the turf is healthy, you can "recycle" it by cutting, repair, or extend the lawn on other parts of your property.

The drawing above shows a technique for removing relatively small areas of strong healthy turf for replanting elsewhere. First, with a sharp shovel, cut it into squares or strips about 1 to 2 ft. square (these small pieces are easy to lift) ❶. Then slice a few inches deep under each square and lift the squares, roots and all, like brownies from a pan ❷. Quickly transplant the squares to a previously prepared site; water them well until the roots are established. You can rent a sod-cutting machine for larger areas you wish to recycle.

If you don't need the turf anywhere else, or if it's straggly or weedy, leave it in place and kill the grass. A single application of herbicide kills some grasses, but you may need to spray vigorous turf twice. Another way to kill grass is to cover it with a tarp or a sheet of black plastic for about four weeks during the heat of summer. After you've killed the grass, dig or till the bed, shredding the turf, roots and all, and mixing it into the soil. This is hard work if the soil is dry but less so if the ground has been softened by a recent rain or watering.

Removing large limbs

If there are large trees on your property now, you may want to remove some of the lower limbs so you can walk and see underneath them and so more light can reach plantings you're planning beneath them. Major pruning of large trees is a job for a professional arborist, but you can remove limbs smaller than 4 in. in diameter and less than 10 ft. above the ground yourself with a simple bow saw or pole saw.

Use the three-step procedure shown below to remove large limbs safely and without harming the tree. First, saw partway through the bottom of the limb, approximately 1 ft. out from the trunk ❶. This keeps the bark from tearing down the trunk when the limb falls. Then make a corresponding cut down through the top of the limb ❷—be prepared to get out of the way when the limb drops. Finally, remove the stub ❸. Undercut it slightly or hold it as you finish the cut, so it doesn't fall away and peel bark off the trunk. Note that the cut is not flush with the trunk but is just outside the thick area at the limb's base, called the branch collar. Leaving the branch collar helps the wound heal quickly and naturally. Wound dressing is considered unnecessary today.

Branch collar

❷ Saw down to remove the limb.

❶ Saw up from the bottom.

❸ Remove the stub just outside the branch collar.

Clearing the Site 117

"Sidebars"
Detailed information on special topics, set within ruled boxes.

Step-by-Step
Illustrations show process; steps are keyed by number to discussion in the main text.

Plant Profiles

Plant Portraits
Photos of selected plants.

Recommended evergreen hollies

Ilex × attenuata
A slim, columnar or conical tree, growing about 25 ft. tall and 10 to 15 ft. wide, with shiny leaves and lots of red berries. 'Foster #2' (pp. 30, 33, 34, 109, 111, *111*) is a popular cultivar with slender leaves. 'Savannah' (pp. 81, 82) is similar but has larger leaves and berries.

I. cornuta
A large, dense, bushy shrub with glossy foliage. 'Burfordii', or Burford holly (pp. 20, 77, *78*, 79), grows 15 to 20 ft. tall, has large leaves with few spines, and bears abundant crops of red berries. 'Needlepoint' (pp. 49, 109, 111, *111*) can reach 10 ft. tall and wide but is often kept smaller by shearing. It has lobed leaves with very sharp spines, and bright red-orange berries.

I. crenata, Japanese holly
A dense twiggy shrub with small dark green leaves and inconspicuous dark berries. 'Compacta' (pp. 24, 30, 50, 101) grows about 6 ft. tall and

wide, with glossier-than-average leaves. 'Helleri' (pp. 21, 24, 30, 65) reaches only 4 ft. tall and wide and has dull leaves. Both are often sheared, but they don't need it, as their natural growth habit is very neat and compact. Japanese hollies need acid soil; where the soil is alkaline, plant dwarf yaupon holly instead.

I. 'Nellie R. Stevens'
A slim, columnar or conical tree with narrow shiny leaves and lots of red berries. Grows quickly, reaching 25 to 30 ft. tall, 10 to 15 ft. wide, but can be kept smaller. Pages: 57, *58*, 79.

I. opaca, American holly
A conical tree, native to the Southeast, with broad leaves that have a few spines. Foliage is typically olive green, but selected cultivars have bright green leaves. Berries are dark red. Can reach 50 ft. tall, 30 ft. wide. Page: 79.

I. vomitoria, Yaupon holly
A native tree with small, shiny,

spineless leaves. Bears huge crops of juicy red berries. Grows about 15 to 20 ft. tall, usually with multiple trunks, and is easily trained and pruned into a picturesque specimen (pp. 101, *102*). Dwarf yaupon holly, 'Nana' (pp. 26, 31, *31*, 49), is a low, compact, shrubby form that grows 3 to 5 ft. tall and wide. It has attractive leaves but bears few berries. Yaupon hollies are very tough, adaptable, and easy to grow.

Ilex crenata 'Compacta'
JAPANESE HOLLY

Iberis sempervirens
EVERGREEN CANDYTUFT. A bushy perennial that forms a low or sprawling mound, about 1 ft. tall and 2 to 3 ft. wide, of slender, glossy evergreen foliage, topped for several weeks in March or April with clusters of bright white flowers. Needs full or partial sun, well-drained soil. Shear off the top half of the plants after they bloom. Needs no other care. Don't try to divide it; buy new plants if you want more. Pages: 33, 34, *35*, 45, 47, 71.

Ilex, Evergreen hollies
A versatile group of evergreen shrubs and trees used for foundation plantings, hedges, and specimens. The stiff-textured leaves can be small or large, smooth or spiny, dull or glossy. Holly plants are either male or female. Females typically bear heavy crops of small round berries that ripen in fall and

last through the next spring. See box above for more information on specific hollies. All tolerate sun or shade. Prune or shear at any season to keep them at the desired size.

Ilex decidua
POSSUMHAW. Also known as winterberry holly. A native small tree or large shrub that grows fairly quickly, reaching 15 to 20 ft. tall. Usually trained with multiple trunks and a rounded crown. Small spineless leaves are deciduous and don't have much fall color, but the large red or orange berries look wonderful all fall and winter. Only females produce berries, and there has to be a male within a few hundred yards. A local nursery can advise whether there's likely to be a male growing wild in your vicinity or if you should plant your own. Needs full or partial sun. Pages: 24, 27.

186 *Iberis sempervirens*

Ilex verticillata
WINTERBERRY HOLLY. A native deciduous shrub with many twiggy stems and soft spineless leaves that turn yellow in fall. Grows about 8 to 12 ft. tall, 6 to 8 ft. wide. Female cultivars such as 'Sparkleberry' and 'Winter Red' bear tremendous crops of small bright red berries, if there's a wild male or a male cultivar such as 'Apollo' or 'Southern Gentleman' growing within a few hundred yards. Slow-growing, so start with the largest, fullest plants you can find and prune only to remove dead or damaged shoots. Needs full or partial sun. Pages: 77, *78*, 79, 98.

Iris
GERMAN OR BEARDED IRIS. Popular perennials that bloom in midspring, with large elegant flowers in shades of blue, purple, pink, yellow, or white, on stalks 1 to 3 ft. tall. Irises form patches of stiff, bladelike, gray-green leaves about 1 ft. tall. They need full sun and well-drained soil. Divide every few years in late summer, cutting the thick finger-like rhizomes into sections with three or four buds

Ilex verticillata
WINTERBERRY HOLLY

or fans of foliage each. When planting, lay the rhizome horizontally right at the surface of the soil. Pages: 24, 52, 106, *107*.

Iris sibirica
SIBERIAN IRIS. A carefree perennial that forms a large, vase-shaped clump of slender green leaves up to 2 ft. long and bears scores of showy flowers in late spring on stalks 2 to 3 ft. tall. 'Caesar's Brother' (pp. 45, 65, *67*, 68) is a popular cultivar with very dark blue-purple flowers. 'White Swirl' (pp. 72, 75) has clear white flowers. Other cultivars have indigo, sky blue, or yellow flowers. Let the seedpods develop if you choose; they look interesting from summer through winter, and setting seed doesn't seem to reduce the next year's display of flowers. Needs full or partial sun. Divide clumps after several years, in early fall. Pages: 24, 93, 109.

Itea virginica 'Henry's Garnet'
'HENRY'S GARNET' VIRGINIA SWEETSPIRE. A native deciduous shrub that forms a clump of erect or arching stems 6 to 8 ft. tall, topped with clusters of fragrant white flowers in early summer. Smooth leaves are glossy green in summer, rich wine red or burgundy throughout the fall. Adapts to sun or shade. Prefers moist soil. Pages: 98, 99.

Juniperus chinensis 'Torulosa'
HOLLYWOOD JUNIPER. A small evergreen tree with an interesting irregular profile and bright green, fine-textured foliage. Grows 15 to 20 ft. tall, 4 to 8 ft. wide. Needs full sun. Prune only if needed to remove damaged shoots. Carefree. Pages: 29, 52, *55*.

Iris sibirica 'White Swirl'
SIBERIAN IRIS

Juniperus chinensis 'Torulosa' 187

Choices
Selections here help you choose from the many varieties of certain popular plants.

Detailed Plant Information
Descriptions of each plant's noteworthy qualities and requirements for planting and care.

10 **Home Landscaping: Southeast Region**

ing for the plants to keep them healthy and attractive year after year.

We've taken care to make installation of built elements simple and straightforward. The paths, trellises, fences, and arbors (elements that landscape designers call "hardscape") all use basic materials available from local suppliers, and they can be assembled by people who have no special skills or tools beyond those commonly used for home maintenance. The designs can easily be adapted to meet specific needs or to fit in with the style of your house or other landscaping features.

Installing different designs requires different techniques. You can find what you need by following the cross-references in the Portfolio to pages in the Guide to Installation, or by skimming the Guide. If you continue to improve your landscape by adding more than one design, you'll find that many basic techniques are reused from one project to the next. You might want to start with one of the smaller, simpler designs. Gradually you'll develop the skills and confidence to do any project you choose.

Most of the designs in this book can be installed in a weekend or two; some will take a little longer. Digging planting beds, building retaining walls, and erecting fences and arbors can be strenuous work. If you lack the time or energy for the more arduous installation tasks, consider hiring a neighborhood teenager to help out; local landscaping services can provide more comprehensive help.

Plant Profiles

The final section of the book includes a description of each of the plants featured in the Portfolio. These profiles outline the plants' basic preferences for environmental conditions, such as soil, moisture, and sun or shade, and provide advice about planting and ongoing care.

Working with the book's landscape designers, we selected plants carefully, follow-ing a few simple guidelines: Every plant should be a proven performer in the region; once established, it should thrive without pampering. All plants should be available from a major local nursery or garden center; if they're not in stock, they could be ordered, or you could ask the nursery staff to recommend suitable substitutes.

In the Portfolio section, you'll note that plants are referred to by their common name but are cross-referenced to the Plant Profiles section by their Latin, or scientific, name. While common names are familiar to many people, they can be confusing. Distinctly different plants can share the same common name, or one plant can have several different common names. Latin names, therefore, ensure greatest accuracy and are more appropriate for a reference section such as this. Although you can confidently purchase most of the plants in this book from local nurseries using the common name, knowing the Latin name allows you to make sure that the plant you're ordering is actually the one that is shown in our design.

Southeast Hardiness Zones

This map is based on one developed by the U.S. Department of Agriculture. It divides the region into "hardiness zones" based on minimum winter temperatures. While most of the plants in this book will survive the lowest temperatures in the region, a few may not. These few are noted in the Plant Profiles descriptions, where we have usually suggested alternatives. When you buy plants, most will have "hardiness" designations, which correspond to a USDA hardiness zone on the map. A Zone 7 plant, for example, can be expected to survive winter temperatures as low as 0°F, and it can be used with confidence in Zones 7 and 8 but not in the colder Zone 6. It is useful to know your zone and the zone designation of any plants that you wish to add to those in this book.

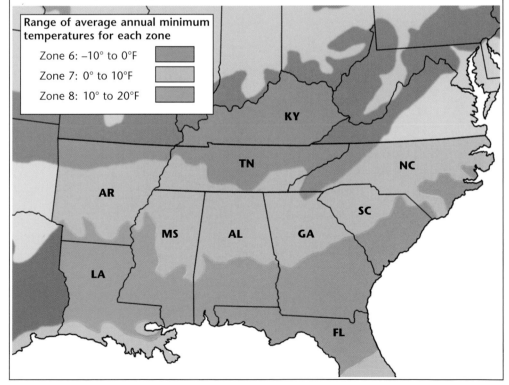

Range of average annual minimum temperatures for each zone

Zone 6: −10° to 0°F

Zone 7: 0° to 10°F

Zone 8: 10° to 20°F

Seasons in Your Landscape

One of the rewards of landscaping is watching how plants change through the seasons. During the dark winter months, you look forward to the bright, fresh flowers of spring. Then the lush green foliage of summer is transformed into the blazing colors of fall. Perennials that rest underground in winter can grow chest-high by midsummer, and hence a flower bed that looks flat and bare in December becomes a jungle in July.

To illustrate typical seasonal changes, we've chosen one of the designs from this book (see pp. 70–71) and shown here how it would look in spring, summer, fall, and winter. As you can see, this planting looks quite different from one season to the next, but it always remains interesting. Try to remember this example of transformation as you look at the other designs in this book. There we show how the planting will appear in one season and call attention to any plants that will stand out at other times of year.

The task of tending a landscape also changes with the seasons. Below we've noted the most important seasonal jobs to summarize the annual work cycle.

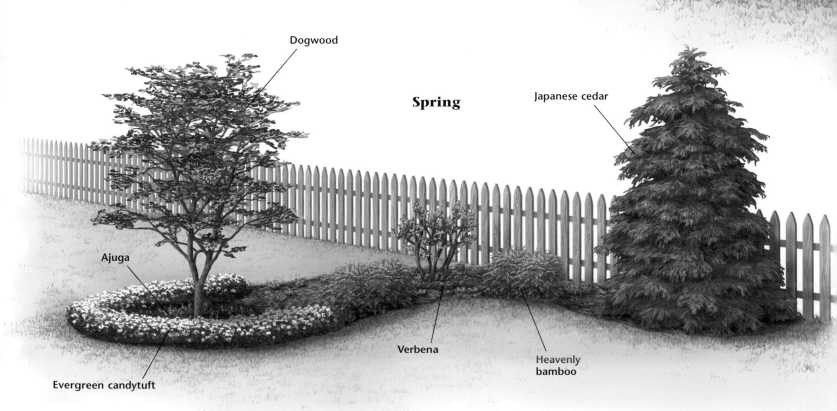

Dogwood

Japanese cedar

Spring

Ajuga

Verbena

Heavenly bamboo

Evergreen candytuft

Summer

Butterfly bush

Veronica

Purple coneflower

Spring

The spring flower season begins in February across most of the Southeast and peaks in March and April, when the dogwoods and azaleas bloom, the lawns turn green, and the trees leaf out. In this garden, a pink dogwood is joined by spring-blooming perennials such as white evergreen candytuft, blue ajuga, and pink verbena. Meanwhile, summer-blooming plants are just starting to grow. The evergreen Japanese cedar and heavenly bamboo have traded their winter colors for plain green. Do a thorough cleanup in early spring. Remove last year's perennial flower stalks and foliage, cut ornamental grasses to the ground, prune shrubs and trees, renew the mulch, and neaten the edges between flower beds and lawn.

Summer

In summer, both evergreen and deciduous trees and shrubs grow new shoots covered with fresh foliage. Flowering perennials and shrubs such as the verbena, veronica, purple coneflower, and butterfly bush shown here add spots of color to the otherwise green landscape. To coax as many flowers as possible from these plants and to keep the garden tidy, cut or shear off older blossoms as they fade. Summer weather is typically hot and humid throughout this region, but droughts are not uncommon. Water new plantings at least once a week during dry spells, and water older plants, too, if the soil gets so dry that they wilt. Pull any weeds that sprout up through the mulch; this is easiest when the soil is moist.

Fall

The bright fall foliage and ripening berries of dogwoods and other trees and shrubs brighten the Southeast landscape in late October or November. Meanwhile, butterfly bush, verbena, and veronica continue blooming from summer into fall, joined in September or so by 'Autumn Joy' sedum, hardy chrysanthemums, and Japanese silver grass. These fall flowers last for many weeks as the weather cools off and the days get shorter. You can leave grasses and perennial stalks standing all winter, if you choose, or clear them away whenever hard frosts or heavy rains turn them brown or knock them down. Toss the stems on the compost pile, along with any leaves that you rake up. After the first frost, replace any summer annuals with pansies or other cold-weather annuals, and plant tulips or other spring-blooming bulbs now. Fall rains usually soak the ground, so you can stop watering.

'Autumn Joy'
sedum

Winter

In winter, when much of the landscape turns tan and brown, you appreciate evergreen plants such as the bronze Japanese cedar, crimson heavenly bamboo, emerald evergreen candytuft, and purple ajuga shown here. Welcome in winter, too, are clumps of rustling grass; dried perennial flower stalks; and shrubs and trees with handsome branch patterns, conspicuous buds or berries, or distinctive bark.

Normally, garden plants need little if any care in winter. If a heavy snow or an ice storm snaps or crushes some plants, you can trim away the broken parts as soon as it's convenient, but if plants get frozen during a severe cold spell, wait until spring to assess the damage before deciding how far to cut them back.

Fall

Butterfly bush

Japanese silver grass

Veronica

Hardy chrysanthemum

Winter

Japanese cedar

Ajuga

Evergreen candytuft

Heavenly bamboo

As Your Landscape Grows

Landscapes change over the years. As plants grow, the overall look evolves from sparse to lush. Trees cast cool shade where the sun used to shine. Shrubs and hedges grow tall and dense enough to provide privacy. Perennials and ground covers spread to form colorful patches of foliage and flowers. Meanwhile, paths, arbors, fences, and other structures gain the patina of age.

Constant change over the years—sometimes rapid and dramatic, sometimes slow and subtle—is one of the joys of landscaping. It is also one of the challenges. Anticipating how fast plants will grow and how big they will eventually get is difficult, even for professional designers, and was a major concern in formulating the designs for this book.

To illustrate the kinds of changes to expect in a planting, these pages show one of the designs at three different "ages." Even though a new planting may look sparse at first, it will soon fill in. And because of careful spacing, the planting will look as good in 10 to 15 years as it does after 3 to 5. It will, of course, look different, but that's part of the fun.

At Planting

Crape myrtle

Carolina jasmine

Spirea

Bluebeard

Barberry

Annuals

Mondo grass

Three to Five Years

Crape myrtle

Carolina jasmine

Spirea

Barberry

Mondo grass

At Planting—Here's how the corner planting (pp. 38–39) might appear in spring immediately after planting. The fence and mulch look conspicuously fresh, new, and unweathered. The crape myrtle is only 4 to 5 ft. tall, with trunks no thicker than broomsticks. It hasn't leafed out yet. The spirea and barberries are 12 to 18 in. tall and wide, and the Carolina jasmine just reaches the bottom rail of the fence. Evenly spaced tufts of mondo grass edge the sidewalk. The bluebeards are stubby now but will grow 2 to 3 ft. tall by late summer, when they bloom. Annuals such as vinca and ageratum start flowering right away and soon form solid patches of color. The first year after planting, be sure to water during dry spells and to pull or spray any weeds that pop through the mulch.

Three to Five Years—Shown in summer now, the planting has begun to mature. The mondo grass has spread to make a continuous, weed-proof patch. The Carolina jasmine reaches partway along the fence. The spirea and barberries have grown into bushy, rounded specimens. From now on, they'll get wider but not much taller. The crape myrtle will keep growing about 1 ft. taller every year, and its crown will broaden. As you continue replacing the annuals twice a year, keep adding compost or organic matter to the soil and spreading fresh mulch on top.

Ten to Fifteen Years—As shown here in late summer, the crape myrtle is now a fine specimen, about 15 ft. tall, with a handsome silhouette, beautiful flowers, and colorful bark on its trunks. The bluebeards recover from an annual spring pruning to form bushy mounds covered with blooms. The Carolina jasmine, spirea, and barberry have reached their mature size. Keep them neat and healthy by pruning out old, weak, or dead stems every spring. If you get tired of replanting annuals, substitute low-growing perennials or shrubs in those positions.

Ten to Fifteen Years

Crape myrtle

Spirea

Carolina jasmine

Bluebeard

Barberry

Mondo grass

Portfolio of Designs

This section presents designs for nearly two dozen situations common in home landscapes. You'll find designs to enhance entrances, decks, and patios. There are gardens of colorful perennials and shrubs, as well as structures and plantings that create shady hideaways, dress up nondescript walls, and even make a centerpiece of a lowly mailbox. Large color illustrations show what the designs will look like, and site plans delineate the layout and planting scheme. Texts explain the designs and describe the plants and projects appearing in them. Installed as shown or adapted to meet your site and personal preferences, these designs can make your property more attractive, more useful, and—most important—more enjoyable for you, your family, and your friends.

Southern Hospitality

Make a pleasant passage to your front door

W hy wait until a visitor reaches the front door to extend a cordial greeting? An entryway landscape of well-chosen plants and a revamped walkway not only make the short journey a pleasant one, they can also enhance your home's most public face and help settle it comfortably in its surroundings.

The curved walk in this design extends a helpful "Please come this way" to visitors, while creating a roomy planting area near the house. The walk bridges a grassy "inlet" created by the free-flowing lines of the beds. The flowing masses of plants, lawn, and pavement nicely complement the journey to the door.

Two handsome trees and a skirting of shrubs form a partial screen between the walk and front door and the street. A striking collection of evergreens transforms a foundation planting near the house into a shrub border. Ground covers edge the walkway with pretty foliage, flowers, and berries. A decorative screen by the stoop marks the entry. Fragrant flowers and colorful foliage cover the screen year-round, enticing visitors to linger awhile by the door.

The rest of the planting contributes to the all-season interest with flowers spring, summer, and fall (several fragrant). Colorful foliage and berries grace the autumn and winter months.

River birch Ⓐ

'Otto Luyken' Ⓔ cherry laurel

Walk Ⓛ

Creeping willowleaf Ⓖ cotoneaster

1 square = 1 ft.

Lawn

Stoop

Lawn

House

Driveway

Plants & Projects

Preparing the planting beds and laying the walk are the main tasks in this design. Comprising mostly trees and shrubs, the planting requires only seasonal cleanup and pruning once it's installed.

Ⓐ **River birch** (use 1 plant)
The multiple trunks of this deciduous tree display pretty peeling bark. Leaves are glossy green in summer, colorful in fall. See *Betula nigra*, p. 176.

Ⓑ **Japanese maple** (use 1)
This small deciduous tree will thrive in the shade of the taller birch, providing colorful delicate leaves and a graceful tracery of branches in winter. See *Acer palmatum*, p. 174.

Ⓒ **Burford holly** (use 1)
This evergreen shrub is easily maintained in a conical form by shearing. Its large leaves are a great backdrop for a fine show of red winter berries. See *Ilex*, Evergreen hollies: *I. cornuta* 'Burfordii', p. 186.

Ⓓ **Heavenly bamboo** (use 1)
An evergreen shrub with leaves that change color each season, white summer flowers, and long-lasting red berries. See *Nandina domestica*, p. 190.

See site plan for **I** **M**.

D Heavenly bamboo

H Jackman clematis

B Japanese maple

Site: Sunny

Season: Fall

Concept: Easy-care plantings and distinctive walkway add year-round interest to a home's main entrance.

F 'Helleri' Japanese holly

J 'Stella d'Oro' daylily

K Creeping lilyturf

C Burford holly

E 'Otto Luyken' cherry laurel

E **'Otto Luyken' cherry laurel** (use 8)
This low, spreading evergreen shrub fits perfectly beneath the birch and the windows of the house. Displayed against the dark green leaves, spikes of fragrant white flowers perfume the entryway in midspring. See *Prunus laurocerasus*, p. 192.

F **'Helleri' Japanese holly** (use 9)
This evergreen shrub won't outgrow its place under the windows, instead filling the space with mounds of small, shiny leaves. See *Ilex*, Evergreen hollies: *I. crenata*, p. 186.

G **Creeping willowleaf cotoneaster** (use 7)
An evergreen ground cover, this shrub displays dark purple leaves and red berries in winter and white flowers in spring. See *Cotoneaster salicifolius* 'Repens', p. 180.

H **Jackman clematis** (use 1)
A graceful deciduous vine, this will cover the screen with striking violet-purple flowers in summer. See *Clematis* × *jackmanii*, p. 179.

I **Carolina jasmine** (use 1)
This evergreen vine offers something year-round. Fragrant

yellow trumpet-shaped flowers greet visitors in early spring. Neat green leaves complement the blooming clematis in summer, then turn maroon for the winter. See *Gelsemium sempervirens*, p. 182.

J **'Stella d'Oro' daylily** (use 11)
This cultivar is one of the longest-blooming daylilies, producing golden yellow flowers from late spring to frost. Even without the glowing flowers, this perennial's grassy light green foliage contrasts nicely with the nearby lilyturf. See *Hemerocallis*, p. 184.

K **Creeping lilyturf** (use 44)
This evergreen perennial makes a grasslike mat of dark green leaves along the walk and under the birch. Small spikes of violet, purple, or white flowers appear in summer. See *Liriope spicata*, p. 189.

L **Walk**
Flagstones of random size and shape are ideal for the curved walk. See p. 118.

M **Screen**
A simple structure with narrow vertical "pickets," this is easy to make and sturdy enough to support the vines. See p. 140.

Plant portraits

Showy flowers brighten an entrance, but the attractive forms and foliage of these trees, shrubs, ground covers, ferns, and vines welcome guests over a long season.

● = First design, pp. 20–21
▲ = Second design, pp. 22–23

Creeping lilyturf (*Liriope spicata*, p. 189) ●

Jackman clematis (*Clematis* × *jackmanii*, p. 179) ●

Vinca (*Vinca minor*, p. 197) ▲

Japanese painted fern
(Ferns: *Athyrium goeringianum* 'Pictum', p. 181) ▲

Leatherleaf mahonia (*Mahonia bealei*, p. 190) ▲

'Elegans' hosta (*Hosta sieboldiana*, p. 184) ▲

A shady welcome

If your entry is shady, receiving less than six hours of sunlight a day, try this planting scheme, which replaces the sun-loving plants from the previous design with others that prefer the shade. Overall, the emphasis is still on year-round good looks.

Shade brings out the best in southern plants. In spring, shown here, the planting is awash with flowers and fragrance. During the summer, the dogwoods make a lovely covered walkway to the front door, while shrubs, hostas, and ferns provide a cool display of attractive foliage. Much of the foliage carries on right through the winter; then the Lenten rose announces the arrival of spring and the cycle begins anew.

Plants & Projects

Ⓐ Dogwood (use 3 plants)
This is one of the finest small trees, with white flowers in spring and lovely green foliage that turns crimson in fall, when bright red berries ripen. You can prune the lower branches to create headroom for the passage to the door. See *Cornus florida*, p. 180.

Ⓑ 'Roseum Elegans' rhododendron (use 1)
This evergreen shrub is a stately presence at the corner of the house, with its glossy leaves and striking clusters of pink flowers in late spring. See *Rhododendron*, p. 192.

Ⓒ Leatherleaf mahonia (use 1)
Leathery horizontal leaflets of this upright evergreen shrub stand out against the vertical pickets of the screen near the door. In early spring it produces fragrant golden yellow flowers, followed by showy clusters of blue berries. See *Mahonia bealei*, p. 190.

See site plan for **J** **L**.

English boxwood **D**

Leatherleaf mahonia **C**

Dogwood **A**

E Pink Gumpo azalea

Japanese painted fern **G**

Walk **K**

Lenten rose **H**

Vinca **I**

'Elegans' hosta **F**

'Roseum Elegans' rhododendron **B**

D **English boxwood** (use 1)
Sheared or pruned to a more "natural" shape, this evergreen shrub joins the mahonia in framing the entry. The dark green leaves exude a distinct fragrance. See *Buxus sempervirens*, p. 177.

E **Pink Gumpo azalea** (use 11)
These low, spreading evergreen shrubs are eye-catching from the street or drive. Mounds of fine-textured foliage are covered by clusters of frilly pink flowers that extend the season of bloom into early summer. See *Rhododendron,* p. 192.

F **'Elegans' hosta** (use 12)
The large, blue-gray, textured leaves of this perennial add color to the shade from spring until frost. White flowers are a bonus in summer. See *Hosta sieboldiana,* p. 184.

G **Japanese painted fern** (use 12)
The loveliest of ferns, its delicately colored deciduous fronds blend green, silver, and ma-

roon. They also add a lush, rich look beneath the dogwoods. See Ferns: *Athyrium goeringianum* 'Pictum', p. 181.

H **Lenten rose** (use 18)
Among the first flowers to appear in spring, this perennial's nodding cuplike blooms range in color from light green to rose, white, or pink. When the flowers have faded, the evergreen foliage continues to justify the plant's prominent place in the garden. See *Helleborus orientalis*, p. 183.

I **Vinca** (use about 130)
Dark green shiny leaves and small blue flowers in spring give this creeping perennial ground cover a dainty look, but it's a tough plant. It will soon spread to carpet the beds. See *Vinca minor*, p. 197.

See p. 21 for the following:

J **Carolina jasmine** (use 1)

K **Walk**

L **Screen**

Site: Shady

Season: Spring

Concept: Lovely flowers and foliage create an enticing entryway on a shady site.

House

Stoop

Lawn

Lawn

Driveway

1 square = 1 ft.

A Foundation with Flair

Flowers and foliage dress up a raised entry

A home with a raised entry invites down-to-earth foundation plants that anchor the house to its surroundings and hide unattractive concrete-block underpinnings. In the hospitable climate of the South, a durable, low-maintenance planting need not mean the usual lineup of clipped junipers. As this design shows, a foundation planting can be more varied, more colorful, and more fun.

Within the graceful arc of a low boxwood hedge is a balanced arrangement of shrubs in sizes that fit under windows and hide the foundation at the same time. Larger shrubs and a small tree punctuate the planting and contribute to the variety of foliage textures and colors.

The predominantly evergreen foliage looks good year-round, and in spring and early summer it is a fine backdrop for a lovely floral display. White flowers sparkle on the trees and shrubs, with irises in blues, purples, pinks, or yellows at their feet. Twining up posts or over railings, the Confederate jasmine greets visitors with its deliciously scented creamy flowers.

Plants & Projects

Once established, the plants in this design require little maintenance beyond seasonal cleanup and a yearly pruning to remove old, weak, or winter-damaged stems. To keep it tidy, the boxwood hedge will need trimming once or twice a year. Clean away the iris leaves when they die down in fall.

A Star magnolia (use 1 plant)
This small, multitrunked deciduous tree perfectly fits the corner of the house. Spring's fragrant white flowers are followed by dark green foliage that looks good all summer. See *Magnolia stellata,* p. 190.

B Possumhaw (use 1)
Brightly colored berries decorate this deciduous shrub in fall and winter. The smooth green leaves are attractive in summer. (Also called winterberry holly.) See *Ilex decidua,* p. 186.

C Loropetalum (use 1)
An elegant presence next to the stoop, this evergreen shrub has layers of arching branches bearing lacy white flowers in spring and may bloom sporadically through the summer. See *Loropetalum chinense,* p. 189.

D Heavenly bamboo (use 3)
A colorful evergreen shrub with straight unbranched stems and layers of lacy leaves tinged gold in spring, changing to summer green and turning orangy red in winter. White flowers in summer and months of red berries, too. See *Nandina domestica,* p. 190.

E Variegated pittosporum (use 8)
This evergreen shrub brings a dressy look and year-round color to the foundation with its rounded mounds of glossy gray-green leaves mottled with white. Creamy white flowers scent the air in early summer. See *Pittosporum tobira* 'Variegata', p. 191.

F 'Compacta' Japanese holly (use 1)
Fill the corner next to the stoop with this handsome evergreen shrub. It can be shaped into a ball or cone by shearing. See *Ilex,* Evergreen hollies: *I. crenata,* p. 186.

G 'Helleri' Japanese holly (use 3)
Smaller than 'Compacta', this evergreen shrub won't outgrow its place, making tidy mounds of small, rounded, dull green leaves. See *Ilex,* Evergreen hollies: *I. crenata,* p. 186.

H Littleleaf boxwood (use 32)
A classic sheared evergreen hedge defines the foundation garden; this compact shrub's small, glossy green leaves give it a fine texture. See *Buxus microphylla,* p. 177.

I Confederate jasmine (use 2)
On early summer evenings you can sit on the stoop and enjoy the fragrance of this evergreen vine's white flowers. Twining stems of glossy dark green leaves can climb and cover the posts. See *Trachelospermum jasminoides,* p. 196.

J Siberian iris (use 8)
For graceful May flowers in shades of blue, yellow, or white, this perennial is a natural choice. After flowering, the erect grassy leaves contrast with the rounded pittosporum. See *Iris sibirica,* p. 187.

K Bearded iris (use 12)
These perennials bear showier flowers than their Siberian cousins in a rainbow of colors. Blooms in midspring; stiff leaves are coarser and shorter than those of Siberian iris, but attractive. See *Iris,* p. 187.

Plant labels on illustration: Loropetalum C, Confederate jasmine I, Heavenly bamboo D, Littleleaf boxwood H, 'Helleri' Japanese holly G, 'Compacta' Japanese holly F

K Bearded iris

H Littleleaf boxwood

Possumhaw B

Variegated E pittosporum

Site: Sunny

Season: Early spring

Concept: Varied foliage and fragrant flowers make this planting a treat.

J Siberian iris

A Star magnolia

1 square = 1 ft.

House

Stoop

Steps

Sidewalk

Lawn

A Foundation with Flair 25

Setting for a shady porch

Porch sitting, one of summer's favorite pastimes, can be made even more pleasurable with this planting. Like the previous design, this one combines deciduous and evergreen plants and mixes handsome foliage and pretty flowers to look good in all four seasons. All the plants will thrive in a shady location.

The central Japanese maple screens the porch from the street without obstructing the view of sitters on the porch. Informal hedges of cherry laurel and holly skirt the porch foundation. Glossy-leaved gardenias flank the stoop behind small patches of annuals, and a grassy edging outlines the beds.

Fragrant flowers perfume the porch for months, beginning in earliest spring with witch hazel, followed by cherry laurel, and then gardenia in summer. Vine-covered porch posts and pots of annuals scattered around the porch decking complete the cozy setting.

Plants & Projects

A Japanese maple (use 1 plant)
This small deciduous tree screens the porch even in winter with eye-catching sculptural branches. Choose a cultivar with cool green leaves in summer; they'll turn a vivid red in fall. See *Acer palmatum*, p. 174.

B Vernal witch hazel (use 1)
Unusual spidery flowers appear on this deciduous native shrub in the earliest days of spring and waft their bewitching fragrance over the porch. Large leaves are golden in fall. See *Hamamelis vernalis*, p. 183.

C 'Otto Luyken' cherry laurel (use 5)
Evergreen shrubs that form a casual low hedge of glossy dark green leaves. The profusion of fragrant white flowers makes a seat at the end of the porch especially desirable in late spring. See *Prunus laurocerasus*, p. 192.

D Dwarf yaupon holly (use 5)
A small evergreen shrub that forms compact mounds of small gray-green leaves and stays just the right size for the base of the porch. See *Ilex*, Evergreen hollies: *I. vomitoria* 'Nana', p. 186.

E Gardenia (use 2)
Evergreen shrubs that flank the steps with low mounds of glossy green leaves all year. The sweet heavy scent of its creamy white flowers will beguile visitors in summer. 'Mystery' and

Site: Shady

Season: Summer

Concept: Foliage, flowers, and fragrance add to the pleasures of a sociable porch.

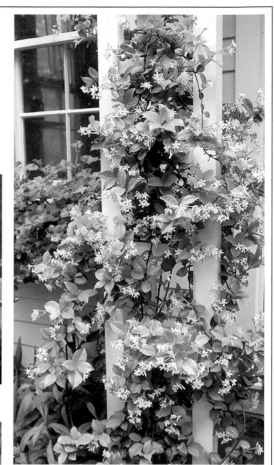

Plant portraits

Handsomely arranged around the foundation or porch, these evergreen and deciduous shrubs and trees and perennials make a four-season display.

● = First design, pp. 24–25
▲ = Second design, pp. 26–27

Variegated pittosporum
(*Pittosporum tobira* 'Variegata', p. 191) ●

Variegated Solomon's seal
(*Polygonatum odoratum* 'Variegatum', p. 192) ▲

Confederate jasmine
(*Trachelospermum jasminoides*, p. 196) ● ▲

Possumhaw (*Ilex decidua*, p. 186) ●

Star magnolia (*Magnolia stellata*, p. 190) ●

J Confederate jasmine
C 'Otto Luyken' cherry laurel

'August Beauty' are good cultivars for this spot. See *Gardenia jasminoides*, p. 182.

F **Jackman clematis** (use 2)
Large violet-purple summer flowers make this deciduous vine a natural choice for the central porch columns. See *Clematis × jackmanii*, p. 179.

G **Variegated Solomon's seal** (use 7)
Fragrant white bell-shaped flowers dangle beneath the arching stems and green-and-white leaves of this perennial in spring. See *Polygonatum odoratum* 'Variegatum', p. 192.

H **Lilyturf** (use 28)
Grasslike clumps of evergreen leaves make an attractive year-round edging. White or purple flowers in late summer. See *Liriope muscari*, p. 189.

I **Annuals**
Impatiens, begonias, and coleus provide color in all seasons in the beds by the steps and the baskets on the porch. See Annuals, p. 175.

See p. 24 for the following:

J **Confederate jasmine** (use 3)

Formal and Friendly

Mix classic symmetry and comfortable plants

A formal garden has a special appeal. Its simple geometry is soothing in a sometimes confusing world, and it never goes out of style. Traditional homes with symmetrical facades are especially suited to the elegant lines and balanced features of this design. The look is formal, but it is an easy formality featuring gentle curves, as well as straight lines, and plants whose tidy forms are produced by nature, not shears.

Unlike many formal gardens whose essentials can be taken in at a glance, this one imparts an air of mystery for visitors approaching from the street. A matching pair of crape myrtles at the corners of the property obscure that view, so that it's only when you approach the gate that the entire garden reveals itself.

A wide brick walkway creates a small courtyard with an eye-catching column of roses at its center. Neat rectangles of lawn are defined by beds of colorful annuals and perennials backed by the graceful curve of a low informal evergreen hedge. Distinctive evergreen shrubs and trees mark the corners of the design and stand guard near the front door. A picket fence reinforces the geometry of the overall design and adds a homey touch. A ground cover of low evergreen shrubs between sidewalk and fence looks good and makes this often awkward area easy to maintain.

'Natchez' crape myrtle Ⓐ

See site plan for Ⓘ Ⓙ .

Dwarf pittosporum Ⓓ

Parson's juniper Ⓕ

Picket fence Ⓜ

Plants & Projects

As formal gardens go, this one is very easy to maintain. The shrubs are chosen for compact forms that need little pruning, and the perennials will bloom happily with little care—just remove the spent flowers to keep things tidy.

Ⓐ **'Natchez' crape myrtle**
(use 2 plants)
These showy, multitrunked, small deciduous trees frame the garden with large clusters of crepe-papery white flowers blooming all summer, colorful leaves in fall, and handsome bark in winter. See *Lagerstroemia indica*, p. 188.

B 'Yoshino' Japanese cedar

Hollywood **C** juniper

Walk and **L** mowing strip

G 'Blaze' climbing rose

K Annual salvia

H Daylily

E Indian hawthorn

F Parson's juniper

B **'Yoshino' Japanese cedar** (use 2)

A pair of these naturally cone-shaped, fine-textured evergreen trees mark the corners of the house. Foliage is rich green in summer, bronze in winter. See *Cryptomeria japonica*, p. 181.

C **Hollywood juniper** (use 2)

An uneven branching pattern gives this small evergreen tree an informal, sculptural look. It's narrow enough to fit on each side of the door. See *Juniperus chinensis* 'Torulosa', p. 187.

D **Dwarf pittosporum** (use 12)

This evergreen shrub makes a lush, dressy but informal hedge with shiny green leaves. Its creamy white flowers scent the air in early summer. See *Pittosporum tobira* 'Wheeleri', p. 191.

E **Indian hawthorn** (use 2)

Pink or white flowers cover the dark foliage of this low, spreading evergreen shrub in spring, followed by blue berries. Select any compact cultivar. See *Rhaphiolepis indica*, p. 192.

F **Parson's juniper** (use 22)

Rugged, gray-green evergreen shrubs edge the sidewalk, their horizontal branches held slightly above the ground. See *Juniperus davurica* 'Expansa', p. 188.

G **'Blaze' climbing rose** (use 1)

This cultivar will cover the central post with glossy green leaves and deep red flowers all summer. Buy a "rose post" at a nursery, or use an old architectural column or other post. Plant salvias around the base. See *Rosa*, p. 194.

H **Daylily** (use 12)

Combine early- and late-blooming cultivars of this useful perennial. Choose orange- and yellow-flowered ones here. See *Hemerocallis*, p. 184.

I **'Stella d'Oro' daylily** (use 10)

From early summer until frost, this hardy perennial's extended show of bright golden yellow flowers can't be beat. The grassy foliage is attractive, too. See *Hemerocallis*, p. 184.

J **Purple verbena** (use 24)

This perennial's clusters of purple flowers keep blooming from early summer to frost. See *Verbena bonariensis*, p. 196.

K **Annual salvia** (use a total of 60)

Red or purple flowers greet visitors for months. Autumn sage (see *Salvia greggii*, p. 194) is a good perennial substitute. See Annuals, p. 175.

L **Walk and mowing strip**

A wide brick walk (p. 118) creates a small courtyard. The brick mowing strip (p. 152) eases lawn maintenance.

M **Picket fence**

Paint or stain the fence to complement the house. See p. 140.

Graceful geometry

A curvaceous formality characterizes this welcoming design. Its outline is reminiscent of a classical amphitheater, with perennials and evergreen shrubs rising from the "stage" (lawn) in graceful ordered tiers. Making use of the existing walkway, the design relies entirely on plants for its effect.

Evergreen foliage gives the planting its structure, while its eye-catching variety of leaf color and texture provides considerable interest. Flowers add color, starting with the fragrant spring blooms of daphne and dianthus, followed by the distinctive globes of hydrangea in early summer and crimson sage blossoms in summer and fall.

Take care during installation to lay out the curving beds precisely. The contrast between sheared hedges and looser "natural" hedges is pleasing to the eye, and it makes maintenance more manageable.

Site: Sunny

Season: Summer

Concept: Colorful curves demonstrate that formal doesn't have to mean rigid or square.

Plants & Projects

A Wax myrtle (use 2 plants)
Airy, open, multitrunked, evergreen trees with silvery bark and fragrant gray-green foliage. See *Myrica cerifera*, p. 190.

B Foster holly (use 2)
These slender evergreen trees are perfect for corner of house. Lots of red berries. See *Ilex*, Evergreen hollies: *Ilex × attenuata* 'Foster #2', p. 186.

C Variegated winter daphne (use 2)
Intensely fragrant white flowers on this compact evergreen shrub greet visitors at the door in spring. Glossy leaves are edged with gold. See *Daphne odora* 'Aureomarginata', p. 181.

D Littleleaf boxwood (use 2)
A classic evergreen for the formal garden that can be sheared into any shape. In this design, it takes the form of two tall, glossy green cones, sentinels at the garden's entrance. See *Buxus microphylla*, p. 177.

E 'Nikko Blue' hydrangea (use 18)
Thick, shiny green leaves of this deciduous shrub make a handsome "natural" hedge. Bears blue or pink snowball-like flowers in June. See *Hydrangea macrophylla*, p. 184.

F 'Compacta' Japanese holly (use 6)
Leathery dark green leaves of this evergreen shrub contrast with the daphne; its mounding form fits below the windows. See *Ilex*, Evergreen hollies: *I. crenata*, p. 186.

G 'Helleri' Japanese holly (use 16)
This evergreen shrub's neat mounds of dull green foliage are just the right height to cre-

A Wax myrtle

B Foster holly

G 'Helleri' Japanese holly

H Dwarf yaupon holly

E 'Nikko Blue' hydrangea

ate a "layered" effect in front of the hydrangeas. See *Ilex,* Evergreen hollies: *I. crenata,* p. 186.

H **Dwarf yaupon holly** (use 10)
An evergreen shrub that forms compact mounds of small, dull green leaves, ideal for a low hedge beneath the crape myrtles. See *Ilex,* Evergreen hollies: *I. vomitoria* 'Nana', p. 186.

I **Autumn sage** (use 30)
This bushy, low-growing perennial brightens the planting from summer through fall with loose clusters of crimson flowers. See *Salvia greggii,* p. 194.

J **'Bath's Pink' dianthus** (use 48)
Mats of grassy blue-gray foliage form an edging around the lawn. Bears wonderfully fragrant pink flowers in spring; sheared after bloom, the foliage looks fresh the rest of the year. See *Dianthus,* p. 181.

Plant portraits

The fine foliage and interesting forms of these trees and shrubs carry these formal gardens beautifully through every season.

● = First design, pp. 28–29
▲ = Second design, pp. 30–31

'Natchez' crape myrtle
(*Lagerstroemia indica,* p. 188) ●

'Nikko Blue' hydrangea
(*Hydrangea macrophylla,* p. 184) ▲

Parson's juniper
(*Juniperus davurica* 'Expansa', p. 188) ●

Dwarf yaupon holly
(*Ilex,* Evergreen hollies: *I. vomitoria* 'Nana', p. 186) ▲

Indian hawthorn (*Rhaphiolepis indica,* p. 192) ●

'Yoshino' Japanese cedar
(*Cryptomeria japonica,* p. 181) ●

Angle of Repose

Make a back-door garden for a sheltered niche

Many homes offer the opportunity to tuck a garden into a protected corner. In the front yard, such spots are ideal for an entry garden or a display that showcases your house when viewed from the street. If the planting is in the backyard, as shown here, it can be a more intimate part of a comfortable outdoor room you can stroll around at leisure or enjoy from a nearby terrace or window.

This planting was designed with spring in mind, so we're showing that season here. (For a look at the planting later on, when perennials and shrubs take over the show, see p. 34.) Dozens of spring bulbs light up the corner from February through May,

assisted by several early-blooming annuals, perennials, and handsome spring-flowered evergreen shrubs. Early flowers aren't the only pleasures of spring. Watch buds fatten and burst into leaf on the Japanese maple, and mark the progress of the season as new, succulent shoots of summer perennials emerge.

Foster holly **L** 'Otto Luyken' cherry laurel **A** Japanese maple **K** 'Otto Luyken' cherry laurel **A** 'Little Princess' spirea **N** Heavenly bamboo **M**

C 'Ebony Knight' black mondo grass

F Crocuses

G 'Spring Beauty' squill

E Grape hyacinths

H Glory-of-the-snow

I Annuals

B Evergreen candytuft

D Red tulips

J Planter

Plants & Projects

Except for the red tulips, the bulb flowers in this planting are small, but they make a splash when blooming in masses. Their foliage will die back unnoticed among the perennial foliage that follows later in the season. Treat the tulips like pansies and other annuals—discard them after they bloom, and replant fresh tulip bulbs every fall.

A **'Otto Luyken' cherry laurel** (use 5 plants)
Glossy dark green leaves and a lovely spreading form make this a choice evergreen to dress up the walls of the house without covering the windows. As a bonus, fragrant white flowers cover this easy-care shrub in midspring. See *Prunus laurocerasus*, p. 192.

B **Evergreen candytuft** (use 8)
An excellent evergreen perennial for the edge of the garden, with a low, rounded form that is not too formal, topped with white flowers in early spring. Shear off the tops of the plants after the flowers fade. See *Iberis sempervirens*, p. 186.

C **'Ebony Knight' black mondo grass** (use 28)
This evergreen grass makes an elegant carpet of thin, purple-black leaves, a striking setting for the small blue flowers of the spring bulbs sprinkled in the patch. See *Ophiopogon planiscapus*, p. 190.

D **Red tulips** (use about 50)
Red tulips add vibrant color to the spring garden like no other plant. Repeated along the edge of the bed and in the planter, they look great with the yellow and blue pansies. Plant five bulbs between each clump of candytuft. Lots of different red cultivars are available; try different ones each year. See Bulbs: *Tulipa*, p. 176.

E **Grape hyacinths** (use 30)
These little bulbs will spread happily beneath the maple tree, flecking the mondo-grass carpet with clusters of fragrant blue flowers. See Bulbs: *Muscari armeniacum*, p. 176.

F **Crocuses** (use 40)
Plant generous clumps (six to eight per square foot) of these bulbs among the sedums (see p. 34), and enjoy their cup-shaped flowers in February. Use yellow or purple varieties, or both. See Bulbs: *Crocus*, p. 176.

G **'Spring Beauty' squill** (use 10)
Clusters of bell-shaped flowers in a lovely shade of clear blue nod above the dianthus foliage in early spring. See Bulbs: *Scilla siberica*, p. 176.

H **Glory-of-the-snow** (use 60)
Starry pale blue flowers with white centers will twinkle in the mondo grass as early as February. See Bulbs: *Chionodoxa luciliae*, p. 176.

I **Annuals** (use about 4 dozen)
Alternating with the evergreen candytuft at the edge of the bed, yellow and blue pansies delight children (and adults) with their personable flowers. See Annuals, p. 175.

J **Planter**
In spring this large planter offers a colorful array of tulips and pansies in a bed of blue-green dianthus foliage. You can build the 5-ft.-long, 2-ft.-wide planter yourself (see p. 142) or purchase one.

See p. 34 for the following:

K Japanese maple (use 1)
L Foster holly (use 1)
M Heavenly bamboo (use 1)
N 'Little Princess' spirea (use 1)

Site: Sunny

Season: Spring

Concept: Spring-flowering bulbs, shrubs, and perennials put on a special show that can be enjoyed from the patio or nearby windows.

1 square = 1 ft.

The scene in summer

There's no drop-off in interest or enjoyment as this planting moves from spring (shown on the previous pages) to summer and fall. Now perennials join woody plants in a tapestry of varied foliage accented by a succession of flowers in shades of white, blue, pink, and red.

Anchoring the planting is a lovely ornamental tree in perfect scale with the house. Foliage textures include a selection of delicate lacy leaves on the maple, heavenly bamboo, and spirea. Grassy dianthus and mondo grass contrast with the more robust foliage of the holly and cherry laurels. New annuals in the planter and edging the bed keep pace with the changing seasons.

Site: Sunny

Season: Summer

Concept: Distinctive, colorful foliage graces the planting from summer through winter.

Plants & Projects

A Japanese maple (use 1 plant)
This elegant small deciduous tree fills the corner beautifully with rich red leaves in summer as well as in fall; sculptural branches and attractive bark stand out in winter. (Many red-leaved cultivars are available.) See *Acer palmatum*, p. 174.

B Foster holly (use 1)
The neat, narrow form and rich color of this broad-leaved evergreen tree add visual weight and balance to the end of the planting. This holly keeps its shape without pruning and bears lots of red berries. See *Ilex*, Evergreen hollies: *Ilex × attenuata* 'Foster #2', p. 186.

C Heavenly bamboo (use 1)
An eye-catching evergreen shrub with pretty leaves that change color each season, fluffy white flowers in summer, and long-lasting red berries. See *Nandina domestica*, p. 190.

D 'Little Princess' spirea (use 1)
This compact deciduous shrub's dainty leaves and neat form are just right for its spot by the planter. In early summer, rosy pink flowers stand out against dark green foliage. See *Spiraea japonica*, p. 195.

E 'Autumn Joy' sedum (use 4)
The gray-green succulent foliage of this tough plant contrasts nicely with the leaves of the nearby cherry laurels. It gives a long and colorful show, with flat-topped pale pink flower clusters that appear in August, maturing to dark pink and then rusty red as autumn progresses. See *Sedum*, p. 195.

F 'Itsaul White' dianthus (use 5)
This perennial's marvelously fragrant white flowers appear in early summer. With a post-bloom shearing, the grassy blue-green foliage will look good through the winter. See *Dianthus*, p. 181.

G Annuals (use about 4 dozen)
When the weather turns hot, discard the pansies and replace them with blue ageratum and white annual vinca, filling the planter and the spaces along the edge of the bed. See Annuals, p. 175.

See p. 33 for the following:

H 'Otto Luyken' cherry laurel

I Evergreen candytuft

J 'Ebony Knight' black mondo grass

Patio

Lawn

1 square = 1 ft.

B Foster holly — Japanese maple A — H 'Otto Luyken' cherry laurel — C Heavenly bamboo

F 'Itsaul White' dianthus — E 'Autumn Joy' sedum — G Annuals

G Annuals — I Evergreen candytuft — J 'Ebony Knight' black mondo grass — D 'Little Princess' spirea

Plant portraits

Bulbs, perennials, shrubs, and trees provide color through every season in this small protected niche.

● = Summer, pp. 32–33
▲ = Spring, p. 34

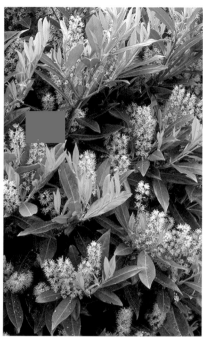

'Otto Luyken' cherry laurel
(*Prunus laurocerasus*, p. 192) ● ▲

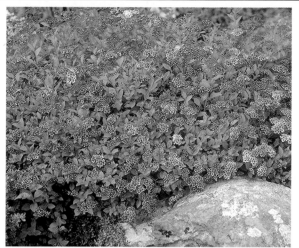

'Little Princess' spirea (*Spiraea japonica*, p. 195) ● ▲

Red tulips (Bulbs: *Tulipa*, p. 176) ●

'Ebony Knight' black mondo grass
(*Ophiopogon planiscapus*, p. 190) ● ▲

Evergreen candytuft
(*Iberis sempervirens*, p. 186) ● ▲

'Autumn Joy' sedum (*Sedum*, p. 195) ▲

Japanese maple (*Acer palmatum*, p. 174) ● ▲

An Eye-Catching Corner
Beautify a boundary with easy-care plants

The corner where your property meets your neighbor's and the sidewalk is often a kind of grassy no-man's-land. This design defines that boundary with a planting that can be enjoyed by both property owners, as well as by passersby. Good gardens make good neighbors, so we've used well-behaved, low-maintenance plants that won't make extra work for the person next door—or for you.

Because of its exposed location, remote from the house and close to the street, this is a less personal planting than those in other more private and frequently used parts of your property. It is meant to be appreciated from a distance. Rising from low-growing plants at the edge of the lawn to the butterfly bush near the sidewalk, the design draws the eye when viewed from the house. An existing split-rail fence along the property line serves as a backdrop for the plants without hiding them from the view of neighbors or passersby. While not intended as a barrier, the planting also provides a modest psychological, if not physical, screen from activity on the street.

There's lots of bloom summer and fall, some of it fragrant, some bearing nectar that's attractive to butterflies. Flowing grasses and the evergreen foliage of shrubs and perennials carry the planting from late fall through winter. For early-spring color, consider planting daffodils among the daylilies, coneflowers, and other perennials, whose rising leaves will quickly cover the fading bulb foliage after bloom.

Goldflame honeysuckle **C**

Chinese abelia **B**

Germander **J**

Plants & Projects

These rugged plants thrive on an open, sunny, dry site and require little care beyond seasonal pruning and removal of spent flowers to encourage further bloom. In spring, cut the fast-growing butterfly bush and the overwintered grasses close to the ground, shear the germander, and thin old growth out of the honeysuckle. During summer, snip off spent flowers from coneflower, daylily, and Asiatic lilies.

A 'White Profusion' butterfly bush (use 1 plant)
The arching branches of this vase-shaped deciduous shrub carry long spikes of fragrant white flowers at their tips. Blooms from midsummer until fall. Butterflies love the flowers. See *Buddleia davidii*, p. 176.

B Chinese abelia (use 1)
Another favorite of butterflies, this evergreen shrub bears white flowers with a de-

Fence

Lawn

Sidewalk

Spade-cut the edges of the planting bed where it meets the lawn.

1 square = 1 ft.

D 'Morning Light' Japanese silver grass

F Dwarf fountain grass

E 'Golden Sword' yucca

A 'White Profusion' butterfly bush

Site: Sunny

Season: Summer

Concept: A colorful planting that looks good year-round marks the property line in a neighborly fashion.

I Asiatic lilies

J Germander

H Daylily

G 'Goldsturm' coneflower

J Germander

---

licious honeysuckle fragrance from early summer to frost. Its mound of glossy leaves contrasts with the grassy neighbors and turns purple-bronze in winter. If this plant isn't available, use glossy abelia (*Abelia × grandiflora*). See *Abelia chinensis*, p. 174.

C Goldflame honeysuckle (use 1)
Beginning in early summer, then off and on until fall, this evergreen vine covers the fence with fragrant pink-and-yellow flowers. The handsome blue-green leaves provide cover and color through the winter. See *Lonicera × heckrottii*, p. 189.

D 'Morning Light' Japanese silver grass (use 1)
Delicate white stripes on the slender arching leaves of this ornamental grass make it glitter in the slightest breeze. Its fluffy seed heads and tawny color add fall and winter interest. See *Miscanthus sinensis*, p. 190.

E 'Golden Sword' yucca (use 3)
This shrubby perennial's sword-shaped evergreen leaves, striped with yellow and gold, bring a strong, spiky form to the corner planting. Tall stems bearing showy clusters of creamy flowers appear in June. See *Yucca filamentosa*, p. 197.

F Dwarf fountain grass (use 3)
Near the front of the planting, this perennial grass produces spreading mounds of green leaves that turn warm shades of orange and tan in autumn. Fluffy flower spikes appear in midsummer. See *Pennisetum alopecuroides* 'Hameln', p. 191.

G 'Goldsturm' coneflower (use 8)
An improved version of the reliable old black-eyed Susan. In late summer an abundance of large, gold-and-brown, daisylike flowers rise on stalks above clumps of dark green leaves. See *Rudbeckia fulgida*, p. 194.

H Daylily (use 6)
For a rugged planting of grassy light green foliage and cheerful summer flowers, this hardy perennial can't be beat. Choose pink-flowered cultivars to blend with the germander and lilies. Use both early and late varieties to extend the season of bloom. See *Hemerocallis*, p. 184.

I Asiatic lilies (use 20)
The large, trumpet-shaped flowers of these regal perennials add color all summer. Plant the bulbs among the daylilies, with which they'll coexist nicely. Choose white and purple cultivars. See *Lilium,* p. 188.

J Germander (use 12)
A great perennial for edging the bed, forming neat mounds of small, shiny evergreen leaves. In late summer, a profusion of tiny pink flowers make a soft pink haze over the foliage. See *Teucrium chamaedrys*, p. 196.

An Eye-Catching Corner   37

Plant portraits

These shrubs, perennials, and bulbs produce attractive foliage and flowers with little effort on your part.

● = First design, pp. 36–37
▲ = Second design, pp. 38–39

'Snowmound' spirea (*Spiraea nipponica*, p. 196) ▲

Asiatic lilies (*Lilium*, p. 188) ●

Miniature daffodils (Bulbs: *Narcissus*, p. 176) ▲

Germander (*Teucrium chamaedrys*, p. 196) ●

Goldflame honeysuckle
(*Lonicera × heckrottii*, p. 189) ●

'Longwood Blue' bluebeard
(*Caryopteris × clandonensis*, p. 178) ▲

Simply shrubs

This design is simpler but no less attractive than the previous one. The crape myrtle flowers all summer long and has fall color and lovely bark. In spring, the Carolina jasmine is covered with deliciously fragrant, golden yellow flowers, and the spirea is a cloud of white. Shrubby bluebeard blooms for weeks in late summer and fall.

Daffodils, both large and small, join with other colorful bulbs in spring. Seasonal plantings of annuals, replaced in spring and fall, bloom throughout the year.

This planting requires only routine pruning and cleanup. Prune the crape myrtle and bluebeard in winter, and the spirea and Carolina jasmine in early summer. Renew the mulch when you replant the annuals.

Plants & Projects

Ⓐ **'Natchez' crape myrtle**
(use 1 plant)
Grown as a small multitrunked specimen, this deciduous tree bears large white flowers for months in summer. Its orangy red fall foliage and attractive bark add to the three-season show. See *Lagerstroemia indica*, p. 188.

Ⓑ **'Crimson Pygmy' Japanese barberry** (use 3)
This colorful deciduous shrub's maroon leaves turn crimson in fall, when they're joined by bright red berries. Its low, rounded form fits well beneath the crape myrtle. See *Berberis thunbergii*, p. 176.

Ⓒ **'Snowmound' spirea** (use 1)
In May, the profusion of white flowers covering the arching branches of this deciduous shrub truly do make it look like

See site plan for **G** **H** **I**.

Site: Sunny

Season: Late summer

Concept: Woody plants, aided by spring bulbs and annuals, create a corner with a different look.

'Natchez' crape myrtle **A**

'Snowmound' spirea **C**

Carolina jasmine **E**

F Mondo grass

J Annuals

J Annuals

'Crimson Pygmy' Japanese barberry **B**

Annuals **J**

D 'Longwood Blue' bluebeard

D 'Longwood Blue' bluebeard

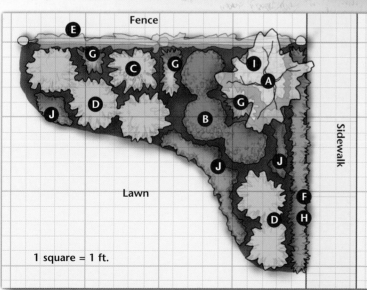

Fence

E

G

C

G

I

A

G

J

D

B

Sidewalk

J

J

Lawn

D

F

H

1 square = 1 ft.

---

a mound of snow. Blue-green leaves and a neat form are attractive the rest of the season. See *Spiraea nipponica*, p. 196.

D **'Longwood Blue' bluebeard** (use 5)
Butterflies like the fringed blue flowers of this deciduous shrub; blooms from late summer to frost. Offers soft gray foliage, a tough nature, and a compact form that fits the front of the planting. See *Caryopteris × clandonensis*, p. 178.

E **Carolina jasmine** (use 1)
In early spring this tough, attractive evergreen vine gives a warm greeting to passersby with its fragrant, yellow, trumpet-shaped flowers. The slender leaves are maroon in winter and will quickly cover the fence. See *Gelsemium sempervirens*, p. 182.

F **Mondo grass** (use 60)
The thin, leathery, grassy leaves of this evergreen perennial create an attractive deep green edging along the sidewalk in four seasons. See *Ophiopogon japonicus*, p. 190.

G **Regular daffodils** (use 3 clumps of 12 each)
Tucked between the bare branches of deciduous shrubs, the cheerful yellow trumpet flowers of this hardy bulb are one of spring's most welcome sights. The shrubs' emerging leaves will hide the bulbs' foliage as it fades after bloom. See Bulbs: *Narcissus*, p. 176.

H **Miniature daffodils** (use 60)
Charming little reproductions of their larger cousins, the flowers of these spring bulbs will rise just above the mondograss foliage that edges the bed along the sidewalk. See Bulbs: *Narcissus*, p. 176.

I **Small bulbs** (use 50)
A colorful spring carpet of crocus, grape hyacinth, or glory-of-the-snow graces the area beneath the crape myrtle. Plant them 3 in. apart; any color will do. See Bulbs, p. 176.

J **Annuals** (use about 50, spaced 1 per sq. ft.)
Three patches of annuals edging the lawn and sidewalk add color to the planting all year. Plant ageratum and annual vinca for a summer show, and blue and yellow pansies for winter. See Annuals, p. 175.

Streetwise and Stylish

Give your curbside strip a new look

Homeowners seldom think much about the area that runs between the sidewalk and street. At best this is a tidy patch of lawn; at worst, a weed-choked eyesore. Yet this is one of the most public parts of many properties. Planting this strip with attractive perennials, shrubs, and trees can give pleasure to passersby and visitors who park next to the curb, as well as enhancing the streetscape you view from the house. (This strip is usually city-owned, so check local ordinances for restrictions before you start a remake.)

It might help to think of this curbside strip as an island bed between two defined boundaries: the street and the sidewalk. These beds are divided further by a wide pedestrian walkway, providing ample room for visitors to get in and out of front and rear car doors. A pair of handsome evergreen trees form a gateway. The diagonal skew of this design keeps the symmetry of the plantings either side from appearing staid. You can expand the beds to fill a longer strip, or plant lawn next to the beds.

This can be a difficult site. Summer drought and heat, pedestrian and car traffic, and errant dogs are the usual conditions found along the street. Plants have to be tough to perform well here, but they need not look tough. These combine colorful foliage and flowers for a dramatic impact from spring until fall. Evergreen foliage and clumps of tawny grass look good through the winter. The plantings beneath the trees won't grow tall enough to block your view of the street as you pull out of the driveway.

Japanese ligustrum **A**

'Little Princess' spirea **B**

'Crimson Pygmy' Japanese barberry **C**

Dwarf fountain grass **E**

'Stella d'Oro' daylily **F**

'Blue Pacific' shore juniper **D**

Sidewalk

B

C

Lawn

E A D

F

G

E

D

A

F

C

B

Driveway

Street

1 square = 1 ft.

A Japanese ligustrum

Dwarf fountain grass **E**

G Walk

F 'Stella d'Oro' daylily

B 'Little Princess' spirea

C 'Crimson Pygmy' Japanese barberry

Site: Sunny

Season: Summer

Concept: Small but varied planting transforms an often neglected area and treats visitors and passersby to a colorful display.

Plants & Projects

Tough as they are, these plants will benefit from a generous bark mulch, which conserves moisture, helps control weeds, and makes the bed look neat in this highly visible location. In addition to seasonal cleanup, you'll need to prune the shrubs occasionally to keep them tidy and healthy. Divide the clumps of daylilies when they get crowded.

A **Japanese ligustrum**
(use 2 plants)
The dark green, waxy leaves of this small broad-leaved evergreen tree are a perfect background for the fragrant white flowers it bears in early summer. Dark blue berries follow in fall and winter. Grows quickly; prune lower branches as necessary to accommodate visitors using the walk. See *Ligustrum japonicum*, p. 188.

B **'Little Princess' spirea** (use 6)
The small fine leaves and rosy pink flowers of this dainty deciduous shrub belie its tough nature. It will bloom happily for weeks in conditions next to the street in early summer. See *Spiraea japonica*, p. 195.

C **'Crimson Pygmy' Japanese barberry** (use 6)
The dark maroon leaves of this deciduous shrub turn crimson in late fall. Naturally forms a broad tidy mound. See *Berberis thunbergii*, p. 176.

D **'Blue Pacific' shore juniper**
(use 2)
This low, trailing evergreen ground cover has handsome blue-green foliage that can stand up to street life. Makes a subtle carpet beneath the trees. See *Juniperus conferta*, p. 188.

E **Dwarf fountain grass** (use 2)
This perennial grass is a year-round presence. Fluffy flower spikes rise above neat clumps of arching green leaves in midsummer. Flowers and foliage turn shades of gold and tan in autumn and last through the winter. See *Pennisetum alopecuroides* 'Hameln', p. 191.

F **'Stella d'Oro' daylily** (use 8)
This very popular perennial produces golden yellow flowers from late spring until frost; quite a feat considering that each flower lasts only a day. The grassy foliage is attractive, too. See *Hemerocallis*, p. 184.

G **Walk**
This design provides interest underfoot. Set the framework of pressure-treated 2x4s on a sand-and-gravel base (see p. 118); position the square precast concrete pavers in the center of each cell; and fill between paver and frame with crushed rock, tamped firm.

Plant portraits

Blessed with fine foliage and flowers, these are also rugged plants that can survive the stress of life beside a busy street.

● = First design, pp. 40–41
▲ = Second design, p. 43

Ajuga (*Ajuga reptans* 'Burgandy Glow', p. 175) ▲

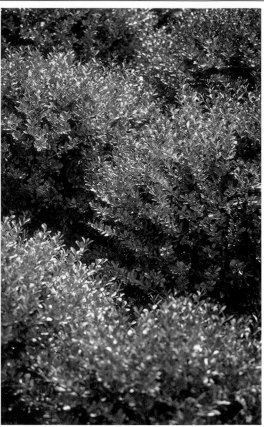

'Crimson Pygmy' Japanese barberry (*Berberis thunbergii*, p. 176) ●

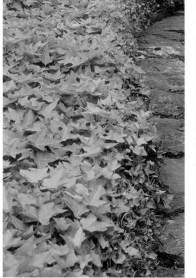

English ivy (*Hedera helix*, p. 183) ▲

Redbud (*Cercis canadensis*, p. 179) ▲

Dwarf fountain grass (*Pennisetum alopecuroides* 'Hameln', p. 191) ●

'Blue Pacific' shore juniper (*Juniperus conferta*, p. 188) ●

Leafy oasis

This design features shade-loving plants for those who live on the cool shady streets that make many neighborhoods so pleasant. Emphasizing foliage more than flowers, the effect is more subdued than the previous design, but still cheerful.

A pair of small trees once again anchor the design. They flower in early spring, followed by the azaleas and ajuga flanking the walk. A mix of rich green foliage, accented by the large blue leaves of the hostas, carries the planting through the summer and fall. The evergreen azaleas and ivy and the handsome form of the redbuds look good through the winter.

Plants & Projects

A **Redbud** (use 2 plants)
Small pink flowers line the branches of this small deciduous tree in early spring. Heart-shaped leaves turn gold in the fall. This fast-growing tree needs little pruning; just remove lower limbs. See *Cercis canadensis*, p. 179.

B **Gumpo azalea** (use 15)
These low, spreading evergreen shrubs form mounds of fine-textured foliage, an ideal background for the lovely display of frilly flowers that brighten the shade in late spring. Use pink or white cultivars, or both. Foliage looks fresh all year. See *Rhododendron*, p. 192.

C **'Elegans' hosta** (use 12)
The huge, blue-gray, textured leaves of this perennial add cool color to the shade from spring until frost, contrasting with the finer-leaved azaleas. In late summer, white flowers peek just above the foliage. See *Hosta sieboldiana*, p. 184.

D **English ivy** (use 100)
A virtually indestructible perennial, this vine quickly spreads to form a dark green mat of glossy lobed leaves beneath the trees. You can choose a cultivar with variegated leaves to provide additional color to the planting. See *Hedera helix*, p. 183.

E **Ajuga** (use 50)
An excellent ground cover for partial shade, this evergreen perennial will quickly spread to carpet the areas next to the walk with dark green or multi-colored leaves. In late spring, the foliage is covered with erect spikes of tiny blue flowers. See *Ajuga reptans*, p. 175.

See p. 41 for the following:

F **Walk**

Site: Shady

Season: Late spring

Concept: Enhance the looks of a shady curb with lovely foliage and a spring flush of flowers.

1 square = 1 ft.

Landscaping a Low Wall
A colorful two-tier garden replaces a bland slope

Some things may not love a wall, but plants and gardeners do. For plants, walls offer warmth for an early start in spring and good drainage for roots. Gardeners appreciate the rich visual potential for composing a garden on two levels, as well as the practical advantage of working on two relatively flat surfaces instead of a single sloping one. If you have a wall, or have a place to put one, grasp the opportunity for some handsome landscaping.

This design places two complementary perennial borders above and below a wall bounded at one end by a set of stairs. While each bed is relatively narrow, when viewed from the lower level the two combine to form a border almost 10 ft. deep, with plants rising to eye level or more. The planting can be extended with the same or similar plants.

Building the wall that makes this impressive sight possible doesn't require the time or skill it once did. Nor is it necessary to scour the countryside for tons of fieldstone or to hire an expensive contractor. Thanks to precast retaining-wall systems, a knee-high do-it-yourself wall can be installed in as little as a weekend. More experienced or ambitious wall builders may want to tackle a natural stone wall, but anyone with a healthy back (or access to energetic teenagers) can succeed with a prefabricated system.

'Snowbank' boltonia A

'David' garden phlox B

Purple coneflower C

'Becky' Shasta daisy G

'Homestead Purple' verbena K

Purple coneflower C

Evergreen candytuft J

'Moonbeam' coreopsis L

'Sunny Border Blue' veronica H

Autumn sage I

'Sunny Border Blue' veronica H

Daylily F

Evergreen candytuft J

Plants & Projects

Drifts of blues, whites, yellows, and pinks, a dash of cherry red, and the flash of butterfly wings keep the garden popping with color from summer through fall. For more color in spring, plant small bulbs like crocus or grape hyacinth throughout the beds. Care is basic: spring and fall clean-up, snipping spent flowers, and dividing a plant now and then.

Ⓐ 'Snowbank' boltonia (use 2 plants)
White daisylike flowers cover this tough perennial for three to five weeks in fall. An upright plant with fine blue-green leaves, it never needs staking. See *Boltonia asteroides*, p. 176.

Ⓑ 'David' garden phlox (use 3)
A sturdy perennial topped with clusters of clear white, fragrant flowers in late summer. It forms a patch of upright stems clothed in healthy green leaves, a pleasing backdrop for the plants in front of it. See *Phlox paniculata*, p. 191.

Ⓒ Purple coneflower (use 9)
Thick flower stalks rise above this perennial's clump of dark green foliage in midsummer, displaying large daisylike blossoms. Each flower has dark pink petals surrounding a dark central cone. Leave some seed heads for winter interest and the finches they attract. See *Echinacea purpurea*, p. 181.

Ⓓ 'Caesar's Brother' Siberian iris (use 4)
The erect grassy leaves of this perennial provide an interesting spiky look along the wall, and the graceful flowers add deep purple color in late spring. See *Iris sibirica*, p. 187.

Ⓔ Gold moneywort (use 4)
Planted at the feet of the irises, the bright yellow coin-shaped leaves of this creeping perennial spill over the wall. Yellow flowers in summer complement the coreopsis in the lower bed. See *Lysimachia nummularia* 'Aurea', p. 190.

Ⓕ Daylily (use 5)
Grassy foliage and colorful trumpet-shaped flowers, fresh every day, make this perennial a lovely centerpiece for the lower bed. Choose a cultivar with maroon flowers to blend with the pink coneflowers, or mix several kinds to give a longer blooming period. See *Hemerocallis*, p. 184.

Ⓖ 'Becky' Shasta daisy (use 9)
This popular perennial's big white daisies bloom all summer on sturdy stalks that never need staking. The shiny foliage looks good through the winter. See *Chrysanthemum × superbum*, p. 179.

Ⓗ 'Sunny Border Blue' veronica (use 6)
Lustrous green crinkled leaves topped with bright blue flower spikes make this perennial a cheerful recurring presence in the garden. It will bloom from early summer to frost if you clip off the spent flowers. See *Veronica*, p. 196.

Ⓘ Autumn sage (use 2)
A bushy low-growing perennial with loose clusters of bright red flowers that keep coming all summer and fall. See *Salvia greggii*, p. 194.

Ⓙ Evergreen candytuft (use 6)
An excellent evergreen perennial for a wall, with a low, rounded form that falls loosely over the edge. It's topped with clusters of white flowers in early spring. See *Iberis sempervirens*, p. 186.

Ⓚ 'Homestead Purple' verbena (use 2)
This perennial also trails over the edge of the wall and bears purple flowers from spring to frost if you clip off the spent blossoms. See *Verbena canadensis*, p. 196.

Ⓛ 'Moonbeam' coreopsis (use 6)
Edging the lower bed, this perennial's tidy mound of fine foliage sparkles with small yellow flowers for months. See *Coreopsis verticillata*, p. 180.

Ⓜ Retaining wall and steps
This 2-ft.-tall wall and the steps are built from a precast concrete block system. Select a color that complements your house. See p. 130.

Ⓝ Path
Gravel is an attractive, informal surface, easy to install and to maintain. See p. 118.

Ⓓ 'Caesar's Brother' Siberian iris

Ⓜ Retaining wall and steps

Ⓔ Gold moneywort

Site: Sunny

Season: Summer

Concept: Low retaining wall creates easy-to-maintain beds for a distinctive two-level planting.

Ⓝ Path

Lawn   1 square = 1 ft.

A late-season treat

This design adds flowers and colorful foliage to the wall garden to bolster its appeal in fall. The backbone of the planting remains the long-flowering summer perennials of the previous plan, but new additions make autumn a satisfying encore to the summer show.

With flowers in blues and pinks, the new plants fit right into the overall color scheme. Bluebeard and pincushion flower attract butterflies, and the pink flowers of sedum are pretty accents at the garden edges. Blazing star's striking purple flower spikes have become distinctive seed heads by fall, when, along with the feathery plumes and golden leaves of dwarf fountain grass, they add mellow color to the scene.

Site: Sunny

Season: Early fall

Concept: New additions enhance the wall garden's appeal during the autumn months.

A 'Longwood Blue' bluebeard

C Blazing star

B Dwarf fountain grass

E 'Butterfly Blue' pincushion flower

Purple F coneflower

J 'Homestead Purple' verbena

I Evergreen candytuft

L Retaining wall and steps

M Path

D 'Vera Jameson' sedum

C Blazing star

E 'Butterfly Blue' pincushion flower

G Daylily

H 'Becky' Shasta daisy

K 'Moonbeam' coreopsis

Plants & Projects

Ⓐ **'Longwood Blue' bluebeard**
(use 3 plants)
The pretty blue fringed flowers on this deciduous shrub bloom from late summer to frost. Soft gray foliage makes a compact mound after the plant is cut back each spring. See *Caryopteris × clandonensis*, p. 178.

Ⓑ **Dwarf fountain grass** (use 2)
This perennial grass is most striking in fall, when its cascading mound of green leaves turns gold or tan beneath fluffy flower spikes held on arching stalks. Looks good far into winter, too. See *Pennisetum alopecuroides* 'Hameln', p. 191.

Ⓒ **Blazing star** (use 6)
This durable perennial's tall dense spikes of purple flowers are eye-catching from midsummer on. It combines beautifully with its garden neighbor and prairie companion, purple coneflower. Flowers are great for cutting and drying. See *Liatris spicata*, p. 188.

Ⓓ **'Vera Jameson' sedum** (use 11)
A low-growing perennial next to the steps, where its distinctive purple-tinged succulent leaves can be appreciated close up. Flat clusters of pink flowers top the floppy stems in late summer and dry to a crisp brown in winter. See *Sedum*, p. 195.

Ⓔ **'Butterfly Blue' pincushion flower** (use 11)
For lots of sky blue color near the steps, you can't beat this little perennial. Bloom begins in May and goes on until frost if you trim spent blossoms. See *Scabiosa columbaria*, p. 195.

See p. 45 for the following:

Ⓕ **Purple coneflower** (use 9)

Ⓖ **Daylily** (use 5)

Ⓗ **'Becky' Shasta daisy** (use 3)

Ⓘ **Evergreen candytuft** (use 6)

Ⓙ **'Homestead Purple' verbena** (use 4)

Ⓚ **'Moonbeam' coreopsis** (use 4)

Ⓛ **Retaining wall and steps**

Ⓜ **Path**

Plant portraits

These perennials will dependably deliver attractive healthy foliage and months of outstanding bloom year after year.

● = First design, pp. 44–45
▲ = Second design, pp. 46–47

'Snowbank' boltonia (*Boltonia asteroides*, p. 176) ●

'Homestead Purple' verbena
(*Verbena canadensis*, p. 196) ● ▲

'Vera Jameson' sedum (*Sedum*, p. 195) ▲

'Moonbeam' coreopsis
(*Coreopsis verticillata*, p. 180) ● ▲

'Becky' Shasta daisy
(*Chrysanthemum × superbum*, p. 179) ● ▲

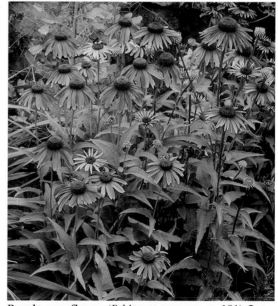
Purple coneflower (*Echinacea purpurea*, p. 181) ● ▲

"Around Back"

Dress up the family's day-to-day entrance

When people think of landscaping the entrance to their home, the public entry at the front of the house comes immediately to mind. It's easy to forget that the back door often gets more use. If you make the journey between back door and driveway or garage many times each day, why not make it as pleasant a trip as possible? For many properties, a simple planting like the one shown here can transform the space bounded by the house, garage, and driveway, making it at once more inviting and more functional.

In a high-traffic area frequented by ball-bouncing, bicycle-riding children as well as busy adults, delicate fussy plants have no place. This design employs durable plants, all of which look good year-round. The holly hedge links the house and the garage and separates the more private backyard from the busy driveway. A Japanese maple anchors the backyard planting, a composi-tion of shrubs and perennials that is equally pleasing whether viewed on your way to and from the back door or while re-laxing on a backyard deck or patio.

There are flowers in yellow, pink, white, and purple from spring through fall, in-cluding gardenias that fill the summer air with sweet scent and cheerful daylilies that bloom for months. And when the flowers fade in autumn, there is plenty of evergreen foliage to enjoy through the winter.

A — Japanese maple

See site plan for F.

E — 'Needlepoint' holly

H — Variegated lilyturf

G — Gardenia

Walk L

D — Heavenly bamboo

'Stella d'Oro' daylily C

Glen Dale azalea B

Moss phlox K

Dwarf yaupon holly I

Plants & Projects

If you don't need the path to the garage door shown here, extend the azaleas and heavenly bamboo to fill in near the garage, and plant additional lilyturf between the azaleas and holly hedge. Maintenance is not demanding—just seasonal pruning and cleanup to keep the shrubs and perennials healthy, and periodic shearing to keep the hedge tidy.

Ⓐ Japanese maple (use 1 plant)
A small deciduous tree with an attractive form and finely cut leaves. For striking summer color, choose from among the cultivars that have red leaves in that season as well as in the fall. See *Acer palmatum*, p. 174.

Ⓑ Glen Dale azalea (use 3)
Lovely broad-leaved evergreen shrubs line the path beneath the maple tree. In spring they bear striking flowers in pink,
white, red, or orange. See *Rhododendron*, p. 192.

Ⓒ 'Stella d'Oro' daylily (use 5)
Numerous golden yellow flowers (each lasting only a day) nod above this remarkable perennial's arching leaves from late spring until hard frost. See *Hemerocallis*, p. 184.

Ⓓ Heavenly bamboo (use 2)
A colorful shrub with straight unbranched stems bearing layers of lacy evergreen leaves, white flowers in summer, and red berries in fall and winter. The leaves change color from gold to green to red with the progress of the seasons. See *Nandina domestica*, p. 190.

Ⓔ 'Needlepoint' holly (use 5)
A tough evergreen shrub, ideal for shearing as a hedge, with shiny dark green leaves and a magnificent show of red berries in winter. See *Ilex*, Evergreen hollies: *I. cornuta*, p. 186.

Ⓕ 'Diana' rose-of-Sharon (use 1)
A deciduous shrub with eye-catching pure white flowers
from July through September. Its size and colorful presence make it effective as an endpoint for this planting or as a transition to an existing foundation planting. See *Hibiscus syriacus*, p. 184.

Ⓖ Gardenia (use 1)
Beloved in the region for the sweet, heavy scent of its creamy white flowers, this evergreen shrub makes the trip down the path a special pleasure in summer. Glossy dark green leaves look good all year. Plant 'Mystery' or 'August Beauty' here. See *Gardenia jasminoides*, p. 182.

Ⓗ Variegated lilyturf (use 50)
This grasslike evergreen perennial makes a colorful edging along the lawn and path, with its dark green leaves striped in yellow and white. In late summer it bears small violet, purple, or white flowers. Space plants 1 ft. apart; they'll soon grow together. See *Liriope muscari* 'Variegata', p. 189.

Ⓘ Dwarf yaupon holly (use 3)
A small evergreen shrub that forms compact mounds of small shiny leaves and stays just the right size for its spot between the path and the house. See *Ilex*, Evergreen hollies: *I. vomitoria* 'Nana', p. 186.

Ⓙ 'David' garden phlox (use 3)
This perennial offers sturdy upright stems of healthy green leaves topped for weeks in late summer with clusters of fragrant white flowers. See *Phlox paniculata*, p. 191.

Ⓚ Moss phlox (use 7)
This evergreen perennial forms a dense mat of prickly foliage next to the path. In spring it is covered with pretty little flowers; a purple-flowered variety will look best in this planting. See *Phlox subulata*, p. 191.

Ⓛ Walk
The texture, color, and irregular shape of this flagstone walk suit this planting well. Large stones look good and make a safe, even surface. See p. 118.

1 square = 1 ft.

Site: Sunny

Season: Summer

Concept: A planting to raise spirits weighed down by shopping bags and to separate activities in the backyard from the driveway.

Ⓙ 'David' garden phlox

Plant portraits

These back-door plants have front-door style, offering eye-catching flowers, handsome foliage, and enticing fragrance.

● = First design, pp. 48–49
▲ = Second design, pp. 50–51

Heavenly bamboo
(*Nandina domestica*, p. 190) ● ▲

Moss phlox (*Phlox subulata*, p. 191) ●

Gardenia (*Gardenia jasminoides*, p. 182) ●

'Diana' rose-of-Sharon (*Hibiscus syriacus*, p. 184) ●

Variegated lilyturf (*Liriope muscari* 'Variegata', p. 189) ●

'David' garden phlox (*Phlox paniculata*, p. 191) ●

A shady passage

This design features a simple vine-covered arbor that makes something special of the journey to and from the back door. (You can extend the arbor and the foundation planting of hydrangeas to suit your site.) A row of handsome shrubs and a picket fence separate the driveway from the backyard.

Evergreen clematis forms a canopy on the arbor year-round, its white flowers adding a lovely fragrance in summer. The planting offers flowers from late winter through fall with few pauses. Hollies, heavenly bamboo, and lilyturf join the clematis to provide evergreen foliage that enlivens the area through the winter months.

Plants & Projects

A Evergreen clematis
(use 1 plant per post)
The glossy green leaves of this vine cover the arbor year-round and serve as a handsome backdrop for the large white flowers that brighten and perfume the path in spring. See *Clematis armandii*, p. 179.

B 'Harbour Dwarf' heavenly bamboo (use 9)
This is a smaller version of the heavenly bamboo that anchors a corner of this planting (and is used in the previous design). Compact and bushy, it makes a colorful low hedge along the fence. The foliage turns bright crimson in winter. Needs little if any pruning. See *Nandina domestica*, p. 190.

C 'Compacta' Japanese holly (use 3)
Evergreen shrub that forms a dense mound of glossy leaves. Needs no pruning to maintain its tidy shape. See *Ilex*, Evergreen hollies: *I. crenata*, p. 186.

Arbor **I**   See site plan for **B** **K**.

Evergreen clematis **A**

'Compacta' Japanese holly **C**

'Compacta' Japanese holly **C**

Herbs **H**

'Black Knight' butterfly bush **F**

'Arp' rosemary **G**

Evergreen clematis **A**

Walk **L**   Fence **J**   Lilyturf **E**   'Nikko Blue' hydrangea **D**

D **'Nikko Blue' hydrangea** (use 3)
This is a handsome cultivar of the popular deciduous shrub. Distinctive ball-shaped clusters of blue (or pink, depending on your soil) flowers cover the glossy foliage in summer. See *Hydrangea macrophylla*, p. 184.

E **Lilyturf** (use 40 or more)
A dark green form of this grassy evergreen ground cover is attractive year-round along the path. Purple or white flowers are showy in late summer. Space plants 1 ft. apart. See *Liriope muscari*, p. 189.

F **'Black Knight' butterfly bush** (use 1)
The arching branches of this vase-shaped deciduous shrub carry long trusses of fragrant dark blue-purple flowers at their tips. Makes a fine focal point for the planting, blooming from midsummer through fall and attracting bevies of butterflies to the backyard. See *Buddleia davidii*, p. 176.

G **'Arp' rosemary** (use 1)
This well-known kitchen herb is also a handsome evergreen shrub. Its gray-green, needle-like leaves are fragrant as well as tasty. Bears small blue flowers in late winter. See *Rosmarinus officinalis*, p. 194.

H **Herbs** (use 1 or more of each)
Anchored by the rosemary at one end, this small garden of culinary herbs includes parsley, chives, basil, thyme, sage, and oregano and so is as useful as it is attractive.

I **Arbor**
A vine-covered wooden arbor shades the path from driveway toward back door. See p. 142.

J **Fence**
A picket fence complements the arbor and encloses the backyard. See p. 142.

See p. 49 for the following:

K **Heavenly bamboo** (use 1)

L **Walk**

Garage   Driveway

Lawn

House

1 square = 1 ft.

Site: Sunny

Season: Summer

Concept: Fence, arbor, and plantings are functional and attractive year-round.

Make a Fresco of Flowers

A vertical garden beautifies a blank wall

Just as you enhance your living room by hanging paintings on the walls, you can decorate blank walls in your outdoor "living rooms." The design shown here transforms a nondescript garage wall into a living fresco, showcasing lovely flowers and foliage. Instead of a view of a plain wall, imagine gazing at this scene from a nearby patio, deck, or kitchen window. A vertical garden like this is also ideal where yard space is limited.

The simple composition spotlights three quite different plants, each striking in its own way. At one end, a deciduous shrub offers colorful leaves and fountainlike form. At the other, an evergreen tree provides balance and contrast with its narrow irregular form and bright green foliage. Between

them, the wall sparkles all summer with red roses highlighted against a backdrop of healthy green leaves. Note how the off-center placement of the trellis on the wall combines with the narrow waist of the curving bed to draw the eye to the roses and blend the three main plants into a coherent whole.

A supporting cast of perennials performs admirably at the feet of the major players. Above a carpet of handsome foliage in a range of textures, these plants provide lovely flowers in red, blue, and white from spring to frost. The planting holds its own in winter, too, with a study in contrasts between the tree and shrub, one with rich evergreen foliage, the other an attractive bouquet of straight bare stems.

Mealy **D** blue sage

Hollywood **B** juniper

Plants & Projects

Designed for a south- or west-facing wall that receives full sun, this planting uses tough plants that thrive in hot dry conditions. They'll need regular watering for the first year (even in winter). Spread a layer of bark mulch to control weeds while the plants are young. From the second year on, the plants require only normal rainfall and little, if any, fertilizing.

A 'Blaze' rose (use 1 plant)
Long a favorite, this rose produces small, mildly fragrant red roses abundantly in spring and then off and on all summer. Foliage is healthy and shouldn't need spraying. As they grow, fix canes to the trellis with twist-ties. Each winter, cut a few of the older canes back to the ground. See *Rosa*, p. 194.

B Hollywood juniper (use 1)
An uneven branching pattern gives this small evergreen tree an interesting, informal look. It is slow-growing and doesn't need pruning to keep it from crowding its space. The bright green foliage is a cheerful sight all year. See *Juniperus chinensis* 'Torulosa', p. 187.

C 'Royal Purple' smoke tree (use 1)
Foliage and flowers vie for top billing on this deciduous shrub. The dark purple leaves turn gold or orange in fall; pink flowers in fluffy plumes last weeks in summer and fall. Cut all stems back to 6-in. stubs each spring to produce a vase-shaped clump of straight, 5-ft.-long stems. See *Cotinus coggygria*, p. 180.

D Mealy blue sage (use 9)
Through summer and fall, this perennial wildflower makes a carpet of glossy green foliage topped by slim spikes of blue flowers. (A medium blue cultivar will look best here.) See *Salvia farinacea*, p. 194.

E Autumn sage (use 6)
This bushy, low-growing perennial forms an evergreen mass to balance the green juniper in winter, and its loose clusters of bright red or pink flowers keep coming from spring until fall. See *Salvia greggii*, p. 194.

F Bearded iris (use 6)
This perennial produces elegant but short-lived flowers in spring, before the rose blooms. (Blue or white flowers will look best here.) The swordlike blue-green foliage is tough and at-

tractive for months, sometimes evergreen in the Deep South. See *Iris*, p. 187.

G 'Itsaul White' dianthus (use 12)
Blue-green, grassy foliage and fragrant white flowers that bloom in spring with the rose make this a stunning perennial for the front of the planting. Shear the foliage after bloom and it will look good all year. See *Dianthus*, p. 181.

H Trellis
This large trellis can be assembled from 1x2s and 2x2s in a few hours. Suspended on hooks, it is easy to remove to paint the wall. See p. 144.

I Mowing strip
A brick edging neatly outlines the bed and makes mowing easier. See p. 152.

H Trellis

A 'Blaze' rose

I Mowing strip

F Bearded iris

Site: Sunny

Season: Late summer

Concept: Flowers, foliage, and a neat trellis make a picture that pleases year-round.

G 'Itsaul White' dianthus

E Autumn sage

C 'Royal Purple' smoke tree

Driveway

Garage

A brick mowing strip separates the planting bed from the lawn.

Lawn

1 square = 1 ft.

A shady wall garden

A cooler, shadier site, such as an east- or north-facing wall, calls for a different palette of plants. The basic design remains the same as the previous one, but here shade-tolerant shrubs, vines, and perennials replace the sun lovers.

Once again, the planting provides interest year-round. Scented flowers are present for months, beginning in late winter with sweet box and mahonia, followed by a summer-long display of honeysuckle on the trellis. Small bulbs in spring and hydrangea, lilyturf, and hostas in summer add to the show.

Varied foliage has its own eye-catching appeal in addition to providing a handsome backdrop for flowers. Winter is graced by evergreen foliage (which may turn purplish) and the mahonia's sky blue berries, which last until the mockingbirds eat them in spring.

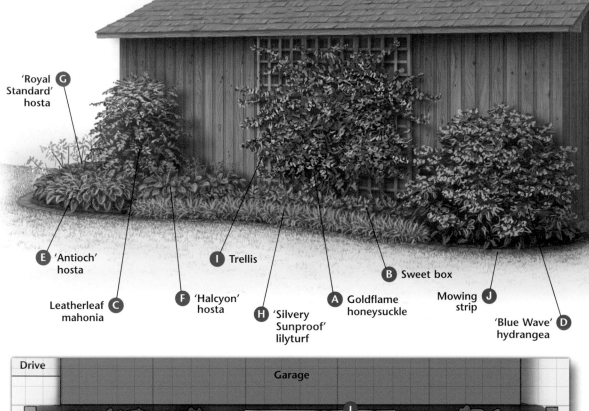

Site: Shady

Season: Summer

Concept: Shade-tolerant vines, perennials, and shrubs make a showpiece of this wall on a cool, shady site.

Plants & Projects

A Goldflame honeysuckle (use 1 plant)
Cover the trellis with color and fragrance from spring through summer with this choice vine. Ruby red flower buds produce sweet-scented flowers that are pink outside, creamy white to yellow inside. The waxy blue-green leaves provide color through mild winters. See *Lonicera × heckrottii*, p. 189.

B Sweet box (use 7)
Small, sweetly scented, white flowers dot the shiny green foliage of this evergreen shrub in late winter. It will spread to form a solid carpet beneath the honeysuckle in about three years. See *Sarcococca hookeriana* 'Humilis', p. 195.

C Leatherleaf mahonia (use 1)
The upright, straight-stemmed form of this evergreen shrub is ideal for this space. Dark blue-green leaves set off the fragrant yellow flowers in late winter and early spring. Pretty sky blue berries ripen in summer and last through the winter. See *Mahonia bealei*, p. 190.

D 'Blue Wave' hydrangea (use 1)
A deciduous shrub with big, shiny green leaves and "lace-cap" summer flowers. Flowers will be pink or blue, depending on your soil. Plant about 50 grape hyacinth bulbs beneath it for spring color; fragrant purple flowers will bloom before the hydrangea leafs out. See *Hydrangea macrophylla*, p. 184.

E 'Antioch' hosta (use 3)
The green-and-white leaves of this tough perennial match the color, but contrast with the shape, of the nearby lilyturf. Lavender flowers are a bonus in midsummer. See *Hosta*, p. 184.

F 'Halcyon' hosta (use 5)
Forms broad clumps of distinctive foliage, powder blue in spring, darkening to blue-green in summer. Pale lavender flowers sway on slender stalks in midsummer. See *Hosta*, p. 184.

G 'Royal Standard' hosta (use 3)
This hosta forms large clumps of green leaves. Lilylike white flowers last for weeks in August and release a lovely sweet aroma on warm evenings. See *Hosta*, p. 184.

H 'Silvery Sunproof' lilyturf (use 15)
A perennial with green-and-white-striped leaves in grasslike clumps that make an attractive edging. Leaves are evergreen in mild winters. It has small purple flowers in late summer. See *Liriope muscari*, p. 189.

See p. 52 for the following:

I Trellis

J Mowing strip

Plant portraits

These perennials and shrubs fill a blank wall with handsome foliage and pretty flowers for months each year.

● = First design, pp. 52–53
▲ = Second design, p. 54

'Royal Standard' hosta (*Hosta*, p. 184) ▲

'Blue Wave' hydrangea (*Hydrangea macrophylla*, p. 184) ▲

'Royal Purple' smoke tree (*Cotinus coggygria*, p. 180) ●

Hollywood juniper (*Juniperus chinensis* 'Torulosa', p. 187) ●

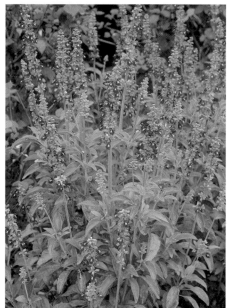

Mealy blue sage (*Salvia farinacea*, p. 194) ●

'Blaze' rose (*Rosa*, p. 194) ●

Sweet box (*Sarcococca hookeriana* 'Humilis', p. 195) ▲

A Shady Hideaway

Create a fragrant oasis in a corner of your backyard

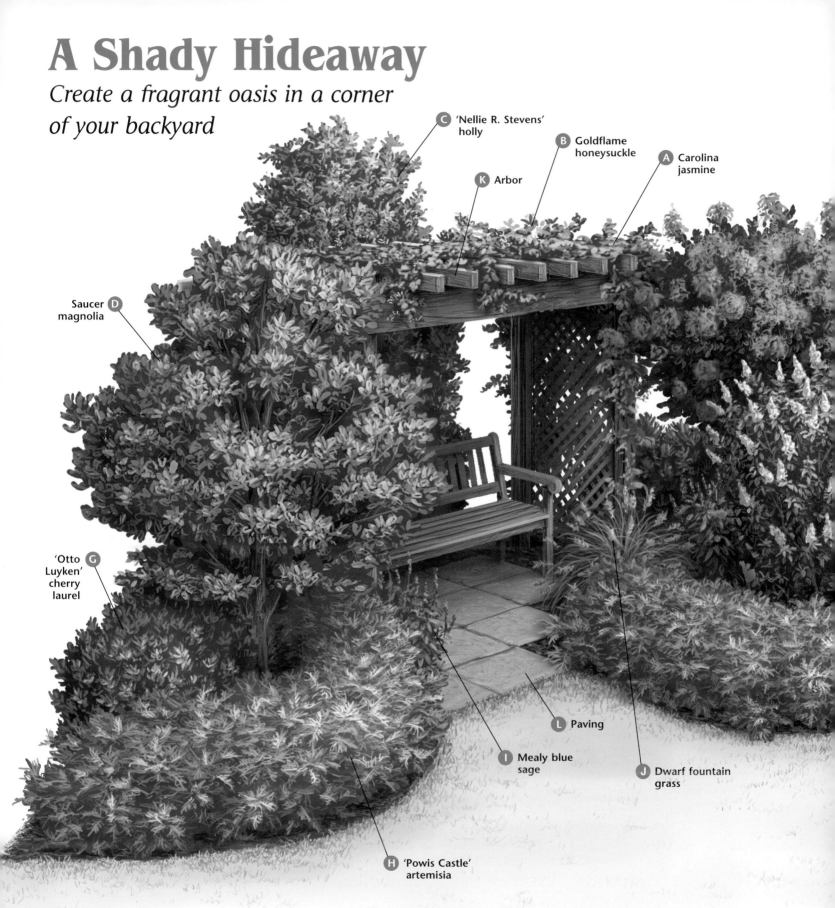

C 'Nellie R. Stevens' holly

B Goldflame honeysuckle

A Carolina jasmine

K Arbor

D Saucer magnolia

G 'Otto Luyken' cherry laurel

L Paving

I Mealy blue sage

J Dwarf fountain grass

H 'Powis Castle' artemisia

One of life's little pleasures is sitting in a shady spot reading a book or newspaper or just looking out onto your garden, relishing the fruit of your labors. If your property is long on lawn and short on shade, a bench under a leafy arbor can provide a cool respite from the heat or the cares of the day. Tucked into a corner of the property and set among attractive shrubs, vines, and perennials, the arbor shown here is a desirable destination even when the day isn't sizzling.

Carefully selected and placed plants create a cozy enclosure. In addition to the vines covering the arbor, evergreen shrubs behind and to each side of it afford year-round screening. Plantings in front of the arbor reinforce the seclusion but don't obscure your view of the rest of the property. As they mature, the magnolia and smoke tree will give the planting a "woodsier" feel.

Whether you're strolling around the planting or relaxing beneath the arbor, you can enjoy flowers and fragrance from spring through fall. Bloom begins early with the magnolia and Carolina jasmine; cherry laurels soon add their heady fragrance. Summer is full of flowers and the creatures attracted to them. Fragrant blossoms of honeysuckle and butterfly bush, the fluffy plumes of smoke tree, and the graceful spikes of mealy blue sage linger until the first hard frost in fall. Take a moment to savor the aromatic foliage of artemisia as you enter the arbor; this perennial stays fresh looking almost year-round.

Plants & Projects

The arbor, paving, and plants can be installed in a few weekends. Pruning is the main chore in this planting. You'll need to trim the bottom limbs from the magnolia and smoke tree. The vines and shrubs will need yearly pruning, mostly to control their size.

A **Carolina jasmine** (use 2 plants)
An evergreen twining vine with fragrant bell-shaped flowers in early spring and slender dark green leaves that turn maroon in winter. See *Gelsemium sempervirens*, p. 183.

B **Goldflame honeysuckle** (use 2)
A fast-growing vine providing summer color, fragrance, and shade. Blooms heavily in early summer, then off and on into fall. Its flowers are yellow on the inside, creamy pink on the outside. The handsome blue-green leaves shelter the arbor through the winter. See *Lonicera × heckrottii*, p. 189.

C **'Nellie R. Stevens' holly** (use 1)
This tough, fast-growing evergreen holly screens the back of the arbor. Heavy crops of dark red berries sparkle on the dark waxy leaves if there is a male Chinese holly nearby. See *Ilex*, Evergreen hollies, p. 186.

D **Saucer magnolia** (use 1)
This popular deciduous tree offers fine form, handsome gray bark, and large oblong leaves. Distinctive white, pink, or purple flowers appear in early spring. Remove the lower branches to accommodate the plants beneath. See *Magnolia × soulangiana*, p. 190.

E **'Royal Purple' smoke tree** (use 1)
Pruned to a tree form by removal of the lower branches, this deciduous shrub provides colorful leaves from spring through fall and fluffy pink flowers in summer and fall. See *Cotinus coggygria*, p. 180.

F **'White Profusion' butterfly bush** (use 1)
Arching branches of this deciduous shrub are tipped with fragrant white flowers from midsummer through fall. See *Buddleia davidii*, p. 176.

G **'Otto Luyken' cherry laurel** (use 6)
Glossy dark green leaves and a spreading habit make this a choice evergreen shrub to frame the arbor. Masses of fragrant white flower spikes make a session on the bench particularly enjoyable in late spring. See *Prunus laurocerasus*, p. 192.

H **'Powis Castle' artemisia** (use 7)
This perennial's mounds of aromatic lacy silver foliage set off the colors of the neighboring sage and cherry laurel. See *Artemisia*, p. 175.

I **Mealy blue sage** (use 12)
From early summer until frost, this perennial adds abundant color with spikes of blue flowers. Glossy green foliage makes attractive clumps. See *Salvia farinacea*, p. 194.

J **Dwarf fountain grass** (use 1)
In summer, arching green leaves and fluffy flower spikes bring a contrast in texture to the planting. In autumn and winter, this perennial grass is tan or gold; its dry leaves rustle musically next to the bench. See *Pennisetum alopecuroides* 'Hameln', p. 191.

K **Arbor**
This substantial structure can be built in a weekend. If you use cedar or cypress, you can let it weather to a handsome silver-gray color. See p. 145.

L **Paving**
Precast concrete pavers make an attractive, sturdy surface for the bench. Choose a color that will complement the flowers or foliage. See p. 118.

E 'Royal Purple' smoke tree

F 'White Profusion' butterfly bush

Property line

Lawn

1 square = 1 ft.

Site: Sunny

Season: Summer

Concept: Make your own shade with an arbor and handsome foliage and fragrant flowers to enjoy while you relax.

Plant portraits

These handsome plants will shelter you in the arbor and provide eye-catching flowers and foliage to enjoy while you're resting in the shade.

● = First design, pp. 56–57
▲ = Second design, pp. 58–59

Saucer magnolia
(*Magnolia* × *soulangiana*, p. 190) ●

'Nellie R. Stevens' holly
(*Ilex*, Evergreen hollies, p. 186) ●

Pink anemone clematis
(*Clematis montana* 'Rubens', p. 179) ▲

'Goldflame' spirea (*Spiraea japonica*, p. 195) ▲

Blue fescue grass
(*Festuca ovina* var. *glauca*, p. 182) ▲

Cleyera (*Ternstroemia gymnanthera*, p. 196) ▲

A cool spot for a hot site

If your site is hot and dry, the planting shown here is for you. Like the design on the previous pages, this one creates a cool, private retreat, but it does so with plants that tolerate heat and drought.

The planting produces flowers in abundance, but the foliage is perhaps even more compelling. The range of texture and color is outstanding—broad leaves, narrow leaves, plump and succulent, thin and flowing leaves in gold, bronze, maroon, blue, silver, and a range of greens. The honeysuckle has it all: evergreen leaves and lovely fragrant flowers. Enjoy the hummingbirds drawn to its flowers; then be serenaded by songbirds dining on the berries that follow.

Plants & Projects

Ⓐ Trumpet honeysuckle
(use 2 plants)
This vigorous evergreen vine produces trumpet-shaped coral, red, or yellow flowers for most of the summer. See *Lonicera sempervirens*, p. 189.

Ⓑ Pink anemone clematis (use 2)
Clouds of fragrant pink dogwoodlike flowers appear in profusion on this deciduous vine in spring. See *Clematis montana* 'Rubens', p. 179.

Ⓒ Cleyera (use 1)
Evergreen shrub with colorful leaves makes a year-round screen behind the arbor. Large red berries heighten fall and winter interest. See *Ternstroemia gymnanthera*, p. 196.

Ⓓ 'Goldflame' spirea (use 5)
Deciduous shrub with arching stems and bright gold foliage that turns red in fall; pale pink summer flowers. See *Spiraea japonica*, p. 195.

Arbor **L**

Bronze canna **G**

'Morning Light' Japanese silver grass **F**

B Pink anemone clematis

A Trumpet honeysuckle

See site plan for **C**.

'Moonshine' yarrow **I**

'Goldflame' spirea **D**

'Stella d'Oro' daylily **K**

'Autumn Joy' sedum **H**

Blue fescue grass **J**

'Crimson Pygmy' Japanese barberry **E**

E **'Crimson Pygmy' Japanese barberry** (use 7)
Low deciduous shrubs edge the front of the planting; maroon leaves turn crimson in fall. See *Berberis thunbergii*, p. 176.

F **'Morning Light' Japanese silver grass** (use 2)
A perennial forming large clumps of narrow, silvery green leaves that are topped from summer on through winter by fluffy seed heads. See *Miscanthus sinensis*, p. 190.

G **Bronze canna** (use 12)
A large perennial with lush bronze leaves and showy summer flowers in bright colors. See *Canna*, p. 178.

H **'Autumn Joy' sedum** (use 6)
The gray-green succulent foliage of this perennial is topped by flat flower clusters that mature from pale pink to rusty red during late summer to fall. See *Sedum*, p. 195.

I **'Moonshine' yarrow** (use 6)
Flat clusters of lemon yellow flowers bloom for weeks in summer atop this perennial. The lacy and aromatic gray-green foliage nicely sets off the colors of the nearby plants. See *Achillea*, p. 174.

J **Blue fescue grass** (use 3)
A perennial whose fine blue leaves form neat tufts that look great against the cannas and barberries. Foliage lasts through winter. See *Festuca ovina* var. *glauca*, p. 182.

K **'Stella d'Oro' daylily** (use 20)
This popular perennial edges the front of the planting with grassy light green foliage and cheerful golden yellow flowers from mid-June until fall. See *Hemerocallis*, p. 184.

See p. 57 for the following:

L Arbor

M Paving

Site: Sunny

Season: Early fall

Concept: A shady retreat made of attractive heat- and drought-tolerant plants.

Lawn

Property line

1 square = 1 ft.

A Shady Hideaway   59

Create a "Living" Room

A patio garden provides privacy and pleasure

A patio can become a true extension of your living space with the addition of plants to screen views and to create an attractive setting. In this design, plants and wooden screens at one end of the patio form a "wall" of three-dimensional and constantly changing floral motifs. The handsome brick floor accommodates a family barbecue or a large gathering. Together, plants and patio nicely commingle the "indoors" with the "outdoors."

Scale is particularly important when you're planting near the house. The small flowering cherry tree will grow large enough to cast welcome shade on the patio without overwhelming the house. The two staggered screen panels are large enough to block views from neighboring yards; covered with the evergreen foliage and lovely flowers of honeysuckle, they blend right into the planting. (Hummingbirds also love the honeysuckle's flowers, and songbirds like to dine on its large red berries.)

Evergreen shrubs are an attractive presence year-round and provide, along with the tree and vines, lovely flowers and fragrance from early spring to fall. Perennials add striking accents of flowers and foliage—flamboyant bronze cannas, colorful hostas, cheery daylilies, and aromatic geraniums with pretty pink flowers.

The design can be adapted to suit patios in a range of sizes. (The drawing extends into the foreground to indicate this possibility.) Just extend the planting of gardenias and pittosporums along the house and, if you like, repeat part or all of the large "wall" planting along the edge of the patio or at the other end.

Plants & Projects

The patio and fence are sizable projects, but their rewards are large, too. Check local codes before building the fence. You'll need to cut some bricks for the angled edges, but the interesting shape is worth it. Once established, the plants require little maintenance beyond seasonal cleanup and simple pruning to remove old, damaged, or diseased stems and to control size.

(A) Yoshino cherry (use 1 plant)
This lovely small deciduous tree brings shade to the patio. Fragrant pink or white flowers cluster along its bare branches in early spring; green leaves turn yellow in fall. See *Prunus × yedoensis*, p. 192.

(B) Trumpet honeysuckle (use 2)
This vigorous evergreen vine will quickly cover the screen panels with glossy blue-green leaves. Trumpet-shaped coral, red, or yellow flowers decorate the vine in early summer and appear off and on the rest of the season. See *Lonicera sempervirens*, p. 189.

(C) Heavenly bamboo (use 6)
A shrub with true four-season appeal. Its slender erect stems bear evergreen leaves that change color from gold to green to red with the seasons. In summer, clusters of white flowers produce red berries that last into winter. See *Nandina domestica*, p. 190.

(D) Dwarf pittosporum (use 7)
This evergreen shrub brings a lush, dressy look to the patio with its neat mounds of shiny dark green leaves. Creamy white flowers scent the air in early summer. See *Pittosporum tobira* 'Wheeleri', p. 191.

(E) 'Radicans' gardenia (use 9)
A dwarf form of the popular evergreen shrub beloved for the sweet, heavy scent of its creamy white flowers. Its low mounds of glossy dark green leaves spill onto the patio, and the flowers perfume the air for weeks in summer. See *Gardenia jasminoides*, p. 182.

(F) Bronze canna (use 8)
The large, lush purple-bronze leaves and showy red or orange flowers keep this popular heat-loving perennial colorful from early summer until fall. See *Canna*, p. 178.

(G) Daylily (use 18)
For an attractive edging of grassy light green foliage and cheerful summer flowers, this durable perennial can't be beat. Sizes vary and flower colors cover the spectrum; you can mix cultivars to extend bloom through most of the summer. See *Hemerocallis*, p. 184.

(H) 'Piedmont Gold' hosta (use 3)
Brighten the shady spot beneath the cherry tree with this perennial's large, golden yellow, heart-shaped leaves. Forms a big clump of foliage, topped with white flowers for a few weeks in mid- to late summer. See *Hosta*, p. 184.

(I) Bigroot geranium (use 9)
Mounds of this perennial's deeply lobed, aromatic leaves edge the patio year-round. (It may die back in cold winters.) It bears pink flowers in late spring; leaves turn red to purple in winter. See *Geranium macrorrhizum*, p. 183.

(J) Patio
Brick pavers edged with 4x4 landscape timbers make a handsome durable patio that goes with almost any architectural style. See p. 124.

(K) Screens
These tall panels provide privacy, while gaps between the boards allow air to circulate among the plants. See p. 146.

Yoshino cherry **(A)**

Trumpet honeysuckle **(B)**

Screen **(K)**

'Piedmont Gold' hosta **(H)**

Heavenly bamboo **(C)**

Daylily **(G)**

House

E   D

K   F

G

B

G

C   C

I

F   K

J

B   A

H   E

C

D

G

Lawn

1 square = 1 ft.

Site: Sunny

Season: Early summer

Concept: Planting provides privacy and colorful, fragrant ambiance on the patio.

F Bronze canna

I Bigroot geranium

'Radicans' E gardenia

Dwarf D pittosporum

Dwarf D pittosporum

'Radicans' E gardenia

Patio J

Plant portraits

This fine selection of woody plants and perennials lends privacy, color, and fragrance to your patio.

● = First design, pp. 60–61
▲ = Second design, pp. 62–63

Yoshino cherry (*Prunus × yedoensis*, p. 192) ●

Florida leucothoe (*Leucothoe populifolia*, p. 188) ▲

Bronze canna
(*Canna*, p. 178) ●

Bigroot geranium
(*Geranium macrorrhizum*, p. 183) ●

'Radicans' gardenia
(*Gardenia jasminoides*, p. 182) ●

Private patio in the shade

If your patio is already blessed with a cool canopy of shade, perhaps from a large tree nearby, consider this planting. The basic design is the same as on the previous pages, but here a garden of shade-loving shrubs and a small understory tree afford screening and ambiance for those on the patio.

The light and airy dogwood is unsurpassed for a patio accent in a shady setting. The deciduous oakleaf hydrangea performs all year round, as do the evergreen shrubs and ground covers that complete the planting. Together they provide a pleasing range of leaf textures and colors. In spring, the planting bursts with flowers in pink and white that delight the eye and freshen the air on the patio with delicious scent.

Plants & Projects

Ⓐ **Dogwood** (use 1 plant)
A popular native, this small deciduous tree produces clouds of white or pink flowers in spring and dark green foliage that turns red in fall, when it is joined by a crop of red berries. See *Cornus florida*, p. 180.

Ⓑ **'Roseum Elegans' rhododendron** (use 4)
Tall enough to serve as a privacy screen for the patio, this evergreen shrub is a stately presence with glossy leaves and pink flowers in late spring. See *Rhododendron*, p. 192.

Ⓒ **Oakleaf hydrangea** (use 1)
An all-season performer, this deciduous shrub offers white flowers in late spring, colorful foliage in fall, and pretty peeling bark in winter. It grows large enough to help screen the patio in summer. See *Hydrangea quercifolia*, p. 185.

See site plan for **G**.

Dogwood **A**

B 'Roseum Elegans' rhododendron

Oakleaf hydrangea **C**

Drooping leucothoe **E**

Gumpo azalea **F**

Florida leucothoe **D**

Gumpo azalea **F**

Drooping leucothoe **E**

Door   House

D   **B**   **G**   **D**   **F**   **A**   **B**   **C**   **E**

F   **E**

H

Lawn

1 square = 1 ft.

Site: Shady

Season: Spring

Concept: A year-round planting screens and enhances a shady patio.

D **Florida leucothoe** (use 4)
One of the best evergreen shrubs for shade, with arching stems of willowy light green leaves that look good with the nearby rhododendrons. In spring, its bell-shaped white flowers waft a honey fragrance over the patio. This is a vigorous plant; an annual pruning will keep it in bounds. See *Leucothoe populifolia*, p. 188.

E **Drooping leucothoe** (use 8)
A lower-growing, spreading cousin of Florida leucothoe, with fragrant white flowers in spring and mounding dark green foliage that turns purplish in winter. See *Leucothoe fontanesiana*, p. 188.

F **Gumpo azalea** (use 7)
The small evergreen leaves give this low, spreading shrub a fine texture. Clusters of frilly pink mor white flowers cover the foliage in late spring. See *Rhododendron*, p. 192.

G **Ground cover** (use 1 per sq. ft.)
When the plants are young, fill bare ground in the bed with evergreen ground covers such as vinca (*Vinca minor*, p. 197) or creeping phlox (*Phlox stolonifera*, p. 191). As the other plants grow to the sizes shown above, the shade will diminish or kill the ground covers.

See p. 60 for the following:

H Patio

Create a "Living" Room   63

Splash Out
Make a handsome water garden in a few weekends

A water garden adds a new dimension to a landscape. It can be the eye-catching focal point of the entire property, a center of outdoor entertainment, or a quiet out-of-the-way retreat. A pond can be a hub of activity—a place to garden, watch birds and wildlife, raise ornamental fish, or stage an impromptu paper-boat race. It just as easily affords an opportunity for some therapeutic inactivity; a few minutes contemplating the ripples on the water's surface provides a welcome break in a busy day.

A pond can't be easily moved, so choose your site carefully. Practical considerations are outlined on pp. 126–129 (along with instructions on installation); think about those first. Then consider how the pond and its plantings relate to the surroundings. Before plopping a pond down in the middle of the backyard, imagine how you might integrate it, visually if not physically, with nearby plantings and structures.

The plantings in this design are intended to settle the pond comfortably into an expanse of lawn. The soil excavated during construction of the pond forms a mound along one side, a subtle change of elevation that adds a surprising amount of interest to a flat site. Seen from a distance, the trees, shrubs, ornamental grasses, and perennials that frame the pond resemble an island bed. Viewed from a comfortable seat at water's edge, however, the mound and plantings provide enclosure, privacy, and a sense of being on the island looking at its flora and fauna.

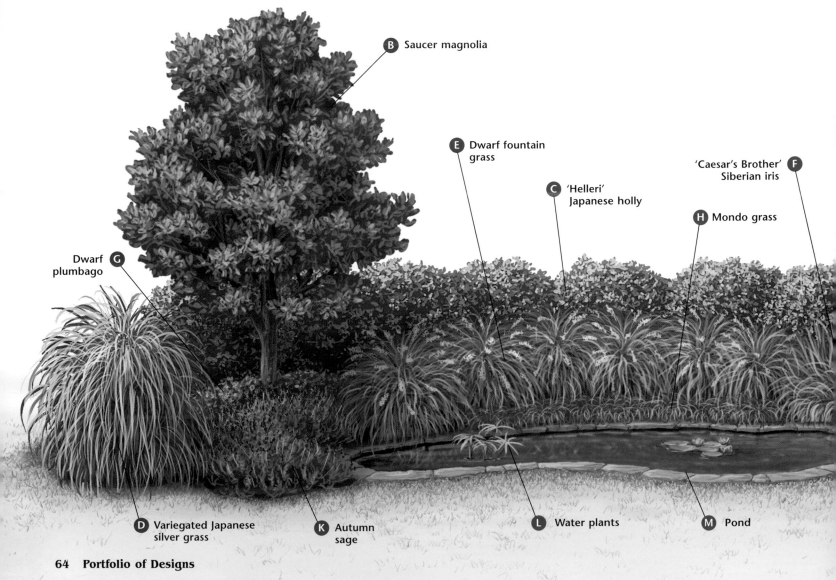

B Saucer magnolia

E Dwarf fountain grass

'Caesar's Brother' Siberian iris F

C 'Helleri' Japanese holly

H Mondo grass

Dwarf plumbago G

D Variegated Japanese silver grass

K Autumn sage

L Water plants

M Pond

Plants & Projects

Once established, the plants take pretty good care of themselves. The pond, however, requires more attention to keep a healthy balance of water plants and fish (if you have them) in order to maintain oxygen levels and to keep algae in check. Consult local or mail-order suppliers to help you get the right mix.

A Japanese maple (use 1 plant)
A small deciduous tree with lovely form and finely cut leaves. Choose a cultivar that has red leaves in summer. See *Acer palmatum*, p. 174.

B Saucer magnolia (use 1)
A deciduous tree prized for its large velvety leaves, handsome gray bark, and (of course) the large showy white, pink, or purple flowers it bears in early spring. See *Magnolia × soulangiana*, p. 190.

C 'Helleri' Japanese holly (use 9)
Planted on the back slope of the soil mound, this compact evergreen shrub makes a fine informal hedge. See *Ilex*, Evergreen hollies: *I. crenata*, p. 186.

D Variegated Japanese silver grass (use 1)
This perennial grass forms a graceful arching mound of green-and-white-striped leaves. Tall fluffy seed heads and tawny foliage are eye-catching all winter. See *Miscanthus sinensis* 'Variegatus', p. 190.

E Dwarf fountain grass (use 6)
Broad mounds of grassy leaves echo the larger holly hedge behind this perennial. Its green leaves and flower spikes are gold and tan through the winter. See *Pennisetum alopecuroides* 'Hameln', p. 191.

F 'Caesar's Brother' Siberian iris (use 3)
A perennial with striking blue-purple flowers in late spring and good-looking slender green leaves the rest of the season. See *Iris sibirica*, p. 187.

G Dwarf plumbago (use 12)
A perennial ground cover with small indigo blue flowers in summer and fall and smooth dark green leaves that turn maroon in fall. See *Ceratostigma plumbaginoides*, p. 178.

H Mondo grass (use 12)
The grassy leaves of this evergreen perennial ground cover edge the pond with dark green through all four seasons. See *Ophiopogon japonicus*, p. 190.

I 'Ebony Knight' black mondo grass (use 20)
The slender purple-black foliage of this evergreen perennial carpets the ground beneath the maple in striking contrast to the adjacent green-and-gold moneywort. See *Ophiopogon planiscapus*, p. 190.

J Moneywort (use 15)
Fast-spreading perennial ground cover with bright green coin-shaped leaves and pretty yellow summer flowers. See *Lysimachia nummularia*, p. 190.

K Autumn sage (use 7)
Bushy perennial makes a bright red accent beside the pond all summer and fall. Glossy foliage can be evergreen in mild winters. See *Salvia greggii*, p. 194.

L Water plants (use 1 each)
Plant a dwarf water lily, a dwarf lotus, and a dwarf papyrus in pots; then set the pots in the pond. (See p. 129.) Add some oxygenating plants to keep the water clear and to sustain fish. See Water plants, p. 197.

M Pond
Installing a pond is arduous but simple work, requiring a weekend or two of energetic digging and a commercially available pond liner. Fieldstone disguises the liner edge and lends a natural look to the pond. See p. 126.

A Japanese maple

I 'Ebony Knight' black mondo grass

J Moneywort

1 square = 1 ft.

Lawn

Fieldstones

Site: Sunny

Season: Summer

Concept: A landscape focal point, the pond nestles among trees, shrubs, and perennials and features attractive water plants.

Mini-pond

This little pond provides the pleasures of water gardening for those without the space or energy required to install and maintain a larger pond. Within its smaller confines you can enjoy one or more water plants as well as a few fish. You might install a small fountain or, as shown here, opt for a simple reflecting pool.

Pond and plantings can stand alone in an expanse of lawn, but they will look their best integrated into a larger scheme. For instance, the scale is just right for use as the focal point of a patio planting.

We've selected plants that dangle and droop, mound and arch to create contours similar to those in the previous design but on a more intimate scale. Their varied foliage and colorful flowers make an attractive display in all four seasons.

Plants & Projects

A **Pink Gumpo azalea** (use 7 plants)
Low, spreading shrubs make neat mounds of small evergreen leaves that are an excellent backdrop for a late-spring display of distinctive pink flowers. See *Rhododendron*, p. 192.

B **Germander** (use 3)
A perennial that forms a low mound of small shiny evergreen leaves. Bears tiny pink-purple flowers in late summer. See *Teucrium chamaedrys*, p. 196.

C **Northern sea oats** (use 1)
This perennial grass has wide green leaves topped from mid-summer by clusters of flat seed heads that droop gracefully beside the pool. Winter color is a lovely warm tan. See *Chasmanthium latifolium*, p. 179.

D **Hardy chrysanthemum** (use 3)
An heirloom perennial to brighten autumn days, forming a broad mound covered with small blossoms in late fall. Choose from cultivars with pink, white, or yellow flowers. See *Dendranthema*, p. 181.

E **'Moonbeam' coreopsis** (use 8)
A durable perennial with delicate-looking foliage and pale yellow flowers that bloom from June to September. See *Coreopsis verticillata*, p. 180.

F **Variegated Japanese sedge** (use 8)
Neat low tufts of grassy evergreen leaves, striped yellow and green, make this perennial grass ideal for a transition to adjacent lawn. See *Carex morrowii* 'Aureo-variegata', p. 178.

G **Creeping lilyturf** (use 9)
This perennial spreads quickly to form a flowing mat of grassy leaves that stay dark green all year. Bears small lavender flower spikes in summer. See *Liriope spicata*, p. 189.

H **Pond**
A small pond like this can be made with a molded fiberglass shell or plastic liner like the one in the previous design. Select edging stones in scale with the pond. See p. 126.

See p. 65 for the following:

I **Variegated Japanese silver grass** (use 1)

J **Dwarf plumbago** (use 12)

K **'Ebony Knight' black mondo grass** (use 5)

1 square = 1 ft.

Lawn

Site: Sunny

Season: Fall

Concept: A miniature pond is the focal point of a small-scale but varied planting.

'Moonbeam' coreopsis **E**

Northern sea oats **C**

Variegated Japanese silver grass **I**

Pink Gumpo azalea **A**

Hardy chrysanthemum **D**

Dwarf plumbago **J**

Variegated Japanese sedge **F**

'Ebony Knight' black mondo grass **K**

Pond **H**

Creeping lilyturf **G**

Germander **B**

Plant portraits

Whether growing in the water or nearby, these plants combine fresh foliage and lovely flowers for your poolside pleasure.

● = First design, pp. 64–65
▲ = Second design, p. 66

Water plants
(*Nymphaea* 'Perry's Fire Opal' shown; p. 197) ●

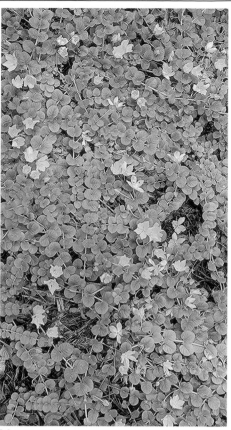

Moneywort
(*Lysimachia nummularia*, p. 190) ●

Dwarf plumbago
(*Ceratostigma plumbaginoides*, p. 178) ● ▲

Variegated Japanese silver grass
(*Miscanthus sinensis* 'Variegatus', p. 190) ● ▲

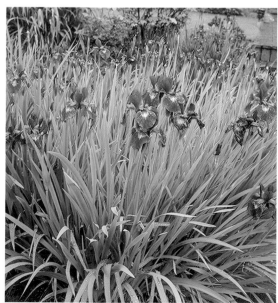

'Caesar's Brother' Siberian iris
(*Iris sibirica*, p. 187) ●

Hardy chrysanthemum
(*Dendranthema* 'Sheffield', p. 181) ▲

Mondo grass
(*Ophiopogon japonicus*, p. 190) ●

Garden in the Round
Create a planting with several attractive faces

Saucer magnolia Ⓐ

'Halcyon' hosta Ⓑ

Plantings in domestic landscapes are usually "attached" to something. Beds and borders hew to property lines, walls, or patios; foundation plantings skirt the house, garage, or deck. Most are meant to be viewed from the front, rather like a wall-mounted sculpture in raised relief.

On the other hand, the planting shown here is only loosely moored to the property line, forming a peninsula jutting into the lawn. It is an excellent option for those who want to squeeze more gardening space from a small lot, add interest to a rectangular one, or divide a large area into smaller "outdoor rooms." Because you can walk around most of the bed, plants can be displayed "in the round," presenting different scenes from several vantage points.

Without a strong connection to a structure or other landscape feature, a bed like this (or its close cousin, the island bed, which floats free of any anchors) requires an active sensitivity to scale. To be successful, the bed must neither dominate its surroundings nor be lost in them. The combination of large and small, subtle and bold plants in this planting is attractive when viewed up close or from a distance, and there's always something to admire as you stroll by.

Spring is the most colorful season, with lots of lovely flowers and fresh new foliage. But evergreen shrubs, summer-flowering perennials, handsome fall foliage, and eye-catching winter berries provide interest through the rest of the year.

Plants & Projects

If you want more flowers, it's easy to add them to this planting. For spring bloom, plant small bulbs in any open space beneath the wax myrtles and daffodils among the perennials. Follow the bulbs with annual impatiens beneath the wax myrtles. You can also substitute annuals for some of the heavenly bamboo along the edge of the bed. Plant pansies in the fall for a winter show and sun-loving annuals in the spring for summer display.

Ⓐ **Saucer magnolia** (use 1 plant)
A classic small deciduous tree, it offers large showy white, pink, or purple flowers in early spring. Large leaves, attractive bark, and pleasing form round out the year. Trim off the lower limbs to accommodate plants below. See *Magnolia × soulangiana*, p. 190.

Ⓑ **'Halcyon' hosta** (use 12)
A shade-loving perennial, it forms a pool of colorful leaves beneath the magnolia, powder blue in spring, darkening to blue-green in summer. See *Hosta*, p. 184.

Ⓒ **'Harbour Dwarf' heavenly bamboo** (use 15)
A small shrub whose evergreen leaves change from gold to green to red from spring to winter. It forms a compact mound and rarely needs pruning. See *Nandina domestica*, p. 190.

Ⓓ **Wax myrtle** (use 2)
Sizable evergreen shrubs with slender stems and glossy leaves provide year-round privacy along the property line. Female plants bear clusters of gray berries in fall and winter. See *Myrica cerifera*, p. 190.

Ⓔ **Lenten rose** (use 7)
Some of the very first flowers to appear in early spring are this evergreen perennial's nodding, cup-shaped blooms in pink, rose, white, or greenish shades. The large lobed leaves complement the slender foliage of the wax myrtles. See *Helleborus orientalis*, p. 183.

Ⓕ **Creeping phlox** (use 17)
A perennial ground cover with fragrant flowers in spring and evergreen foliage. It will spread among the Lenten rose in front of the wax myrtles. See *Phlox stolonifera*, p. 191.

Ⓖ **Bengal tiger canna** (use 3)
A striking perennial with a lush tropical look. Large yellow-and-green-striped leaves and eye-catching orange flowers from early summer to fall. See *Canna* 'Pretoria', p. 178.

Ⓗ **'Caesar's Brother' Siberian iris** (use 3)
The erect grassy leaves of this perennial contrast with the rounded forms of spirea and pincushion flower. Bears elegant deep purple flowers in late spring. See *Iris sibirica*, p. 187.

Ⓘ **'Snowmound' spirea** (use 1)
A deciduous shrub that is aptly named for its look in spring when covered with clusters of pure white flowers. Its neat mound of arching stems and dark blue-green foliage is attractive the rest of the season. See *Spiraea nipponica*, p. 196.

Ⓙ **Double Japanese aster** (use 7)
This easy perennial forms an upright clump of small leaves and produces numerous, tiny, white double flowers with yellow centers in summer and again (if cut back) in fall. See *Kalimeris pinnatifida*, p. 188.

Ⓚ **'Butterfly Blue' pincushion flower** (use 7)
For months of misty blue color (and lots of butterflies) in the middle of the bed, you can't beat this little perennial. Round flowers on wiry stems appear in late winter and go right on until frost if you keep picking off spent blossoms. See *Scabiosa columbaria*, p. 195.

See site plan for **J** **K** .

Bengal tiger canna **G**

'Caesar's Brother' Siberian iris **H**

D Wax myrtle

I 'Snowmound' spirea

C 'Harbour Dwarf' heavenly bamboo

F Creeping phlox

E Lenten rose

Site: Sunny

Season: Late spring

Concept: Mix of perennials and woody plants looks good from several vantage points, at a distance, or as you stroll close by.

Property line

Lawn

1 square = 1 ft.

Favoring fall

This planting is designed to lift your spirits after a long summer. Butterfly bush, veronica, verbena, and chrysanthemum will all be blooming then, in shades of blues, purples, pinks, and whites. The ornamental grass, sedum, and coneflowers add rich golds, tans, and bronzy hues to the autumn scene.

Other seasons aren't slighted here. The pink dogwood will be the focal point of the spring garden, joined by a carpet of purple ajuga and white candytuft. There are plenty of flowers during the summer; several attract clouds of butterflies as a bonus. Colorful dried foliage and seed heads complement evergreen foliage in winter.

Property line

Lawn

1 square = 1 ft.

Site: Sunny

Season: Fall

Concept: At its height of bloom in fall, this island bed saves the best for last.

Plants & Projects

A Dogwood (use 1 plant)
A small deciduous tree offering spring flowers, light green foliage that turns crimson in fall, and bright red berries in autumn. Buy a pink-flowered cultivar. See *Cornus florida*, p. 180.

B 'Burgundy Glow' ajuga (use 25)
A perennial ground cover with foliage mixing shades of purple, green, and white. Spikes of blue flowers add color beneath the dogwood in spring. See *Ajuga reptans*, p. 175.

C 'Yoshino' Japanese cedar (use 1)
The fine-textured foliage of this handsome, fast-growing evergreen tree is bright green in summer, bronzy in winter. See *Cryptomeria japonica*, p. 181.

D 'White Profusion' butterfly bush (use 1)
The arching branches of this deciduous shrub carry long clusters of fragrant white flow-

See site plan for **E**.

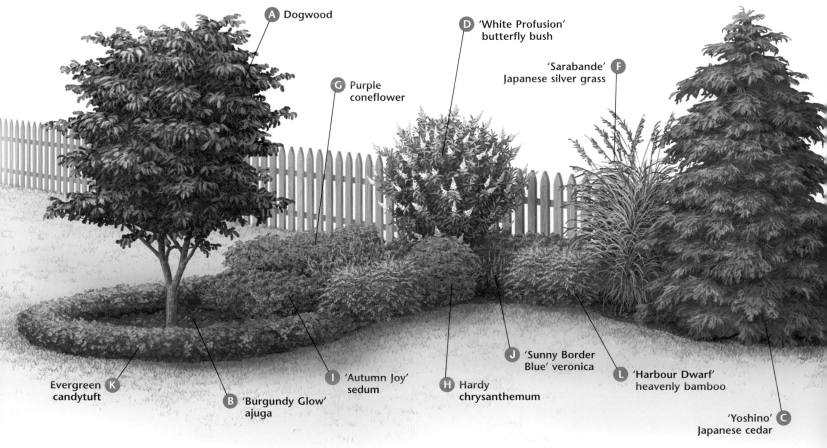

A Dogwood

D 'White Profusion' butterfly bush

F 'Sarabande' Japanese silver grass

G Purple coneflower

J 'Sunny Border Blue' veronica

L 'Harbour Dwarf' heavenly bamboo

I 'Autumn Joy' sedum

H Hardy chrysanthemum

K Evergreen candytuft

B 'Burgundy Glow' ajuga

C 'Yoshino' Japanese cedar

ers at their tips. It blooms in summer and fall, providing a focal point for the bed and nectar for butterflies. See *Buddleia davidii*, p. 176.

E **'Homestead Purple' verbena** (use 6)
A low-growing and spreading perennial with evergreen foliage. Blooms steadily from summer until late fall, bearing round clusters of rosy purple flowers that look lovely beneath the white butterfly bush. See *Verbena canadensis*, p. 196.

F **'Sarabande' Japanese silver grass** (use 1)
An elegant perennial grass with arching white-striped leaves and tall plumes of flowers that appear in late summer and look good through the winter. See *Miscanthus sinensis*, p. 190.

G **Purple coneflower** (use 5)
A durable prairie perennial that bears dark pink daisylike flowers with dark centers above a mound of dark foliage. Blooms in summer; dried seed heads last through the winter. See *Echinacea purpurea*, p. 181.

H **Hardy chrysanthemum** (use 4)
A much-loved perennial, its broad mound of aromatic foliage is covered with small, clear pink or white blossoms in fall. See *Dendranthema*, p. 181.

I **'Autumn Joy' sedum** (use 8)
Flat-topped pale pink flower clusters appear above this perennial's fleshy foliage in August. They mature to dark pink and are attractive through the winter. See *Sedum*, p. 195.

J **'Sunny Border Blue' veronica** (use 5)
The lustrous green, crinkled leaves of this perennial are topped with bright blue flower spikes from early summer to frost if you clip off spent flowers. See *Veronica*, p. 196.

K **Evergreen candytuft** (use 11)
An evergreen perennial with a loose rounded form. It is covered with bright white flowers in spring and may bear some scattered blooms in fall. See *Iberis sempervirens*, p. 186.

See p. 68 for the following:

L **'Harbour Dwarf' heavenly bamboo** (use 5)

Plant portraits

These lovely plants make an island visit a pleasure any time of year, and they cruise through the seasons without demanding much care.

● = First design, pp. 68–69
▲ = Second design, pp. 70–71

'Harbour Dwarf' heavenly bamboo (*Nandina domestica*, p. 190) ● ▲

Bengal tiger canna (*Canna* 'Pretoria', p. 178) ●

'Butterfly Blue' pincushion flower (*Scabiosa columbaria*, p. 195) ●

Double Japanese aster (*Kalimeris pinnatifida*, p. 188) ●

'White Profusion' butterfly bush (*Buddleia davidii*, p. 176) ▲

Creeping phlox (*Phlox stolonifera*, p. 191) ●

A Beginning Border

Flowers and a fence make a traditional design

'Arp' rosemary **C**

Bengal tiger canna **F**

'Homestead Purple' verbena **J**

A mixed border can be one of the most delightful of all gardens. Indeed, that's usually its sole purpose. Unlike many other types of landscape plantings, a traditional border is seldom yoked to any function beyond that of providing as much pleasure as possible. From the first neat mounds of foliage in the spring to the fullness of summer bloom and autumn color, the mix of flowers, foliage, textures, tones, and hues brings enjoyment.

This border is designed for a beginning or busy gardener, using durable plants that are easy to establish and care for. Behind the planting, screening out distraction, is a simple fence. The border is meant to be viewed from the front, so tall plants go at the back. The arrangement is symmetrical but not repetitive; the plants on each side of the centerline are different but of similar size and shape.

The plants here provide three seasons of staggered bloom and attractive foliage to carry interest through the winter months. Spring highlights include striking purple and yellow flowers of verbena and daylily and elegant white irises. During the long months of summer and fall, butterflies flit among the blue flowers on the butterfly bush and pincushion flower, and stately lilies join raucous coneflowers and daisies. Winter offers evergreen foliage of rosemary and Shasta daisy and the silvers and golds of the butterfly bush and flowing grass.

Plants & Projects

The plants chosen here all perform admirably in the high heat and humidity of the region, conditions that can pose problems for many traditional border plants. Removing spent flowers and seasonal pruning (cutting stems to the ground) are the main chores. Don't cut back the grass until spring, or you'll miss its buff and brown winter hues. And be sure to mark where the lilies are planted with labels, so you won't damage them in spring cleanup. Place a few steppingstones in the bed for easy access. For a larger border, just plant more of each plant to fit the space, or repeat parts of the design.

A **Evergreen clematis**
(use 1 plant)
Clambering along the top of the fence, the glossy leaves of this evergreen vine create a shimmering backdrop. Large white flowers add fragrance in spring. Stretch thin wires between eyebolts fixed to the fence to help the vine climb. See *Clematis armandii*, p. 179.

B **'Nanho Blue' butterfly bush**
(use 1)
A fine focal point, with arching branches tipped with long trusses of fragrant blue flowers from midsummer until fall. Underplant with daffodils and evergreen ajuga for additional color from spring through winter. See *Buddleia davidii*, p. 176.

C **'Arp' rosemary** (use 1)
A small, bushy evergreen shrub whose needlelike silver-green leaves have a delicious aroma and taste. Tiny blue flowers appear in late winter and last through spring. See *Rosmarinus officinalis*, p. 194.

D **'Morning Light' Japanese silver grass** (use 1)
Delicate white stripes on the narrow leaves of this perennial grass make it shimmer in the slightest breeze. Fluffy seed heads and tawny color look good in fall and winter. See *Miscanthus sinensis*, p. 190.

E **Oriental lilies** (use 2 clumps of 3 bulbs each)
In late summer these much-loved perennials will scent the entire border with the rich perfume of their large elegant flowers. Try one clump of 'Stargazer', with white-edged crimson blooms, and one of 'Casablanca', with pure white flowers. See *Lilium*, p. 188.

F **Bengal tiger canna** (use 3)
Stunning, large, yellow-and-green-striped leaves are eye-catching from spring through fall. Bears equally spectacular orange flowers in midsummer. See *Canna* 'Pretoria', p. 178.

G **'Coronation Gold' yarrow** (use 1)
This perennial's flat heads of bright yellow-gold flowers bloom for months atop gray-green ferny foliage. An attractive contrast to the nearby silver grass. See *Achillea*, p. 174.

H **'Becky' Shasta daisy** (use 3)
Big white daisies with yellow centers bloom all summer on this perennial's sturdy stalks. The foliage is dark green and shiny year-round. See *Chrysanthemum × superbum*, p. 179.

I **Purple coneflower** (use 3)
Mirroring the Shasta daisy, this perennial's daisylike flowers are dark with a dark center. Blooms in midsummer. See *Echinacea purpurea*, p. 181.

J **'Homestead Purple' verbena** (use 6)
This low-growing, evergreen, ground-cover perennial blooms steadily from late spring to frost if spent blossoms are removed. Its rosy purple flowers look lovely next to the white daisies. See *Verbena canadensis*, p. 196.

K **'White Swirl' Siberian iris** (use 1)
These rugged perennials form clumps of graceful grassy foliage at the front of the border, but the distinctive large white flowers are the main attraction. See *Iris sibirica*, p. 187.

N Fence

B 'Nanho Blue' butterfly bush

Oriental lilies **E**

D 'Morning Light' Japanese silver grass

A Evergreen clematis

G 'Coronation Gold' yarrow

M 'Butterfly Blue' pincushion flower

L 'Stella d'Oro' daylily

I Purple coneflower

K 'White Swirl' Siberian iris

H 'Becky' Shasta daisy

L **'Stella d'Oro' daylily** (use 3)
Fresh golden yellow flowers appear daily from late spring to frost on this remarkable perennial. The healthy grasslike foliage complements that of the iris. See *Hemerocallis*, p. 184.

M **'Butterfly Blue' pincushion flower** (use 6)
This perennial's tidy mounds of bright green foliage are covered with round blue flowers on wiry stems from late spring to frost (if you remove the spent flowers). Aptly named—butterflies like them. See *Scabiosa columbaria*, p. 195.

N **Fence**
Clean arching lines and decorative finials atop the posts transform this simple, 6-ft.-high fence into a worthy backdrop for a handsome planting. See p. 146.

Site: Sunny

Season: Summer

Concept: Even a novice can make a flower border flourish. A simple fence, carefree plants, and a ready-made design make this border both fetching and fail-safe.

1 square = 1 ft.

Lawn

Now, add annuals

Here we've altered the design on the previous pages to include a large planting of annuals. The Southeast region's long growing season and mild winters allow two completely different plantings of annuals a year. The cool-season planting is depicted in the rendering at right, shown in the spring after the old perennial foliage has been cut back in anticipation of new growth.

As the spring and summer progress, the perennials reappear and fill in the border (as shown in the site plan). The continual color provided by the flowers and foliage of the annuals fills any gaps in the sequence of perennial bloom during the summer and fall. And it enlivens the winter garden immeasurably.

Planted in November, the cool-season annuals (and the neighboring daffodils) produce attractive foliage and flowers through May. Then it's time to replace them with warm-season annuals, colorful heat lovers that perform until November, when the cycle begins again.

Plants & Projects

See site plan for **E** and **G** through **M**.

1 square = 1 ft.

A Annuals (use about 3 dozen plants)

Buy cool-season annuals in the fall. Check the labels and choose compact varieties that stay under 1 ft. tall. Space the plants about 1 ft. apart; they will soon grow together. The popular cool-season annuals shown here include dusty miller, with silver-gray foliage; pansies, with large blue flowers; dwarf snapdragons, with white flowers; Iceland poppies, with peachy pink flowers; and violas, with yellow flowers that resemble pansies flowers but are smaller. When the weather turns hot, replace the cool-season annuals with salvias, pentas, lantanas, gomphrenas, zinnias, or other hot-season annuals. Work some compost into the soil every time you replace the annual planting, and add fresh mulch, too. See Annuals, p. 175.

B Daffodils (use 12)

Daffodils add color to the back of the border in spring, when the butterfly bush has been cut short and the perennials in the border are still dormant. 'Ice Follies', shown here, has lovely large flowers that open pale yellow and turn creamy white. Substitute other daffodils or other spring bulbs if you prefer. See Bulbs: *Narcissus*, p. 176.

C Ajuga (use 1 per sq. ft.)

This low-growing perennial makes a good "filler" that spreads under and around other plants, offering bright blue flowers in spring and glossy evergreen foliage. 'Catlin's Giant' is a vigorous, fast-growing cultivar with large purple-bronze leaves. See *Ajuga reptans*, p. 175.

See p. 72 for the following:

D Evergreen clematis (use 1)

E 'Nanho Blue' butterfly bush (use 1)

F 'Arp' rosemary (use 1)

G 'Morning Light' Japanese silver grass (use 1)

D Evergreen clematis

N Purple coneflower

A Dwarf snapdragons

Site: Sunny

Season: Spring

Concept: Mixing perennials and annuals makes a border even more colorful and interesting all year.

H Oriental lilies (use 2 groups of 3 bulbs each)

I Bengal tiger canna (use 3)

J 'Coronation Gold' yarrow (use 1)

K 'Becky' Shasta daisy (use 2)

L 'White Swirl' Siberian iris (use 3)

M 'Stella d'Oro' daylily (use 3)

N Purple coneflower (use 2)

O Fence

Plant portraits

Whether you are a beginning gardener or an old hand, you'll appreciate the lovely foliage and masses of bloom these plants provide.

● = First design, pp. 72–73
▲ = Second design, pp. 74–75

'Arp' rosemary (*Rosmarinus officinalis*, p. 194) ● ▲

'Stella d'Oro' daylily
(*Hemerocallis*, p. 184) ● ▲

Oriental lilies (*Lilium*, p. 188) ● ▲

'Morning Light' Japanese silver grass (*Miscanthus sinensis*, p. 190)
● ▲

Evergreen clematis
(*Clematis armandii*, p. 179) ● ▲

'Coronation Gold' yarrow
(*Achillea*, p. 174) ● ▲

Back to Nature

Create a wooded retreat in your backyard

The open spaces and squared-up property lines in many new developments (and some old neighborhoods as well) can make a homeowner long for the seclusion of a wooded landscape. It may come as a surprise that you can create just such a retreat on a property of even modest size. With a relatively small number of carefully placed trees and shrubs, you can have your own backyard nature park.

Trees and shrubs take time to reach the sizable proportions we associate with a woodland. The plants in this design were chosen in part because they make an attractive setting in their early years, too. Here we show the young planting a few years after installation. On the following pages you'll see the planting as it appears at maturity.

The grassy peninsula extending into the planting is an open "room" in the early years, with the juvenile trees and shrubs functioning as a large mixed border. While the woody plants are small, a selection of durable perennials and wildflowers provides a focal point for the planting. Arrayed along the front of the bed, colorful perennials enliven the summer months. Two low-growing native wildflowers, both self-seeding annuals, carpet the ground between the small trees and shrubs.

Property line

Lawn

1 square = 2 ft.

Loblolly pine **F**

'Black Knight' **K**
butterfly bush

Oakleaf **I**
hydrangea

E Annual
wildflowers

I Oakleaf
hydrangea

B 'Goldsturm'
coneflower

Plants & Projects

Although this is a large planting, you can install it in several weekends. The biggest job is tilling and amending the soil of the entire area for planting; the healthy vigorous growth of the plants will repay the effort. Annual maintenance includes pruning away dead or damaged branches of the trees and shrubs and cleaning up the spent flowers and foliage of the perennials and wildflowers in spring and fall.

While the young trees and shrubs are growing, the plants described here will provide their full range of attractions in just a few years. You can arrange the perennials as shown here or intermix them, using a few plants of each perennial in each of the three areas. Include some daylilies, scarlet sage, or Siberian iris if you want more variety. Space any of these perennials about 2 ft. apart.

Ⓐ Blazing star (use 8 plants)
Spikes of small purple flowers rise on tall leafy stalks above a small mound of stiff grassy foliage in midsummer. Flowers attract butterflies and look good in dried arrangements. There are white-flowered cultivars, too; combine white with purple if you choose. See *Liatris spicata*, p. 188.

Ⓑ 'Goldsturm' coneflower (use 8)
Bears dozens of large, golden yellow, "black-eyed Susans" in late summer. Let the seeds ripen to feed the birds in winter. It forms a large mound of rich green foliage that is attractive all season. See *Rudbeckia fulgida*, p. 194.

Ⓒ Northern sea oats (use 5)
A clump-forming ornamental grass with wide, light green leaves and, from midsummer on, interesting seed heads that dance in the wind. Cut the foliage back in spring so you can enjoy its lovely russet or tan color in winter. See *Chasmanthium latifolium*, p. 179.

Ⓓ Purple coneflower (use 5)
This prairie perennial produces an irregular mound of coarse dark green leaves topped by stiff branching flower stalks that carry large pink daisylike flowers with dark centers in midsummer. There are white-flowered cultivars too, and both pink and white would look good here. Leave some seed heads for winter interest and the finches they attract. See *Echinacea purpurea*, p. 181.

Ⓔ Annual wildflowers (sow seeds)
You can use native wildflowers to form a low ground cover under trees and shrubs. Annual phlox (*Phlox drummondii*), with pink, red, or white flowers, and Indian blanket (*Gaillardia pulchella*), with red-and-yellow flowers, are shown here. Both grow less than 1 ft. tall, so they won't shade or compete with the young shrubs. Both bloom from early summer through most of the season, attracting butterflies. These plants bear seeds and die in the fall; new seedlings will sprout the next spring. See Annuals, p. 175.

See p. 79 for the following:

Ⓕ Loblolly pine (use 3)
Ⓖ Burford holly (use 6)
Ⓗ Winterberry holly (use 3)
Ⓘ Oakleaf hydrangea (use 5)
Ⓙ Chokeberry (use 6)
Ⓚ 'Black Knight' butterfly bush (use 6)

Site: Sunny

Season: Summer

Concept: Mixed planting across the back of a lot attracts birds and wildlife. Shown here just a few years after installation.

Ⓙ Chokeberry
Ⓖ Burford holly
Ⓗ Winterberry holly
Ⓕ Loblolly pine
Ⓙ Chokeberry
Ⓒ Northern sea oats
Purple coneflower Ⓓ
'Black Knight' butterfly bush Ⓚ
Blazing star Ⓐ
Oakleaf hydrangea Ⓘ
Annual wildflowers Ⓔ

Plant portraits

These plants provide privacy, shade, and color for you and habitat to entice birds and other wildlife.

● = Young planting, pp. 76–77
▲ = Older planting, pp. 78–79

Chokeberry (*Aronia arbutifolia*, p. 175) ● ▲

Loblolly pine (*Pinus taeda*, p. 191) ● ▲

Burford holly (*Ilex*, Evergreen hollies: *I. cornuta* 'Burfordii', p. 186) ● ▲

Winterberry holly (*Ilex verticillata*, p. 187) ● ▲

Northern sea oats (*Chasmanthium latifolium*, p. 179) ● ▲

The mature woodland

Change and growth are the essence of living things, but when plants are small, it's not easy to imagine what they'll look like in about 15 years. So we've done it for you.

The grassy peninsula is now a small woodland meadow framed by sturdy trees rising up to 30 ft. Beneath them, shrubs that once seemed to stand too far apart create leafy masses 6 to 8 ft. tall, providing the sense of enclosure and privacy you longed for. Birds and small wildlife abound.

Along the sunny edge of the planting, the perennials continue to provide their colorful summer display. Where sun penetrates between the shrubs, the same native annuals cover the ground; in shadier spots they've been replaced by vinca or other low-growing, shade-tolerant ground covers.

Site: Sunny

Season: Fall

Concept: After about 15 years, the planting is a private shady woodland retreat.

Plants & Projects

Ⓐ Loblolly pine (use 3 plants)
This fast-growing evergreen tree is a regional favorite, ideal for this planting. Cone-shaped at first, it assumes a handsome open layered form. Trim off lower branches to accommodate shrubs below. See *Pinus taeda*, p. 191. Equally suitable here would be longleaf pine (*Pinus palustris*) or Eastern white pine (*Pinus strobus*), both discussed on p. 191.

Ⓑ Burford holly (use 6)
A large shrub or small tree, this evergreen forms a tall screen across the back corner of the yard. Its leathery, glossy green leaves make a great backdrop for the magnificent show of red berries. See *Ilex*, Evergreen hollies: *I. cornuta* 'Burfordii', p. 186. You could substitute 'Nellie R. Stevens' holly or American holly (*I. opaca*). See p. 186 for both.

Ⓒ Winterberry holly (use 3)
An abundance of bright red berries shine through the fall and winter days after this upright deciduous shrub drops its leaves. Dark green foliage turns yellow in fall. Plant one male cultivar as a pollinator to ensure a good berry crop. See *Ilex verticillata*, p. 187.

Ⓓ Oakleaf hydrangea (use 5)
This native deciduous shrub is eye-catching year-round. Clusters of papery flowers that appear in spring change color and last through fall. Dark green leaves turn red and purple in fall. Peeling bark in shades of cinnamon and rust ornament the winter scene. See *Hydrangea quercifolia*, p. 185.

Ⓔ Chokeberry (use 6)
Another four-season performer, this deciduous shrub offers shiny dark green leaves and small white flowers in spring, crimson foliage in fall, and a crop of small red berries all through the winter. A good companion for the hollies. See *Aronia arbutifolia*, p. 175.

Ⓕ 'Black Knight' butterfly bush (use 6)
Butterflies love this deciduous shrub, and you will, too. The arching branches carry long clusters of fragrant deep purple flowers from summer into fall. See *Buddleia davidii*, p. 176.

See p. 77 for the following:

Ⓖ Blazing star

Ⓗ 'Goldsturm' coneflower

Ⓘ Northern sea oats

Ⓙ Purple coneflower

Ⓚ Annual wildflowers

See site plan on p. 76 for Ⓚ.

Make a No-Mow Slope

A terraced planting transforms a steep site

A River birch

'Zabelliana' cherry laurel E

'Savannah' holly B

C Wax myrtle

G Daylily

D Forsythia

F Creeping willowleaf cotoneaster

H Retaining wall

Common features of houses like the one at left, steep slopes can be a landscape nightmare. They're a chore to mow, and they can present problems of erosion and maintenance if you try to establish other ground covers or plantings. One solution to this dilemma is shown here—tame the slope by building a low retaining wall and planting the area with interesting low-care trees, shrubs, and perennials.

Steep slopes near the foundation are typically found around houses with walk-out basements or lower-level garages. Here, the low wall creates two terraces that mirror the curve of the driveway. On the lower level,

shapely woody evergreens rise above a carpet of colorful daylilies. On the top level, massed ranks of deciduous and evergreen shrubs define the gentle curve of the remaining slope. Farther from the house an attractive tree punctuates the end of the wall. Low-growing shrubs spill down the hill, uniting the upper and lower planting terraces and marking the transition to the front lawn.

The planting provides good-looking flowers in spring and summer and handsome foliage, pretty berries, and striking bark in fall and winter. It is attractive whether viewed from above or below. Seen

from the sidewalk, it frames the house and directs attention to the front entrance. It also screens the semiprivate area of drive and garage from the more public entrance. As the large shrubs grow, they overlap, tying the planting together and creating horizontal layers that further reduce the visual impact of the once-dominant slope.

The planting can easily be altered to accommodate existing foundation plants along the facade of the house. Or you can extend it to create a new foundation planting by adding more cherry laurels and cotoneasters, with perhaps a wax myrtle or two where you need some height.

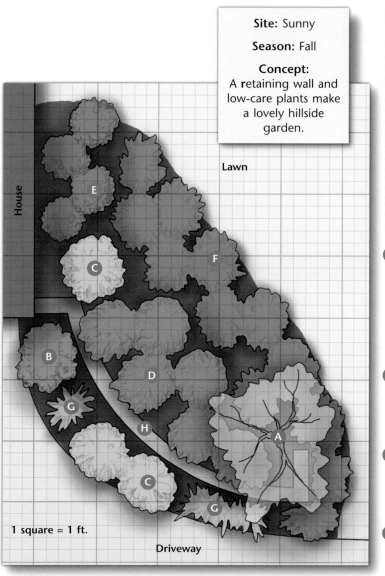

Site: Sunny

Season: Fall

Concept:
A retaining wall and low-care plants make a lovely hillside garden.

Lawn

House

1 square = 1 ft.

Driveway

Plants & Projects

Building the retaining wall, reshaping the slope, and preparing the planting beds is a big job—you might want to line up some energetic helpers or hire someone with a small earthmover like a Bobcat. Once that job is done and the plants are established, this design will provide years of enjoyment with a minimum of maintenance. If you'd like extra flowers, plant small bulbs (crocus, squill, grape hyacinth, small daffodils) in clumps of six or more, scattered among the shrubs.

A River birch (use 1 plant)
The multiple trunks of this fast-growing tree transform winter days with their exquisite bark, which peels back to reveal orange, tan, and creamy white layers. Medium green leaves cast a light summer shade. See *Betula nigra*, p. 176.

B 'Savannah' holly (use 1)
This pyramidal tree with shiny evergreen leaves and red berries makes a fine accent by the garage. See *Ilex*, Evergreen hollies: *I. × attenuata*, p. 186.

C Wax myrtle (use 3)
An evergreen shrub with aromatic leaves and a graceful form. Birds like the clusters of gray berries in fall and winter. See *Myrica cerifera*, p. 190.

D Forsythia (use 6)
With cheery yellow flowers in early spring, this deciduous

shrub covers lots of ground with its arching branches. Foliage is green in summer, purple in fall. See *Forsythia × intermedia*, p. 182.

E 'Zabelliana' cherry laurel (use 4)
Narrow, glossy dark green leaves and a spreading habit make this a choice evergreen shrub to dress up the foundation. In midspring it's covered with fragrant white flowers. See *Prunus laurocerasus*, p. 192.

F Creeping willowleaf cotoneaster (use 12)
This tough, low-growing evergreen shrub is an excellent ground cover for a slope—its stems root where they touch ground, holding the soil in place. Bears white flowers in spring, red berries in fall, and its shiny leaves turn purple in cold weather. See *Cotoneaster salicifolius* 'Repens', p. 180.

G Daylily (use about 3 dozen)
For an extended show of lovely lilylike flowers, combine early- and late-blooming cultivars of this useful perennial in your favorite colors. Its grassy foliage and cheerful blooms make a bright informal edging for the drive. See *Hemerocallis*, p. 184.

H Retaining wall
Using a precast concrete wall system, you can build a curved wall like the one shown here in a weekend. See p. 130.

Design for a shady slope

If your slope is shaded by the house or a large tree nearby, here's a design similar to that on the previous pages but with a selection of shade-tolerant trees, shrubs, and perennials.

Once again, evergreen and deciduous foliage gives the planting a year-round presence. But spring (shown here) is the prettiest season, beginning with dogwood blossoms and early bulbs. At the base of the wall, the delicate fiddleheads of the ferns emerge. Then all the shrubs chime in—papery white hydrangea blossoms, striking trusses of pink rhododendrons, and, right by the lawn and drive where you can enjoy them best, the fragrant white flowers of the drooping leucothoe.

Site: Shady

Season: Late spring

Concept: Shade-tolerant plants make a handsome display on a shady site.

'Savannah' holly (H)

Oakleaf (B) hydrangea

Drooping (D) leucothoe

Cinnamon fern (E)

(A) Dogwood

(C) 'Roseum Elegans' rhododendron

(D) Drooping leucothoe

(B) Oakleaf hydrangea

(I) Retaining wall

See site plan for (F) (G).

House

Lawn

Driveway

1 square = 1 ft.

Plants & Projects

(A) Dogwood (use 1 plant)
This small deciduous tree is a central focal point with beauty in every season: white flower-like bracts in spring, lovely light green foliage that turns crimson in fall, and bright red winter berries. Remove the lower limbs to accommodate nearby shrubs. See *Cornus florida*, p. 180.

(B) Oakleaf hydrangea (use 4)
Oakleaf-shaped leaves and attractive reddish bark distinguish this deciduous shrub. It forms a handsome thicket at the base of the slope, with white flowers in spring and purple to red fall foliage. See *Hydrangea quercifolia*, p. 185.

(C) 'Roseum Elegans' rhododendron (use 3)
This fast-growing evergreen shrub graces the top of the slope with its glossy leaves and rosy pink May flowers. See *Rhododendron*, p. 192.

(D) Drooping leucothoe (use 13)
A spreading evergreen shrub whose mounds of dark green foliage are a perfect companion for the rhododendrons. Fragrant white spring flowers. See *Leucothoe fontanesiana*, p. 188.

(E) Cinnamon fern (use 24)
The interesting fiddleheads of this hardy fern unfurl into broad, pale green, plumelike fronds that create a woodland feel at the base of the wall. Fronds turn gold, then brown, in autumn. See Ferns: *Osmunda cinnamomea*, p.181.

(F) English ivy (use about 100)
Fill any open ground in the planting with this ground-covering evergreen vine. Spaced about 16 in. apart, it carpets the area with a dense mat of glossy green, lobed leaves. See *Hedera helix*, p. 183.

(G) Bulbs
Scatter crocus, squill, grape hyacinth, and small daffodils among the shrubs for bright spring color. Plant groups of three to six bulbs per square foot. See Bulbs, p. 176.

See p. 81 for the following:

(H) 'Savannah' holly (use 1)

(I) Retaining wall

Plant portraits

Transform your slope with the layers of texture and color offered through four seasons by these durable woody plants and perennials.

● = First design, pp. 80–81
▲ = Second design, p. 82

Creeping willowleaf cotoneaster
(*Cotoneaster salicifolius* 'Repens', p. 180) ●

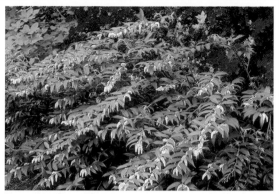

Drooping leucothoe
(*Leucothoe fontanesiana*, p. 188) ▲

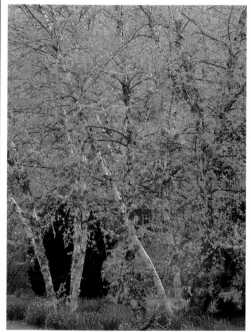

River birch (*Betula nigra*, p. 176) ●

Daylily (*Hemerocallis*, p. 184) ●

Cinnamon fern (Ferns: *Osmunda cinnamomea*, p. 181) ▲

Wax myrtle (*Myrica cerifera*, p. 190) ●

Under the Old Shade Tree

Create a cozy garden in a cool spot

This planting is designed to help homeowners blessed with a large shade tree make the most of their good fortune. A bench is provided, of course. What better spot to rest on a hot summer day? But why stop there? The tree's high, wide canopy affords an ideal setting for a planting of understory shrubs and perennials. The result is a woodland garden that warrants a visit any day of the year.

The planting roughly coincides with the pool of shade cast by the tree. Evergreen shrubs and masses of mostly evergreen perennials extend around the perimeter. You can position the large mahonias to provide privacy, screen a view from the bench, or block early-morning or late-afternoon sun. Smaller plants (hostas, sedge, and other perennials) are placed nearer the path and bench, where they can be appreciated at close range.

The planting is colorful in spring, when the blossoms of Lenten rose are joined by fragrant yellow mahonia flowers and the scented white blooms of daphne. Pretty as these flowers are, the real attraction here is foliage. As summer heats up, the little woodland is a cool oasis of leaves in a range of textures and colors that brighten the shade. Bands of gold edge the puckered blue-green leaves of hosta and the dark green daphne foliage, while golden flecks sparkle on the aucuba's leathery leaves.

Because almost all of the plants are evergreen, the display continues throughout the year. As fall shifts to winter, the tracery of bare branches of the shade tree in the canopy overhead is nicely balanced by the evergreen tapestry below.

Plants & Projects

For best results, thin the tree canopy, if necessary, to produce dappled rather than deep shade. Also remove limbs to a height of 8 ft. or more to provide headroom. The tree's roots compete for moisture with anything planted nearby. The plants here normally do well in these conditions, but need watering during any prolonged dry spells. Also, mulch generously and add fresh mulch every year or two. (For more on planting under a shade tree, see pp. 152 and 159.) If desired, you can fill in bare spots between the shrubs with ajuga, foamflower, or creeping phlox, all of which spread quickly.

A **Leatherleaf mahonia**
(use 7 plants)
A large evergreen shrub forming an erect clump of stout stems and leathery dark green foliage. Fragrant yellow spring flowers produce showy blue fruit clusters that attract birds. See *Mahonia bealei*, p. 190.

B **Gold-dust aucuba** (use 3)
These striking evergreen shrubs with shiny, leathery green leaves flecked with bright yellow provide a colorful backdrop for the bench. See *Aucuba japonica* 'Variegata', p. 176.

C **Prostrate Japanese plum yew**
(use 7)
A low-growing evergreen shrub that spreads to form a wide, fine-textured cushion of dark green needles that contrasts handsomely with the mahonia. See *Cephalotaxus harringtonia* 'Prostrata', p. 178.

D **Variegated winter daphne**
(use 1)
The intensely fragrant bursts of starry white flowers that appear on this compact evergreen shrub will scent the entire area in spring. Glossy green leaves edged with gold are lovely near the path. See *Daphne odora* 'Aureomarginata', p. 181.

E **Lenten rose** (use 20)
In early spring this evergreen perennial bears nodding, cuplike blooms on a clump of large, shiny dark green leaves. Flower colors range from white to rose to shades of pink and green. See *Helleborus orientalis*, p. 183.

F **Cast-iron plant** (use 7)
This tough evergreen perennial thrives with little light or water. It will spread to form a mass of stiff green leaves at the base of the tree trunk. See *Aspidistra elatior*, p. 175.

G **Japanese sacred lily** (use 10)
An evergreen perennial forming an arching clump of dark green swordlike leaves. Insignificant yellow flowers produce pretty red berries. See *Rohdea japonica*, p. 194.

H **'Frances Williams' hosta** (use 3)
A stately presence, this hardy perennial offers huge yellow-edged blue-green leaves with a seersucker texture. White flowers float on stiff stalks above the foliage in mid- to late summer. See *Hosta*, p. 184.

I **Variegated Japanese sedge**
(use 10)
This perennial's neat low tufts of grasslike evergreen leaves, striped yellow and green, create a colorful ground cover along the path. See *Carex morrowii* 'Aureo-variegata', p. 178.

J **Gold moneywort** (use 25)
A quickly spreading perennial ground cover with golden yellow, coin-shaped leaves. It bears little yellow flowers in summer. See *Lysimachia nummularia* 'Aurea', p. 190.

K **Path**
Wood chips make an easy, informal surface for the short path and "clearing" in front of the bench. See p. 118.

Site: Shady

Season: Summer

Concept: A shade garden beneath a venerable old tree makes a lovely spot for sitting or strolling.

Prostrate Japanese **C** plum yew

Gold moneywort **J**

A Leatherleaf mahonia

B Gold-dust aucuba

Lenten **E** rose

H 'Frances Williams' hosta

D Variegated winter daphne

G Japanese sacred lily

F Cast-iron plant

I Variegated Japanese sedge

K Path

Bench

Lawn

1 square = 1 ft.

Plant portraits

These plants offer foliage in a range of shapes, textures, and colors sufficient to enliven any shady spot. And several have lovely flowers as well.

● = First design, pp. 84–85
▲ = Second design, pp. 86–87

Japanese sacred lily (*Rohdea japonica*, p. 194) ●

Cast-iron plant (*Aspidistra elatior*, p. 175) ●

Prostrate Japanese plum yew
(*Cephalotaxus harringtonia* 'Prostrata', p. 178) ● ▲

Variegated winter daphne
(*Daphne odora* 'Aureomarginata', p. 181) ● ▲

Japanese autumn fern (Ferns: *Dryopteris erythrosora*, p. 181) ▲

Variegated lacecap hydrangea
(*Hydrangea macrophylla* 'Mariesii Variegata', p. 184) ▲

A piney woodland

A mature pine tree—its lower limbs either shed naturally or trimmed off, its upper branches forming a graceful spreading crown—can shelter a distinctive shade garden. Casting lighter shade and with less competitive roots than many shade trees, it allows a wider range of understory plants.

This planting replaces several tall shrubs in the previous design with ferns to produce the feel of an open woodland. There are flowers and fragrance in spring; the astilbes and hostas add mid- to late-summer bloom; and there is still plenty of evergreen foliage.

If you prefer more screening than provided here, work in a clump of mahonias or gold-dust aucuba. As in the previous design, fill gaps with ajuga, foamflower, or creeping phlox.

Plants & Projects

Ⓐ **Variegated lacecap hydrangea**
(use 1 plant)
This deciduous shrub makes a fine accent next to the bench. Its shiny green leaves are edged with creamy white stripes. Blue or pink flowers are scattered in lacy clusters. Blooms in summer. See *Hydrangea macrophylla* 'Mariesii Variegata', p. 184.

Ⓑ **Tassel fern** (use 15)
Planted in a large mass, the glossy evergreen fronds of this fern contrast with the nearby hosta and plum yew foliage. It forms impressive clumps. See Ferns: *Polystichum polyblepharum*, p. 181.

Ⓒ **Japanese autumn fern** (use 5)
Fronds of this fern start out copper-colored in spring and mature to a rich green. It forms narrow, erect clumps. May stand up through mild winters.

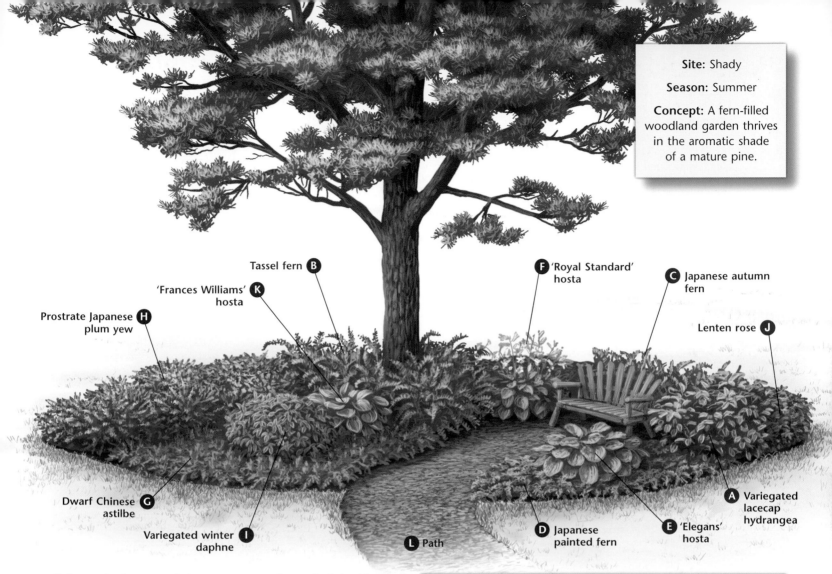

Tassel fern **B**

'Frances Williams' **K**
hosta

'Royal Standard' **F**
hosta

Japanese autumn **C**
fern

Prostrate Japanese **H**
plum yew

Lenten rose **J**

Dwarf Chinese **G**
astilbe

Variegated winter **I**
daphne

Japanese **D**
painted fern

'Elegans' **E**
hosta

Variegated **A**
lacecap
hydrangea

Path **L**

If frozen to the ground, it recovers in spring. See Ferns: *Dryopteris erythrosora*, p. 181.

D **Japanese painted fern** (use 9) One of the prettiest foliage plants, with delicately painted fronds blending green, silver, and maroon, this deciduous fern is displayed in front of the bench, where you can really enjoy it. See Ferns: *Athyrium goeringianum* 'Pictum', p. 181.

E **'Elegans' hosta** (use 1) The huge, blue-gray, textured leaves of this perennial are a marvelous centerpiece among the ferns. White summer flowers are a bonus. See *Hosta sieboldiana*, p. 184.

F **'Royal Standard' hosta** (use 3) Placed next to the bench, where you can get full benefit from the scent of its large white August flowers. Large, medium

green leaves look healthy and glossy from spring to fall. See *Hosta*, p. 184.

G **Dwarf Chinese astilbe** (use 15) Fluffy spires of tiny mauve flowers blanket this low-growing perennial in late summer. Used here as a ground cover, its lacy foliage complements the deeply cut ferns nearby and sets off the hosta and daphne planted in its midst. See *Astilbe chinensis* var. *pumila*, p. 175.

See p. 84 for the following:

H **Prostrate Japanese plum yew** (use 7)

I **Variegated winter daphne** (use 1)

J **Lenten rose** (use 20)

K **'Frances Williams' hosta** (use 3)

L **Path**

Lawn

Bench

1 square = 1 ft.

A Pleasant Passage

Reclaim a narrow side yard for a shade garden

Many residential lots include a slim strip of land between the house and a property line. Usually overlooked by everyone except children and dogs racing between the front yard and the back, this often shady corridor can become a valued addition to the landscape.

In the design shown here, a flagstone path curves gently through a selection of trees, shrubs, and perennials to make a garden that invites adults, and even children, to linger as they stroll from one part of the property to another.

The wall of the house and a tall, opaque fence on the property line shade the space most of the day and give it a closed-in feeling, like a long empty hallway or a narrow room. The curved path makes the corridor seem wider, and the plants clustered at the bends create cozy "garden rooms." Entrances at each end are marked by pretty broad-leaved evergreens whose flowers entice visitors in early summer and fall. The handsome foliage and striking flowers of azaleas form the "walls" of the garden rooms. An edging of painted ferns, mondo grass, and astilbes adds color at their feet, while a magnolia about halfway along the path provides a light roof of fragrant flowers and flashing silvery leaves.

Plants & Projects

Lay the flagstone path first, taking time to make graceful curves—they're instrumental in making the space seem larger than it is. Upkeep is minimal: just spring and fall cleanup, pruning shrubs to size and shape, and renewing the mulch every year or two.

Ⓐ Sweet bay magnolia (use 1 plant)
Sheltering the path in the middle of the garden, this graceful deciduous tree blooms with fragrant creamy white flowers in early summer. Its glossy silver-green leaves sparkle in the breeze and can be evergreen in areas with mild winters. See *Magnolia virginiana*, p. 190.

Ⓑ Japanese ligustrum (use 2)
These small trees mark the entrances to the garden with glossy evergreen leaves that showcase fragrant white flowers in early summer and dark blue-black berries in fall and winter. Grows narrowly upright, with multiple trunks. Remove the lower limbs so you can walk underneath. See *Ligustrum japonicum*, p. 188.

Ⓒ 'Jean May' camellia (use 1)
From late fall into early winter, this popular evergreen shrub produces masses of lovely pink double flowers. Glossy green leaves and compact upright form are attractive year-round. See *Camellia sasanqua*, p. 178.

Ⓓ 'George Lindley Taber' azalea (use 7)
Noted for its large, light pink spring flowers, this evergreen azalea also offers a loose, soft form that is pleasing beside the path throughout the year. See *Rhododendron*, p. 192.

Ⓔ Plumleaf azalea (use 4)
This deciduous shrub adds as much as a month of midsummer color to the garden with its large clusters of orange-red flowers. Delicately textured foliage shows well against the fence, too. See *Rhododendron prunifolium*, p. 192.

Ⓕ Gold-dust aucuba (use 3)
Large leathery green leaves speckled with bright yellow make this rugged evergreen a bright spot in the shade next to the house. See *Aucuba japonica* 'Variegata', p. 176.

Ⓖ Japanese painted fern (use 14)
Lovely deciduous ferns add a lush, rich touch beneath the ligustrums, their delicately painted fronds blending green, silver, and maroon. See Ferns: *Athyrium goeringianum* 'Pictum', p. 181.

Ⓗ White astilbe (use 5)
Mounds of dark green, deeply divided leaves of this perennial dress up the edge of the path all season and are a perfect backdrop for the plumelike flowers that appear in June. Choose a white-flowered cultivar. See *Astilbe*, p. 175.

Ⓘ Mondo grass (use 1 per sq. ft.)
The thin, leathery, grassy leaves of this evergreen perennial create an attractive ground cover edging the path. See *Ophiopogon japonicus*, p. 190.

Ⓙ Path
Providing just the right touch of informality, flagstones in random sizes trace a gracefully curving route through the planting. See p. 118.

Site: Partial shade

Season: Early summer

Concept: Enticing foliage and flowers create a stroll garden in a frequently neglected area.

1 square = 1 ft.

A Sweet bay magnolia

B Japanese ligustrum

F Gold-dust acuba

D 'George Lindley Taber' azalea

J Path

H White astilbe

I Mondo grass

C 'Jean May' camellia

G Japanese painted fern

B Japanese ligustrum

E Plumleaf azalea

A Pleasant Passage 89

Plant portraits

The noteworthy foliage and eye-catching flowers of these plants help transform a narrow site into a lovely stroll garden.

● = First design, pp. 88–89
▲ = Second design, pp. 90–91

Gold-dust aucuba (*Aucuba japonica* 'Variegata', p. 176) ● ▲

White astilbe (*Astilbe*, p. 175) ● ▲

Holly fern (Ferns: *Cyrtomium falcatum*, p. 181) ▲

'Delaware Valley White' azalea (*Rhododendron*, p. 192) ▲

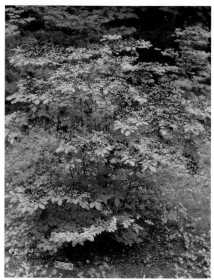

Plumleaf azalea
(*Rhododendron prunifolium*, p. 192) ●

Sweet bay magnolia
(*Magnolia virginiana*, p. 190) ●

Evergreen privacy

If you like hedges and have a wide enough space to accommodate one, try this design. Here, a bank of evergreen wax myrtles helps enclose an equally appealing stroll garden. Other additions include crape myrtles at the entrances, white-flowering azaleas beside the house, holly ferns tucked along the hedge, and hostas with striking blue leaves edging the walk. For more color in spring, plant clusters of your favorite bulbs beneath the crape myrtles and wherever space allows along the path.

1 square = 1 ft.

Site: Partial shade

Season: Late spring

Concept: An evergreen hedge forms a living wall for this attractive corridor garden.

'Natchez' **A** crape myrtle

G Gold-dust aucuba

'Halcyon' **E** hosta

Wax myrtle **B**

See site plan for **H** .

Mondo grass **I**

Holly fern **D**

Path **J**

C 'Delaware Valley White' azalea

F 'Jean May' camellia

Plants & Projects

A 'Natchez' crape myrtle (use 2 plants)
A small deciduous tree with large clusters of crepe-papery white flowers all summer, bright fall color, and handsome flaking bark. Trim off lower limbs to better display plantings behind. See *Lagerstroemia indica,* p. 188.

B Wax myrtle (use 5)
This evergreen shrub's stems of slender glossy aromatic leaves make a dense and tidy "natural" (not sheared) hedge. See *Myrica cerifera,* p. 190.

C 'Delaware Valley White' azalea (use 3)
Its upright growth habit makes this evergreen shrub an excellent choice for the narrow spot between the house and path. Showy clusters of single white flowers light up the center of the garden in midspring. See *Rhododendron,* p. 192.

D Holly fern (use 5)
The shiny coarse-toothed leaflets of this evergreen fern do look like holly leaves. Their color and texture make a nice contrast with the wax myrtles behind. See Ferns: *Cyrtomium falcatum,* p. 181.

E 'Halcyon' hosta (use 5)
The leaves of this low-mounding perennial are powder blue in spring, then turn darker blue in summer. In late summer, lilac-colored flowers wave above the foliage on slim stalks. See *Hosta,* p. 184.

See p. 88 for the following:

F 'Jean May' camellia (use 1)

G Gold-dust aucuba (use 5)

H White astilbe (use 3)

I Mondo grass (use 1 per sq. ft.)

J Path

Down to Earth

Harmonize your deck with its surroundings

A second-story deck is a perfect spot for viewing your garden and yard. Too often, however, the view of the deck from the yard is less pleasing. Perched atop skinny posts, towering over a patch of lawn, an elevated deck looks out of place, an ungainly visitor that is uncomfortable in its surroundings.

In the design shown here, attractive landscaping brings the deck, house, and yard into balance. Plants, combined with a simple homemade lattice skirting attached to the posts, form a broad pedestal of visual support for the deck. Framed by lovely maples, a planting of shrubs and perennials decreases in height from deck to lawn, making it easier for the eye to move between the levels.

In not too many years, the fast-growing native maples will cast shade over the deck. Next to the house, two sweet olives can stand on their own or tie into existing foundation plantings. In autumn their sweetly scented flowers will perfume the entire area. Across the front of the deck, a row of handsome oakleaf hydrangeas forms a hedgelike screen. The slender foliage of iris and sedge makes a grassy ruffle at their feet. Cherry laurels wrap around the corners in a flowing curve that broadens the deck's base when viewed from the lawn. Their flowers are a fragrant treat in spring.

Grass paths lead to the area beneath the deck. Enclosed by the plantings and lattice, this area is ideal for storing garden tools, lawn furniture, and bicycles.

Red maple (A)

'Otto Luyken' (D)
cherry laurel

Site: Sunny

Season: Early summer

Concept: A pleasing mix of woody plants and perennials leads the eye comfortably from ground to deck.

B

B

Grass path

H (beneath deck)

G

D

D

C

E

A

F

A

Lawn

1 square = 1 ft.

Plants & Projects

The lattice can be assembled and installed in a weekend, the planting in another. The curving bed is free-form, but it will look best if you take some care to make the curves "fair," with no awkward flat spots or pronounced bulges. The woody plants will take a few years to reach the sizes we've shown here. When the shrubs are small, mulching the beds with 3 to 4 in. of chipped or shredded bark will control weeds and retain moisture. Other than seasonal cleanup and pruning, the planting requires little maintenance.

Ⓐ **Red maple** (use 2 plants)
A popular deciduous tree for its quick growth and blazing red fall color. It is also

Storage area H

Lattice G

F **Variegated Japanese sedge**

E **Siberian iris**

C **Oakleaf hydrangea**

D **'Otto Luyken' cherry laurel**

B **Sweet olive**

colorful in spring, when the red flower clusters line the bare twigs. As the trees grow, remove lower limbs to accommodate the shrubs below and to encourage the trees to form a shady canopy over the deck. See *Acer rubrum*, p. 174.

B Sweet olive (use 2)
A slow-growing evergreen shrub with a dense compact form and glossy dark green leaves that resemble those of holly. Bears very sweet-scented flowers in late summer and fall. See *Osmanthus × fortunei*, p. 191.

C Oakleaf hydrangea (use 5)
Native to the South, this deciduous shrub offers colorful foliage that turns from pale to dark green to red and purple as the sea-

son progresses. Papery flowers appear in spring and persist until fall, when the plant's flaky cinnamon-colored bark gives you something to look at through the winter. See *Hydrangea quercifolia*, p. 185.

D 'Otto Luyken' cherry laurel (use 11)
A curving band of these low evergreen shrubs forms a fine informal hedge with little or no pruning. In spring it bears white flowers with a powerful fragrance. See *Prunus laurocerasus*, p. 192.

E Siberian iris (use 7)
The graceful flowers of this perennial add late-spring color to the front of the planting. The slender foliage looks good all summer. See *Iris sibirica*, p. 187.

F Variegated Japanese sedge (use 16)
This perennial's neat tufts of grasslike evergreen leaves, striped yellow and green, are an effective edging for the central bed. See *Carex morrowii* 'Aureo-variegata', p. 178.

G Lattice
Easy to make and attach to the deck posts, this lattice dresses up the deck when the shrubs are small (you might train morning glories on it) and provides a nice peek-a-boo background for mature shrubs. See p. 148.

H Storage area
For a durable tidy surface, cover the ground beneath the deck with 2 in. of crushed stone. Use a wooden edging to keep the stone out of the surrounding beds.

Plant portraits

These plants can enhance a deck with lovely foliage textures and colors as well as pretty flowers.

● = First design, pp. 92–93
▲ = Second design, pp. 94–95

Dwarf Chinese astilbe (*Astilbe chinensis* var. *pumila*, p. 175) ▲

Variegated Japanese sedge
(*Carex morrowii* 'Aureo-variegata', p. 178) ●

Red maple (*Acer rubrum*, p. 174) ●

'Antioch' hosta (*Hosta*, p. 184) ▲

Oakleaf hydrangea
(*Hydrangea quercifolia*, p. 185) ●

'George Lindley Taber' azalea
(*Rhododendron*, p. 192) ▲

Skirting a shady deck

This planting also integrates the deck with its surroundings, but it does so in a shady environment, produced perhaps by large trees nearby. The design includes a banquet of azaleas and rhododendrons that make a wonderful feast in spring, whether viewed from the deck or the lawn.

During the summer, a supporting cast of shade lovers provides lovely, if more subdued, color. Fall features the brilliant leaves of the maple; then the evergreen azaleas carry the planting through the winter.

Plants & Projects

Ⓐ Japanese maple (use 1 plant)
On a site with no need of additional shade, this small deciduous tree is a lovely accent. Choose a selection that has green leaves in summer and red or scarlet leaves in fall. See *Acer palmatum*, p. 174.

Ⓑ Wax myrtle (use 2)
Glossy aromatic leaves cover the slender stems of this graceful evergreen shrub. Birds like the gray berries that it bears in fall and winter. A fast grower, it will need yearly pruning to keep it from outgrowing its spot. See *Myrica cerifera*, p. 190.

Ⓒ 'George Lindley Taber' azalea (use 6)
Large light pink flowers grace this shrub in spring. A vigorous plant, it grows quickly to produce a year-round evergreen screen for the storage area beneath the deck. See *Rhododendron*, p. 192.

Ⓓ 'Fiedlers White' azalea (use 6)
Filling the corners between house and deck, these shrubs are a mound of white blossoms in spring and a lovely evergreen presence the rest of the year. See *Rhododendron*, p. 192.

Japanese maple (A)

(L) Lattice

(M) Storage area

Pink Gumpo azalea (F)

Tassel fern (K)

Pink astilbe (I)

Dwarf Chinese astilbe (J)

(G) 'Elegans' hosta

(B) Wax myrtle

(C) 'George Lindley Taber' azalea

(H) 'Antioch' hosta

(E) 'Amagasa' Satsuki azalea

(D) 'Fiedlers White' azalea

(E) 'Amagasa' Satsuki azalea (use 10)
A low evergreen shrub with a spreading form and large deep pink flowers in late spring. See *Rhododendron,* p. 192.

(F) Pink Gumpo azalea (use 12)
Another low, spreading shrub. Mounds of its fine-textured evergreen foliage curve around the front edge of the planting. It bears clusters of large pink flowers in late spring. See *Rhododendron,* p. 192.

(G) 'Elegans' hosta (use 2)
A large perennial with the stature of a small shrub. Its huge blue, textured leaves look great with the nearby azaleas. White flowers on short stiff stems bloom in summer. See *Hosta sieboldiana,* p. 184.

(H) 'Antioch' hosta (use 10)
Forming smaller but still impressive clumps, this hosta edges part of the bed with green-and-white leaves and has lavender flowers in summer. See *Hosta,* p. 184.

(I) Pink astilbe (use 6)
This perennial's dark green, deeply divided leaves make an effective transition from the azaleas behind them to the ferns in front. It bears plumes of pink flowers for weeks in early summer. Choose a tall cultivar for this spot. See *Astilbe,* p. 175.

(J) Dwarf Chinese astilbe (use 10)
A smaller version of the previous plant, this perennial makes pretty patches of lacy foliage with pink flowers in late summer. See *Astilbe chinensis* var. *pumila,* p. 175.

(K) Tassel fern (use 12)
An evergreen fern with upright, finely divided, glossy green fronds. It adds a woodland feel to the front of the planting. See Ferns: *Polystichum polyblepharum,* p. 181.

See p. 93 for the following:

(L) Lattice

(M) Storage area

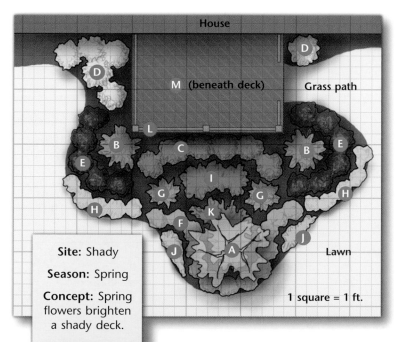

House

M (beneath deck)

Grass path

Lawn

Site: Shady

Season: Spring

Concept: Spring flowers brighten a shady deck.

1 square = 1 ft.

At Woods' Edge

Shrub border borrows a backdrop from nature

The woodlands and forests of the Southeast are treasured by all who live in the region. Many subdivisions, both new and old, incorporate woodland areas, with homes bordering landscapes of stately trees and large shrubs. (In some older neighborhoods, mature trees on adjacent lots create almost the same woodland feeling.)

The planting shown here integrates a domestic landscape with a woodland at its edge. It makes a pleasant transition between the open area of lawn, with its sunny entertainments, and the cool, secluded woods beyond. The design takes inspiration from the buffer zone of small trees and shrubs nature provides at the sunny edge of a wood, and it should have the same attraction to birds and wildlife

(and the people who enjoy them) as its natural counterpart does.

Small deciduous trees, rising to about 15 ft., mingle with lower-growing shrubs and a carpet of perennial ground covers and spring-blooming bulbs. A path accommodates quiet woodland strolls and provides access to the larger woods beyond.

Whether viewed from the path or the distant house, the planting is attractive all year. Spring offers a range of lovely flowers in white and pink, though chances are you'll find something in bloom any time of the year. Summer puts on a lush show of handsome foliage dappled with flowers. Brilliant leaves light up the fall display, while colorful bare branches and evergreen foliage distinguish the winter scene.

Sweet bay magnolia **B**

'Diana' rose-of-Sharon **A**

Path **M**

Plants & Projects

Even though this design calls for relatively few plants in a large area, preparing the entire planting bed by tilling and amending the soil will pay off in the long run with healthy vigorous growth (see p. 150). A deep mulch of bark or pine straw and regular watering the first summer will speed establishment. Then just devote a weekend each spring and fall to mulching and basic pruning.

A **'Diana' rose-of-Sharon**
(use 1 plant)
An updated version of an old-fashioned favorite, this deciduous shrub puts forth large pure white flowers that are a treat from July through September. See *Hibiscus syriacus*, p. 184.

B **Sweet bay magnolia** (use 1)
This graceful tree blooms with fragrant white flowers in early summer. Its silvery green leaves provide flickering color in a breeze and can remain on the tree through mild winters. See *Magnolia virginiana*, p. 190.

C **Glossy abelia** (use 3)
Pale pink flowers stand out against the glossy green leaves of this evergreen shrub from early summer to frost. See *Abelia × grandiflora*, p. 174.

D **Coral bark maple** (use 1)
A four-season tree for the path, an attractive vase shape, scarlet fall foliage, and striking coral-red bark to brighten winter days. See *Acer palmatum* 'Sango Kaku', p. 174.

E **Fringe tree** (use 1)
A small, slow-growing deciduous tree, bushy and typically multistemmed. In May, clusters of spicy-smelling frilly white flowers dangle from every branch. See *Chionanthus virginicus*, p. 179.

F **'Magnoliaeflora' Japanese camellia** (use 1)
A handsome evergreen shrub with glossy dark green leaves and elegant, semidouble, light pink flowers that bloom much of the winter and spring. See *Camellia japonica*, p. 178.

G **'Hummingbird' summersweet** (use 3)
A compact deciduous shrub with wonderfully fragrant white flowers in midsummer and golden fall foliage. See *Clethra alnifolia*, p. 180.

H **Oakleaf hydrangea** (use 1)
A four-season deciduous shrub with papery flowers in late spring, distinctive leaves that are red and purple in fall, and reddish bark for the winter. See *Hydrangea quercifolia*, p. 185.

I **Loropetalum** (use 1)
Elegant at the front of the border, this evergreen shrub forms layers of arching branches that bear lacy white flowers in spring and may bloom sporadically through summer. See *Loropetalum chinense*, p. 189.

J **'Delaware Valley White' azalea** (use 7)
This evergreen shrub is ideal for the front of the planting, where its large white spring flowers are in full display. See *Rhododendron*, p. 192.

K **Autumn cherry** (use 1)
This small deciduous tree earns its central role by producing a cloud of light pink flowers in late fall and again in early spring. See *Prunus subhirtella* 'Autumnalis', p. 192.

L **Ground-cover "fillers"**
Fill in between the shrubs and trees with evergreen ground covers such as ajuga, creeping phlox, dwarf plumbago, vinca, or ferns, and patches of spring-blooming bulbs. As the woody plants mature, some ground covers may be shaded out.

M **Path**
Simply extend the mulch on the beds to form a path, or install a gravel base if drainage is a concern. See p. 118.

F 'Magnoliaeflora' Japanese camellia

H Oakleaf hydrangea

C Glossy abelia

J Delaware Valley White' azalea

K Autumn cherry

E Fringe tree

G 'Hummingbird' summersweet

D Coral bark maple

L Ground-cover "fillers"

I Loropetalum

Site: Sunny

Season: Summer

Concept: Small trees and a variety of shrubs make a pleasing transition between lawn and adjacent woodland.

Existing woodland

Property line

1 square = 2 ft.   Lawn

Scented shade

If your lot is on the shady side of a woodland, try this design (shown here in early spring). The layout is much the same in both plantings, but here smaller shade-tolerant trees and shrubs replace some of the previous design's sun lovers.

Once again there are flowers, foliage, berries, and colorful bark to please year-round. The decorative maple moves to the front, where it receives the most sun. Deciduous plants predominate and in fall produce a splendid array of golds, yellows, reds, and purples. The planting's most distinctive feature, however, is fragrance, provided in abundance from early to late spring and again in late summer and fall.

The ground covers listed in the main plan will also perform well in shade, but you might grow more ferns. Consider adding a bench along the path to provide a restful place to sit.

'Magnoliaeflora' Japanese camellia **I**

Sweet olive **C**

B Piedmont azalea

A Leatherleaf mahonia

G 'Jean May' sasanqua camellia

Ground-cover "fillers" **L**

Coral bark maple **K**

'Nikko Blue' hydrangea **H**

'Arnold Promise' witch hazel **D**

Site: Shady

Season: Very early spring

Concept: Selected for a shady site, these trees and shrubs entice strollers to the shrub border with fragrant flowers and bright fall foliage.

Existing woodland

Property line

1 square = 2 ft.

Lawn

Plants & Projects

A **Leatherleaf mahonia** (use 3 plants)
An evergreen shrub with holly-like foliage, fragrant yellow flowers in early spring, and bird-attracting blue berries. See *Mahonia bealei*, p. 190.

B **Piedmont azalea** (use 3)
Fragrant white or pink blooms appear in spring on this native deciduous shrub. See *Rhododendron canescens*, p. 192.

C **Sweet olive** (use 1)
This compact shrub bears sweet-scented white flowers in late summer and fall on dense evergreen foliage. See *Osmanthus × fortunei*, p. 191.

D **'Arnold Promise' witch hazel** (use 1)
Spidery, fragrant flowers of clear yellow appear in early spring on this small deciduous tree. Fall foliage is gold. See *Hamamelis × intermedia*, p. 183.

E **Winterberry holly** (use 3)
A deciduous native shrub with yellow fall foliage. Use one male and two females, so the female plants will bear bright red berries that attract birds. See *Ilex verticillata*, p. 187.

F **'Henry's Garnet' Virginia sweetspire** (use 5)
Glossy green leaves of this de-

Piedmont azalea (*Rhododendron canescens*, p. 192) ▲

Plant portraits

These trees and shrubs offer enticing flowers, foliage, berries, and bark for a shrub border in sun or shade.

● = First design, pp. 96–97
▲ = Second design, pp. 98–99

E Winterberry holly

J Oakleaf hydrangea

M Path

F 'Henry's Garnet' Virginia sweetspire

Coral bark maple
(*Acer palmatum* 'Sango Kaku', p. 174) ● ▲

Autumn cherry (*Prunus subhirtella* 'Autumnalis', p. 192) ●

Fringe tree (*Chionanthus virginicus*, p. 179) ●

ciduous shrub turn a deep scarlet in fall. Bears fragrant white flowers in early summer. See *Itea virginica*, p. 187.

G 'Jean May' sasanqua camellia (use 1)
From fall into winter, this compact evergreen shrub welcomes strollers with lovely double pink flowers displayed against glossy leaves. See *Camellia sasanqua*, p. 178.

H 'Nikko Blue' hydrangea (use 4)
Pink or blue snowball-shaped flower clusters cover this deciduous shrub in midsummer. The smooth glossy leaves look great all season. See *Hydrangea macrophylla*, p. 184.

See p. 96 for the following:

I 'Magnoliaeflora' Japanese camellia (use 1)

J Oakleaf hydrangea (use 1)

K Coral bark maple (use 1)

L Ground-cover "fillers"

M Path

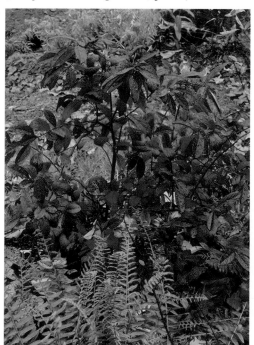
'Henry's Garnet' Virginia sweetspire
(*Itea virginica*, p. 187) ▲

'Arnold Promise' witch hazel
(*Hamamelis* × *intermedia*, p. 183) ▲

Gateway Garden
Arbor and plantings make a handsome entry

Entrances are an important part of any landscape. They can welcome visitors onto your property; highlight a special feature, such as a rose garden; or mark the passage between two areas with different character or function. The design shown here can serve in any of these situations. A waist-high hedge of evergreen hollies creates a friendly attractive barrier, just enough to signal the confines of the front yard. The simple wisteria-covered arbor provides welcoming access, particularly when it is enveloped in the pleasing aroma of the vine's striking flowers.

Curved planting beds face the house, defined by a lower, more informal hedge of evergreen azaleas. At one end, a picturesque multitrunked holly forms a canopy for shade-loving astilbes, with their feathery foliage and long summer display of white flower plumes. Flanking the arch, verbena adds months of purple flowers in summer and fall. Spring, however, offers the most bloom, with pink flowers covering the azaleas, low patches of moss phlox, and lavender flower clusters dangling from the wisteria like bunches of aromatic grapes.

Arbor **H**

A Chinese wisteria

'Compacta' **C** Japanese holly

'Compacta' **C** Japanese holly

D Pink Gumpo azalea

Moss **G** phlox

See site plan for **E F**.

Sidewalk

C · A · C

F · H · F · D · E

D · B

G · G

Existing walkway

Lawn

1 square = 1 ft.

B Yaupon holly

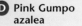
D Pink Gumpo azalea

Site: Sunny

Season: Spring

Concept: An arbor, hedge, and simple plantings define boundaries and provide an inviting entry.

Plants & Projects

On the planting plan shown here, the small bed could be tucked between the arbor and a driveway or the wall of a house or garage. You can easily expand the design in either direction by extending the hedges and adding more perennials. The structures and plantings are easy to build, install, and care for. After the tree, hedges, and wisteria are trained and shaped to your taste, seasonal pruning will keep them tidy.

A Chinese wisteria (use 1 plant)
A vigorous deciduous vine with spectacular clusters of fragrant purple, blue, or white flowers in spring. Prune in midsummer to control its size and to stimulate abundant bloom. See *Wisteria sinensis*, p. 197.

B Yaupon holly (use 1)
A small, tough, easy-to-grow evergreen tree with glossy dark green leaves and masses of red berries. Buy a multitrunked specimen and prune it to best display the interesting crooked trunks and branches. See *Ilex*, Evergreen hollies: *I. vomitoria*, p. 186.

C 'Compacta' Japanese holly (use 8)
The dense twiggy habit and small evergreen leaves make this an excellent shrub for a sheared hedge, as we've shown here, or you can prune it more lightly for an informal effect. Either way, prune it in summer. See *Ilex*, Evergreen hollies: *I. crenata*, p. 186.

D Pink Gumpo azalea (use 16)
This low-growing evergreen shrub is well suited to the informal hedge that defines the curved edge of the bed. Clusters of large pink flowers are a splendid sight in late spring. Prune in early summer. See *Rhododendron*, p. 192.

E White astilbe (use 5)
The white plumelike flowers of this hardy perennial shine out from the shade of the holly tree in summer. When not blooming, mounds of dark green, deeply divided leaves are an effective ground cover. See *Astilbe*, p. 175.

F Purple verbena (use 14)
This perennial's clusters of small purple flowers seem to float in the air above mats of low foliage. Blooms from early summer to frost, attracting butterflies as a bonus. See *Verbena bonariensis*, p. 196.

G Moss phlox (use 10)
Edging the walkway, this tough evergreen ground cover will creep under the azaleas to form a mat of prickly leaves covered with flowers in spring. Choose a pale pink cultivar that complements the azaleas. See *Phlox subulata*, p. 191.

H Arbor
You can build this simple arbor in a weekend. Its 2x6 posts are sturdy enough to support the vigorous growth of the wisteria. Let the wood weather to gray-brown, or stain it to complement your house. See p. 148.

Plant portraits

Combined with an arbor or fence, these handsome plants define boundaries and welcome visitors with their flowers and foliage.

● = First design, pp. 100–101
▲ = Second design, pp. 102–103

Chinese wisteria
(*Wisteria sinensis*, p. 197) ●

Trumpet creeper (*Campsis radicans*, p. 178) ▲

Lady Bank's rose (*Rosa × banksiae*, p. 194) ▲

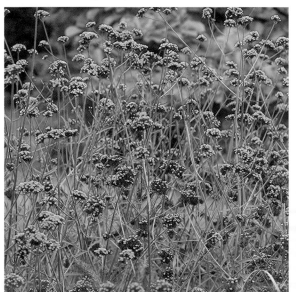

Purple verbena
(*Verbena bonariensis*, p. 196) ● ▲

Yaupon holly (*Ilex*, Evergreen hollies:
I. vomitoria, p. 186) ●

Fancy a fence?

For many people, a picket fence and vine-covered arbor represent old-fashioned neighborly virtues. The fence here is a natural extension of the arbor presented in the previous pages. A narrower barrier than the hedge, it leaves room in the curving beds for larger shrubs and provides something for roses and jasmine vine to scramble over.

This design features camellias whose flowers and evergreen foliage keep the entry beautiful all year. Trumpet creeper attracts hummingbirds to the arbor, while purple coneflower offers bright blossoms during the dog days of summer.

Plants & Projects

Ⓐ Trumpet creeper
(use 2 plants)
This vigorous deciduous vine will quickly cover the arbor with thick stems and large dark green leaves. Bears large clusters of coral-red flowers all summer long. See *Campsis radicans*, p. 178.

Ⓑ Lady Bank's rose (use 2)
Trained along the top of the fence, this climbing rose bears clusters of double yellow flowers that are a charming sight in spring. Glossy green leaves look good for many months. See *Rosa × banksiae*, p. 194.

Ⓒ Confederate jasmine (use 2)
This evergreen vine has stiff woody stems that form bushy mounds against the fence. Sweetly fragrant white flowers bloom for weeks in early summer among glossy dark green leaves. See *Trachelospermum jasminoides*, p. 196.

Ⓓ 'Royal Purple' smoke tree
(use 1)
The dark purple foliage of this large deciduous shrub turns

gold or orange in the fall. Bears fluffy plumes of pink flowers in summer, a striking sight in combination with the purple leaves. Remove lower limbs to accommodate underplanting. See *Cotinus coggygria*, p. 180.

E **Carolina jasmine** (use 2)
This tough evergreen vine spreads to form a ground cover beneath the smoke tree. Its fragrant yellow flowers are a treat in early spring. Prune as needed in midsummer to keep it from outgrowing its spot. See *Gelsemium sempervirens*, p. 182.

F **Camellia** (use 3)
These large evergreen shrubs are a handsome presence here, with their glossy dark green leaves and elegant white, pink, or rose flowers. Combine dif-

ferent cultivars for color and to distribute bloom from late fall to spring. See *Camellia*, p. 178.

G **'Goldsturm' coneflower** (use 8)
An improved version of the reliable perennial sometimes called "black-eyed Susan," this cultivar has large, golden yellow, daisylike blooms with black central cones. It produces masses of flowers in late sum-

mer above compact mounds of deep green foliage. See *Rudbeckia fulgida*, p. 194.

H **Vinca** (use about 12)
A perennial ground cover whose dense mats of shiny dark green leaves will quickly fill the space beneath the camellias and out to the walkway. Bears small blue flowers in spring. See *Vinca minor*, p. 197.

I **Fence**
Alternating wide and narrow "pickets," this low fence varies slightly from the classic pattern but is very easy to build. See p. 148.

See p. 101 for the following:

J **Purple verbena** (use 8)

K **Arbor**

Site: Sunny

Season: Summer

Concept: A fence joins the entry arbor, along with a variety of lovely flowering plants.

1 square = 1 ft.

'Royal Purple' smoke tree **D**

K Arbor

A Trumpet creeper

C Confederate jasmine

F Camellia

B Lady Bank's rose

Purple verbena **J**

Carolina jasmine **E**

Vinca **H**

'Goldsturm' coneflower **G**

Fence **I**

A Postal Planting

Make your daily mail run a perennial pleasure

For some, the lowly mailbox may seem a surprising candidate for landscaping. But posted like a sentry by the driveway entrance, the mailbox is highly visible to visitors and passersby. And it is one of the few places on your property that you visit nearly every day. A handsome planting like the one shown here pleases the passing public and rewards your daily journey, as well as that of your friendly letter carrier.

Plantings around mailboxes too often suffer from timidity—too few plants in too little space. This design makes a bold display, covering a good-size area with color for many months. The long-blooming perennials here are all well suited to the hot, sunny, and often dry conditions that prevail by most streetside mailboxes.

Mail arrives year-round, and no season is overlooked in this planting. Summer is the most colorful, with cheery flowers in blue, pink, red, and gold, highlighted by the yucca's eye-catching spires of creamy white blossoms. Sage, sedum, and asters continue the show through the fall. Then the evergreen foliage of many of the plants comes into its own, making the planting look fresh for visits through the winter and spring, when pink dianthus and blue phlox begin the cycle anew.

'Golden Sword' yucca **A**

Stone edging **J**

Plants & Projects

These are all tough, heat-tolerant plants, but they do best if you add a deep bark mulch to help conserve moisture. Maintenance is minimal. In early spring, cut back the old stems and renew the mulch. Then enjoy your trips to the mailbox.

A **'Golden Sword' yucca**
(use 1 plant)
This shrubby perennial offers sword-shaped evergreen leaves striped with yellow and gold. Bears showy clusters of creamy flowers on tall stems in summer. See *Yucca filamentosa*, p. 197.

B **'Powis Castle' artemisia** (use 1)
A perennial that forms a large mound of lacy gray-green aromatic foliage. Can be evergreen in areas with mild winters. See *Artemisia*, p. 175.

C **'Cherry Chief' autumn sage** (use 1)
Loose clusters of cherry red flowers cover this bushy perennial from summer through fall. Evergreen in mild winters. See *Salvia greggii*, p. 194.

D **'Goldsturm' coneflower** (use 3)
This perennial makes a late-summer show of large, golden yellow, daisylike flowers with black centers, above a mound of dark green foliage. See *Rudbeckia fulgida*, p. 194.

E **'Appleblossom' yarrow** (use 6)
A tough perennial with aromatic, delicate-looking gray-green foliage. It bears flat clusters of tiny clear pink flowers through the summer months. A fine companion for the neighboring sedum and autumn sage. See *Achillea*, p. 174.

F **'Autumn Joy' sedum** (use 3)
A perennial with interesting fleshy gray-green leaves topped by flat clusters of flowers that appear in August and mature from pink to rusty red as autumn progresses. See *Sedum*, p. 195.

G **Stoke's aster** (use 3)
From June to frost, this perennial produces pretty blue flowers atop evergreen foliage. See *Stokesia laevis*, p. 196.

H **'Bath's Pink' dianthus** (use 2)
Pick a few of this perennial's fragrant pink flowers on late-spring mail runs; enjoy the grassy evergreen foliage the rest of the year. See *Dianthus*, p. 181.

I **Moss phlox** (use 3)
Choose a pale blue-flowered variety of this evergreen perennial ground cover to creep around the yucca. Blooms prolifically for several weeks in spring. See *Phlox subulata*, p. 191.

J **Stone edging**
Keep the lawn and bed separate with an edging of small fieldstones, installed using the method described for installing a brick edging on p. 152.

Site: Sunny

Season: Early summer

Concept: Drought-tolerant perennials enhance your trips to the mailbox.

See site plan for Ⓒ Ⓖ.

Ⓔ 'Appleblossom' yarrow

Ⓓ 'Goldsturm' coneflower

'Powis Castle' Ⓑ artemisia

Ⓕ 'Autumn Joy' sedum

Ⓗ 'Bath's Pink' dianthus

Ⓘ Moss phlox

1 square = 1 ft.

Lawn

Driveway

Mailbox

Street

Mostly foliage

Foliage can create as much fanfare as flowers, with even less fuss. Here, a dark green carpet of mondo grass replaces the flowering ground covers in the previous design. Two forms of heavenly bamboo provide colorful foliage year-round and add to the variety of leaf textures offered by the sedum, sage, yucca, and artemisia that repeat from the previous design. The spiky foliage of the tall spring-blooming irises alongside the mailbox looks good long after the elegant flowers have passed. Once established, these tough plants require only seasonal care and cleanup.

Site: Sunny

Season: Late fall

Concept: Foliage rivals flowers for eye-catching interest in this planting.

See site plan for **G**.

F 'Powis Castle' artemisia

E 'Golden Sword' yucca

A 'Moon Bay' heavenly bamboo

B 'Harbour Dwarf' heavenly bamboo

H 'Autumn Joy' sedum

C Bearded iris

D Mondo grass

I Stone edging

1 square = 1 ft.

Lawn

Driveway

Mailbox

Street

Plants & Projects

A **'Moon Bay' heavenly bamboo** (use 3 plants)
A small evergreen shrub whose lacy leaves change color with the seasons: gold in spring, green in summer, and a lovely red or burgundy in fall and winter. Forms an upright clump about 2 ft. tall and rarely needs pruning. See *Nandina domestica*, p. 190.

B **'Harbour Dwarf' heavenly bamboo** (use 5)
Another dwarf cultivar, this evergreen shrub has a lower, more spreading growth habit than 'Moonbay', with the same striking foliage. See *Nandina domestica*, p. 190.

C **Bearded iris** (use 2)
In midspring this perennial's large showy flowers rise on stiff stalks above a clump of thick, swordlike green foliage. Choose a cultivar with blue flowers, which will stand out against the artemisia. See *Iris*, p. 187.

D **Mondo grass** (use 50 sprigs)
Carpet the planting with the rich dark green, grassy leaves of this evergreen perennial, which will highlight the colors of the other plants. See *Ophiopogon japonicus*, p. 190.

See p. 104 for the following:

E **'Golden Sword' yucca** (use 1)

F **'Powis Castle' artemisia** (use 1)

G **'Cherry Chief' autumn sage** (use 1)

H **'Autumn Joy' sedum** (use 1)

I **Stone edging**

Plant portraits

Send (and receive) a cheerful message with this selection of rugged flowering plants.

● = First design, pp. 104–105
▲ = Second design, p. 106

Bearded iris (*Iris*, p. 187) ▲

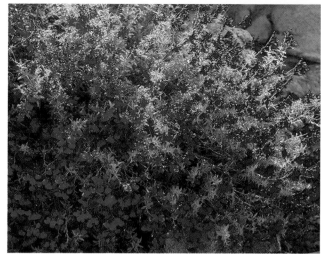

'Cherry Chief' autumn sage (*Salvia greggii*, p. 194) ● ▲

'Powis Castle' artemisia (*Artemisia*, p. 175) ● ▲

'Bath's Pink' dianthus (*Dianthus*, p. 181) ●

'Appleblossom' yarrow (*Achillea*, p. 174) ●

Stoke's aster (*Stokesia laevis*, p. 196) ●

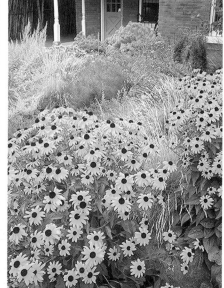

'Goldsturm' coneflower (*Rudbeckia fulgida*, p. 194) ●

Elegant Symmetry
Make a formal garden for the backyard

Formal landscaping often lends dignity to the public areas around a home (see p. 28). Formality can also be rewarding in a more private setting. There, the groomed plants, geometric lines, and symmetrical layout of a formal garden can help to organize the surrounding landscape, provide an elegant area for entertaining, or simply be enjoyed for their own sake.

A series of hedges and edgings define this small garden, punctuated by tidy evergreen trees and shrubs at the corners. Flowers contribute color and fragrance for months from summer through autumn. The foliage looks good year-round.

Formal gardens like this one look self-contained on paper. But even more than other types of landscaping, actual formal gardens work well only when carefully correlated with other elements in the landscape, such as the house, garage, patio, and major plantings. Transitions between formal and more casual areas are particularly important. Separating areas with expanses of lawn, changes of level, or plantings that screen sight lines helps formal and informal elements coexist comfortably.

Site: Sunny

Season: Summer

Concept: This self-contained formal planting could fill a small backyard or join other features on a larger property.

Lawn

Ornament

1 square = 1 ft.

See site plan for **J**.

Foster holly **A**

Blazing star **I**

'Needlepoint' holly **B**

Hybrid tea rose **E**

Sweet olive **C**

Lilyturf **K**

Littleleaf boxwood **D**

Plants & Projects

Shaping plants for a formal garden takes patience and persistence. The holly hedge will need a few years to fill in, and it and the abelia will require regular shearing to look their best. The other trees and shrubs can have loosely formal shapes as shown here or be sheared to a more rigid geometry. Prune the roses in late winter.

A Foster holly (use 2 plants)
The pyramidal form and deep green leaves of this broadleaved evergreen tree add visual weight to the design. Needs little pruning and bears lots of rich red winter berries. See *Ilex,* Evergreen hollies: *I. × attenuata* 'Foster #2', p. 186.

B 'Needlepoint' holly (use 14)
A dense evergreen shrub ideal for a hedge, with shiny leaves and a magnificent show of red winter berries. See *Ilex,* Evergreen hollies: *I. cornuta,* p. 186.

C Sweet olive (use 2)
An evergreen shrub with a dense compact form. Its holly-like leaves are glossy dark green. In autumn the sweetly scented flowers perfume the entire garden. See *Osmanthus × fortunei,* p. 191.

D Littleleaf boxwood (use 4)
This evergreen shrub naturally forms a compact globe. Small, bright green, glossy leaves give it a fine texture. See *Buxus microphylla,* p. 177.

E Hybrid tea rose (use 10)
The classic rose, elegant, fragrant, and right at home in a formal setting. Choose your favorites for months of bloom. See *Rosa,* p. 194.

F 'Edward Goucher' abelia (use 4)
An evergreen shrub that bears rosy purple flowers from early summer to frost. Dark green leaves turn bronze in winter. Can be pruned to any shape. See *Abelia,* p. 174.

G Siberian iris (use 10)
An aristocratic perennial with striking flowers in late spring and slender arching foliage that looks good all summer. See *Iris sibirica,* p. 187.

H Dwarf fountain grass (use 8)
A perennial offering graceful tufts of slender leaves that are green in summer, gold or tan in fall and winter. Fluffy flowers rise above the foliage from summer on. See *Pennisetum alopecuroides* 'Hameln', p. 191.

I Blazing star (use 6)
A prairie native, this durable perennial bears lavender flower spikes on leafy stems, making a colorful, upright accent in midsummer. Attracts butterflies, too. See *Liatris spicata,* p. 188.

J Scarlet sage (use 8)
A bushy perennial often grown as an annual. Bright red flowers heat up the garden's corners for months in the summer. See *Salvia coccinea,* p. 194.

K Lilyturf (use 90)
Spiky grasslike clumps of evergreen leaves make this perennial an ideal edging. It bears small purple flowers in late summer. Space 1 ft. apart. See *Liriope muscari,* p. 189.

L Path
Crushed stone looks just right here. Flagstones across the entries help keep stones out of the lawn. See p. 118.

D Littleleaf boxwood

G Siberian iris

H Dwarf fountain grass

A Foster holly

B 'Needlepoint' holly

E Hybrid tea rose

C Sweet olive

L Path

F 'Edward Goucher' abelia

K Lilyturf

D Littleleaf boxwood

A formal terrace

In this design, a small terrace with table and chairs is given a formal setting, providing a lovely spot for an intimate lunch or a restful hour with a favorite book.

The geometry of this patio garden is similar to that of the previous plan, with several tiers of hedges and edging along the sides and strong accents at the corners. Here an avenue of lawn approaches the terrace. In summer, the planting abounds in flowers offering vivid colors, delicious fragrance, and the gentle companionship of butterflies. On the terrace, containers with lively warm-season annuals augment the sights and scents of the summer garden. Abundant evergreen foliage and containers of cool-season annuals make the garden an inviting spot on sunny days from fall to spring.

Site: Sunny

Season: Summer

Concept: A formal setting for intimate gatherings, enhanced by colorful scented flowers and handsome foliage.

1 square = 1 ft.

Lawn

Foster holly **I**

Gardenia **C**

'Longwood Blue' bluebeard **F**

'Needlepoint' holly **J**

Glossy abelia **B**

Purple coneflower **D**

Foster holly **I**

Gardenia **C**

'Needlepoint' holly **J**

'Longwood Blue' bluebeard **F**

Container **G**

'Stella d'Oro' daylily **E**

Terrace **H**

Littleleaf boxwood **L**

Sweet olive **K**

'Black Knight' butterfly bush **A**

'Black Knight' butterfly bush **A**

Sweet olive **K**

Plants & Projects

Ⓐ 'Black Knight' butterfly bush
(use 2 plants)
Arching branches of this deciduous shrub carry long spikes of fragrant deep purple flowers at their tips from midsummer to fall. See *Buddleia davidii*, p. 176.

Ⓑ Glossy abelia (use 5)
Pale pink flowers cover this evergreen shrub all summer. Dark green leaves turn purple-bronze in winter. See *Abelia × grandiflora*, p. 174.

Ⓒ Gardenia (use 6)
An evergreen shrub with heavily scented creamy white flowers in summer. The cultivar 'Mystery' or 'August Beauty' would work well here. See *Gardenia jasminoides*, p. 182.

Ⓓ Purple coneflower (use 10)
Large pink daisylike flowers with dark centers float above this perennial's mound of dark green foliage in summer. See *Echinacea purpurea*, p. 181.

Ⓔ 'Stella d'Oro' daylily (use 12)
This popular perennial edges the terrace with grassy foliage and bright golden yellow flowers from early summer until frost. See *Hemerocallis*, p. 184.

Ⓕ 'Longwood Blue' bluebeard
(use 10)
Fringed blue flowers and the butterflies they attract grace the soft gray-green foliage of this deciduous shrub from late summer to frost. See *Caryopteris × clandonensis*, p. 178.

Ⓖ Containers
For bright accents on the terrace, fill pots with long-blooming annuals. Replace the plantings in fall and spring. See Annuals, p. 175.

Ⓗ Terrace
A terrace 10 ft. square accommodates a small table and chairs and can be built in a weekend or two. We've shown brick here; select paving material to complement your home. See p. 124.

See p. 109 for the following:

Ⓘ Foster holly (use 2)

Ⓙ 'Needlepoint' holly (use 14)

Ⓚ Sweet olive (use 2)

Ⓛ Littleleaf boxwood (use 20)

Plant portraits

Sheared or left in nature's own tidy forms, offering flowers or foliage or both, these plants bring a fresh look to formal designs.

● = First design, pp. 108–109
▲ = Second design, pp. 110–111

Lilyturf (*Liriope muscari*, p. 189) ●

Littleleaf boxwood (*Buxus microphylla*, p.177) ● ▲

Sweet olive (*Osmanthus × fortunei*, p. 191) ● ▲

Foster holly (*Ilex*, Evergreen hollies: *I. × attenuata* 'Foster #2', p. 186) ● ▲

Hybrid tea rose (*Rosa*, p. 194) ●

'Needlepoint' holly
(*Ilex*, Evergreen hollies: *I. cornuta*, p. 186) ● ▲

Guide to Installation

In this section, we introduce the hard but rewarding work of landscaping. Here you'll find information on all the tasks you need to install any of the designs in this book, organized in the order in which you'd most likely tackle them. Clearly written text and numerous illustrations help you learn how to plan the job; clear the site; construct paths, patios, ponds, fences, arbors, and trellises; and prepare the planting beds and install and maintain the plantings. Roll up your sleeves and dig in. In just a few weekends you can create a landscape feature that will provide years of enjoyment.

Organizing Your Project

If your gardening experience is limited to mowing the lawn, pruning the bushes, and growing some flowers and vegetables, the thought of starting from scratch and installing a whole new landscape feature might be intimidating. But in fact, adding one of the designs in this book to your property is completely within reach, if you approach it the right way. The key is to divide the project into a series of steps and take them one at a time. This is how professional landscapers work. It's efficient and orderly, and it makes even big jobs seem manageable.

On this and the facing page, we'll explain how to think your way through a landscaping project and anticipate the various steps. Subsequent topics in this section describe how to do each part of the job. Detailed instructions and illustrations cover all the techniques you'll need to install any design from start to finish.

The step-by-step approach

Choose a design and adapt it to your site. The designs in this book address parts of the home landscape. In the most attractive and effective home landscapes, all the various parts work together. Don't be afraid to change the shape of beds; alter the number, kinds, and positions of plants; or revise paths and structures to bring them into harmony with their surroundings.

To see the relationships with your existing landscape, you can draw the design on a scaled plan of your property. Or you can work on the site itself, placing wooden stakes, pots, tricycles, or whatever is handy to represent plants and structures. With a little imagination, either method will allow you to visualize basic relationships.

Lay out the design on site. Once you've decided what you want to do, you'll need to lay out the paths and structures and outline the beds. Some people are comfortable laying out a design "freehand," pacing off distances and relying on their eye to judge sizes and relative positions. Others prefer to transfer the grid from the plan full size onto the site in order to place elements

Digging postholes

Amending soil

precisely. (Garden lime, a grainy white powder available at nurseries, can be used like chalk on a blackboard to "draw" a grid or outlines of planting beds.)

Clear the site. (See pp. 116–117.) Sometimes you have to work around existing features—a nice big tree, a building or fence, a sidewalk—but it's usually easiest to start a new landscaping project if you clear as much as possible down to ground level. That means removing unwanted structures or pavement and killing, cutting down, or uprooting all the plants. Needless to say, this can generate a lot of debris, and you'll need to figure out how to dispose of it all. Still, it's often worth the trouble to make a fresh start.

Build the "hardscape." (See pp. 118–149.) "Hardscape" means anything you build as part of a landscape—a fence, trellis, arbor, retaining wall, walkway, edging, outdoor lighting, or whatever. If you're going to do

any building, do it first, and finish the construction before you start any planting. That way you won't have to worry about stepping on any of the plants, and they won't be in the way as you work.

Prepare the soil. (See pp. 150–153.) On most properties, it's uncommon to find soil that's as good as it should be for growing plants. Typically, the soil around a house is shallow, compacted, and infertile. It may be rocky or contain buried debris. Some plants tolerate such poor conditions, but they don't thrive. To grow healthy, attractive plants, you need to improve the quality of the soil throughout the entire area that you're planning to plant.

Do the planting and add mulch. (See pp. 154–159.) Putting plants in the ground usually goes quite quickly and gives instant gratification. Spreading mulch over the soil makes the area look neat and "finished" even while the plants are still small.

Maintain the planting. (See pp. 159–171.) Most plantings need regular watering and occasional weeding for the first year or two. After that, depending on the design you've chosen, you'll have to do some routine maintenance—pruning, shaping, cutting back, and cleaning up—to keep the plants looking their best. This may take as little as a few hours a year or as much as an hour or two every week throughout the growing season.

Planting

Setting flagstones

Clearing the Site

The site you've chosen for a landscaping project may or may not have any man-made objects (fences, old pavement, trash, etc.) to be removed, but it will almost certainly be covered with plants.

Before you start cutting plants down, try to find someone—a friend or neighbor who enjoys gardening—to identify them for you. As you walk around together, make a sketch that shows which plants are where, and attach labels to the plants, too. Determine if there are any desirable plants worth saving—mature shade trees that you should work around, shapely shrubs that aren't too big to dig up and relocate or give away, worthwhile perennials and ground covers that you could divide and replant, healthy sod that you could lay elsewhere. Likewise, decide which plants have to go—diseased or crooked trees, straggly or overgrown shrubs, weedy brush, invasive ground covers, tattered lawn.

You can clear small areas yourself, bundling the brush for pickup and tossing soft-stemmed plants on the compost pile, but if you have lots of woody brush or any trees to remove, you might want to hire someone else to do the job. A crew armed with power tools can turn a thicket into a pile of wood chips in just a few hours. Have them pull out the roots and grind the stumps, too. Save the chips; they're good for surfacing paths or you can use them as mulch.

Working around a tree

If there are any large, healthy trees on your site, be careful as you work around them. It's okay to prune off some of a tree's limbs, as shown on the facing page, but respect its trunk and its roots. Try never to cut or wound the bark on the trunk (don't nail things to a tree), as that exposes the tree to disease organisms. Don't pile soil or mulch against the trunk, since that keeps the bark wet and can make it rot.

Killing perennial weeds

Some common weeds that sprout back from perennial roots or runners are bindweed, blackberry and other briers, Johnson grass, kudzu, nutsedge, and poison ivy. Garden plants that can become weedy include ajuga, akebia, bamboo, bishop's weed, bouncing Bet, comfrey, English ivy, Japanese climbing fern, Japanese honeysuckle, loosestrife, and mint. Once they get established, perennial weeds are hard to eliminate. You can't just cut off the tops, because they keep sprouting back. You need to dig the weeds out, smother them with mulch, or kill them with an herbicide, and it's better to do this before rather than after you plant a bed.

Digging. In many cases, you can do a pretty good job of removing a perennial weed if you dig carefully where the stems enter the ground, find the roots, and follow them as far as possible through the soil, pulling out every bit of root that you find. Some plant roots go deeper than you can dig, and most plants will sprout back from the small bits that you miss, but these leftover sprouts are easy to pull.

Smothering. This technique is easier than digging, particularly for eradicating large infestations, but much slower. First mow or cut the tops of the weeds as close to the ground as possible ❶. Then cover the area with sections from the newspaper, overlapped like shingles ❷, or flattened-out cardboard boxes. Top with a layer of

Smothering weeds

❶ Smothering kills weeds by depriving them of light. Cut the tops off close to the ground.

❷ Cover with thick newspaper or cardboard.

❸ Top with several inches of mulch. Wait a few months to be sure weeds are dead; then till rotted newspaper and mulch into the soil.

Moving turf

❶ With a sharp shovel, cut healthy turf into squares or strips of manageable size.

❷ Slice a few inches deep under each square, lift it, and place as soon as possible in a new spot.

mulch, such as straw, grass clippings, tree leaves, wood chips, or other organic material spread several inches deep ❸.

Smothering works by excluding light, which stops photosynthesis. If any shoots reach up through the covering and produce green leaves, pull them out immediately. Wait a few months, until you're sure the weeds are dead, before you dig into the smothered area and plant there.

Spraying. Herbicides are easy, fast, and effective weed killers when chosen and applied with care. Look for those that break down quickly into more benign substances, and make sure the weed you're trying to kill is listed on the product label. Apply all herbicides exactly as directed by the manufacturer. After spraying, you usually have to wait from one to four weeks for the weed to die completely, and some weeds need to be sprayed a second or third time before they give up. Some weeds just "melt away" when they die, but if there are tough or woody stems and roots, you'll need to dig them up and discard them.

Replacing turf

If the area where you're planning to add a landscape feature is currently part of the lawn, you have a fairly easy task ahead—easier than clearing brush or killing weeds,

anyway. How to proceed depends on the condition of the turf and on what you want to put in its place. If the turf is healthy, you can "recycle" it to replace, repair, or extend the lawn on other parts of your property.

The drawing above shows a technique for removing relatively small areas of strong healthy turf for replanting elsewhere. First, with a sharp shovel, cut it into squares or strips about 1 to 2 ft. square (these small pieces are easy to lift) ❶. Then slice a few inches deep under each square and lift the squares, roots and all, like brownies from a pan ❷. Quickly transplant the squares to a previously prepared site; water them well until the roots are established. You can rent a sod-cutting machine for larger areas you wish to recycle.

If you don't need the turf anywhere else, or if it's straggly or weedy, leave it in place and kill the grass. A single application of herbicide kills some grasses, but you may need to spray vigorous turf twice. Another way to kill grass is to cover it with a tarp or a sheet of black plastic for about four weeks during the heat of summer. After you've killed the grass, dig or till the bed, shredding the turf, roots and all, and mixing it into the soil. This is hard work if the soil is dry but less so if the ground has been softened by a recent rain or watering.

Removing large limbs

If there are large trees on your property now, you may want to remove some of the lower limbs so you can walk and see underneath them and so more light can reach plantings you're planning beneath them. Major pruning of large trees is a job for a professional arborist, but you can remove limbs smaller than 4 in. in diameter and less than 10 ft. above the ground yourself with a simple bow saw or pole saw.

Use the three-step procedure shown below to remove large limbs safely and without harming the tree. First, saw partway through the bottom of the limb, approximately 1 ft. out from the trunk ❶. This keeps the bark from tearing down the trunk when the limb falls. Then make a corresponding cut down through the top of the limb ❷—be prepared to get out of the way when the limb drops. Finally, remove the stub ❸. Undercut it slightly or hold it as you finish the cut, so it doesn't fall away and peel bark off the trunk. Note that the cut is not flush with the trunk but is just outside the thick area at the limb's base, called the branch collar. Leaving the branch collar helps the wound heal quickly and naturally. Wound dressing is considered unnecessary today.

❷ Saw down to remove the limb.

Branch collar

❶ Saw up from the bottom.

❸ Remove the stub just outside the branch collar.

Making Paths and Walkways

Every landscape needs paths and walkways if for no other reason than to keep your feet dry as you move from one place to another. A path can also divide and define the spaces in the landscape, orchestrate the way the landscape is viewed, and even be a key element enhancing its beauty.

Whether it is a graceful curving garden path or a utilitarian slab leading to the garage, a walk has two main functional requirements: durability and safety. It should hold up through seasonal changes. It should provide a well-drained surface that is easy to walk on and to maintain.

A path's function helps determine its surface and its character. In general, heavily trafficked walkways leading to a door, garage, or shed need hard, smooth (but not slick) surfaces and should take you where you want to go fairly directly. A path to a backyard play area could be a strip of soft wood bark, easy on the knees of impatient children. A relaxed stroll in the garden might require only a hopscotch collection of flat stones meandering from one prized plant to another.

Before laying out a walk or path, spend some time observing existing traffic patterns. If your path makes use of a route people already take (particularly children), they'll be more likely to stay on the path and off the lawn or flowers. Avoid areas that are slow to drain. When determining path width, consider whether the path must accommodate rototillers and wheelbarrows or two strollers walking abreast, or just provide steppingstone access for maintaining the plants.

Dry-laid paths

You can make a path simply by laying bricks or spreading wood chips on top of bare earth. While quick and easy, this method has serious drawbacks. Laid on the surface, with no edging to contain them, loose materials are soon scattered, and solid materials are easily jostled out of place. If the earth base doesn't drain very well, the path will be a swamp after a rainstorm. And in cold-winter areas, repeated expansion and contraction of the soil will heave bricks or flagstones out of

alignment, making the path unsightly and potentially dangerous.

The method we recommend—laying surface material on an excavated sand-and-gravel base—minimizes these problems. The sand and gravel improve drainage and provide a cushion against the freeze-thaw movement of the soil. Excavation can place the path surface at ground level, where the surrounding soil or an installed edging can contain loose materials and prevent hard materials from shifting.

All styles, from a "natural" wood-bark path to a formal cut-stone entry walk, and all the materials discussed here can be laid on an excavated base of gravel and sand.

Drainage

Few things are worse than a path dotted with puddles or icy patches. To prevent these from forming, the soil around and beneath the path should drain well. The path's location and construction should ensure that rainwater does not collect on the surface. Drainage also affects frost heaving. In cold-winter areas, the soil expands and contracts as the water in it freezes and

Hard-surface walks

Edging

Flagstone or precast pavers

2 in. builder's sand

Bricks

4 in. coarse gravel or crushed rock

Loose-surface paths

Edging

Water-permeable landscape fabric

Pea gravel, fine crushed rock, bark, or wood chips

4 in. coarse gravel or crushed rock

Choosing a surface

Walkways and paths can be made of either hard or soft material. Your choice of material will depend on the walkway's function, your budget, and your personal preferences.

Soft materials, including bark, wood chips, pine needles, and loose gravel, are best for informal and low-traffic areas. Inexpensive and simple to install, they settle, scatter, or decompose and must be replenished or replaced every few years.

Hard materials, such as brick, flagstone, and concrete pavers, are more expensive and time-consuming to install, but they are permanent, requiring only occasional maintenance. (Compacted crushed stone can also make a hard-surface walk.) Durable and handsome, they're ideal for high-traffic, "high-profile" areas.

Bark, wood chips, and pine needles

Perfect for a "natural" look or a quick temporary path, these loose materials can be laid directly on the soil or, if drainage is poor, on a gravel bed. Bagged materials from a nursery or garden center will be cleaner, more uniform, and considerably more expensive than bulk supplies bought by the cubic yard. Check with local tree services to find the best prices on bulk material.

Gravel and crushed rock

Loose rounded gravel gives a bit underfoot, creating a "soft" but somewhat messy path. The angular facets of crushed stone eventually compact into a "hard" and tidier path that can, if the surrounding soil is firm enough, be laid without an edging. Gravel and stone type and color vary from area to area within a region. Buy these materials by the ton or cubic yard.

Concrete pavers

Precast concrete pavers are versatile, readily available, and often the least expensive hard-surface material. They come in a range of colors and shapes, including interlocking patterns. Precast edgings are also available. Most home and garden centers carry a variety of precast pavers, which are sold by the piece.

Precast pavers

Brick

Widely available in a range of sizes, colors, and textures, brick complements many design styles, both formal and informal. When carefully laid on a well-prepared sand-and-gravel base, brick provides an even, safe, and long-lasting surface. Buy paving brick instead of the softer "facing" brick, which may break up after a few freeze-thaw cycles. (If you buy used brick, pick the densest and hardest.) Avoid brick with glazed faces; the glaze traps moisture and salts, which eventually damage the brick.

Running bond

Two-brick basket weave

Herringbone

Diagonal herringbone

Flagstone

"Flagstone" is a generic term for stratified stone that can be split to form pavers. Limestone, sandstone, and bluestone are common paving materials. The surfaces of marble and slate are usually too smooth to make safe paving because they are slippery when wet. Cut into squares or rectangles, flagstone can be laid as individual stepping-stones or in interesting patterns. Flags with irregular outlines present other patterning opportunities. Flagstones come in a range of colors, textures, and sizes. Flags for walks should be at least 2 in. thick; thinner stones fracture easily. Purchased by weight, surface area, or pallet load, flagstones are usually the most expensive paving choice.

Cut flagstone

Cut and irregular flagstone

Irregular flagstone

Edgings

All walk surfaces need to be contained in some fashion along their edges. Where soil is firm or tightly knit by turf, neatly cut walls of the excavation can serve as edging. An installed edging often provides more effective containment, particularly if the walk surface is above grade. It also prevents damage to bricks or stones on the edges of paths. Walkway edgings are commonly made of 1- or 2-in.-thick lumber, thicker landscaping timbers, brick, or stone.

Wood edging

Wood should be rot-resistant redwood, cedar, or cypress or pressure-treated for ground-contact use. If you're working in loose soils, fix a deep wooden edging to support stakes with double-headed nails. When the path is laid, pull the nails, and fill and tamp behind the edging. Then drive the stakes below grade. In firmer soils, or if the edging material is not wide enough, install it on top of the gravel base. Position the top of the edging at the height of the path. Dimension lumber 1 in. thick is pliable enough to bend around gradual curves.

Treated dimensional lumber
with support stakes

Landscape timbers with
crossties laid on gravel base

Brick and stone edging

In firm soil, a row of bricks laid on edge and perpendicular to the length of the path adds stability. For a more substantial edging, stand bricks on end on the excavated soil surface, add the gravel base, and tamp earth around the base of the bricks on the outside of the excavation. Stone edgings laid on end can be set in the same way. "End-up" brick or stone edgings are easy to install on curved walks.

Bricks on edge, laid on gravel base

Bricks on end, laid on soil

thaws. As the soil moves, so do path and walkway materials laid on it. The effect is minimal on loose materials such as wood chips or gravel, but frost heaving can shift brick and stone significantly out of line.

Before you locate a path, observe runoff and drainage on your property during and after heavy rains. Avoid routing a path through areas where water courses, collects, or is slow to drain.

While both loose and hard paving can sometimes be successfully laid directly on well-drained soil, laying surface materials on a base of gravel and sand will help improve drainage and minimize frost heaving. In most situations, a 4-in. gravel bed topped with 2 in. of sand will be sufficient. Water moves through these materials quickly, and they "cushion" the surface materials from the expansion and contraction of the underlying soil. Very poorly drained soils may require more gravel, an additional layer of coarse rock beneath the gravel, or even drain tiles. If you suspect your site has serious drainage problems, consult a specialist for advice.

Finally, keep water from pooling on a walk by making its surface higher in the center than at the edges. The center of a 4-ft.-wide walk should be at least $1/2$ in. higher than its edges. If you're using a drag board to level the sand base, curve its lower edge to create this "crown." Otherwise crown the surface by eye.

Preparing the base

Having decided on location and materials, you can get down to business. The initial steps of layout and base preparation are much the same for all surface materials.

Layout

Lay out straight sections with stakes and string. You can plot curves with stakes and "fair" the curve with a garden hose, or you can outline the curve with the hose alone, marking it with lime or sand **❶**.

Preparing the base

❶ Lay out the path with stakes, string, garden hose, and lime.

❷ Dig out path between layout string and lime lines.

❸ Install the edging.

❹ Rake out gravel base.

Lay out free-form curved sections with garden hose and mark with lime.

Mark straight sections with 1x2 stakes and string.

Drag board

Edging

❺ Level sand base with a drag board.

Excavation

The excavation depth depends on how much sand-and-gravel base your soil's drainage calls for, the thickness of the surface material, and its position above or below grade ❷. Mark the depth on a stake or stick and use this to check depth as you dig. Walking surfaces are most comfortable if they are reasonably level across their width. Check the bottom of the excavation with a level as you dig. If the walk cuts across a slope, you'll need to remove soil from the high side and use it to fill the low side to produce a level surface. If you've added soil or if the subsoil is loose, compact it by tamping.

Edging installion

Some edgings can be installed immediately after excavation; others are placed on top of the gravel portion of the base ❸. (See the sidebar "Edgings" on the facing page.) If the soil's drainage permits, you can lay soft materials now on the excavated, tamped, and edged soil base. To control

weeds, and to keep bark, chips, or pine needles from mixing with the subsoil, you can spread water-permeable landscape fabric over the excavated soil base.

Laying the base

Now add gravel (if required), rake it level, and compact it ❹. Use gravel up to 1 in. in diameter or $1/4$- to $3/4$-in. crushed stone, which drains and compacts well. You can rent a hand tamper (a heavy metal plate on the end of a pole) or a machine compactor if you have a large area to compact.

If you're making a loose-gravel or crushed-stone walk, add the surface material on top of the base gravel. (See "Loose materials" below.) For walks of brick, stone, or pavers, add a 2-in. layer of builder's sand, not the finer sand masons use for mixing mortar.

Rake the sand smooth with the back of a level-head rake. You can level the sand with a wooden drag board, also called a screed ❺. Nail together two 1x4s or notch a 1x6 to place the lower edge at the desired

height of the sand, and run the board along the path edging. To settle the sand, dampen it thoroughly with a hose set on fine spray. Fill any low spots, rake or drag the surface level, then dampen it again.

Laying the surface

Whether you're laying a loose or hard material, take time to plan your work. Provide access for delivery trucks, and have material deposited as close to the worksite as possible.

Loose materials

Install water-permeable landscape fabric over the gravel base to prevent gravel from mixing with the surface material. Spread bark or wood chips 2 to 4 in. deep. For a pine-needle surface, spread 2 in. of needles on top of several inches of bark or chips. Spread loose pea gravel about 2 in. deep. For a harder, more uniform surface, add 1/2 in. of fine crushed stone on top of the gravel. You can let traffic compact crushed-rock surfaces, or compact them by hand or with a machine.

Bricks and precast pavers

Take time to figure out the pattern and spacing of the bricks or pavers by laying them out on the lawn or driveway, rather than disturbing your carefully prepared sand base. When you're satisfied, begin in a corner, laying the bricks or pavers gently on the sand so the base remains even ❶. Lay full bricks first; then cut bricks to fit as needed at the edges. To produce uniform joints, space bricks with a piece of wood cut to the joint width. You can also maintain alignment with a straightedge or with a string stretched across the path between nails or stakes. Move the string as the work proceeds.

As you complete a row or section, bed the bricks or pavers into the sand base with several firm raps of a rubber mallet or a hammer on a scrap 2x4. Check with a level or straightedge to make sure the surface is even ❷. (You'll have to do this by feel or eye across the width of a crowned path.) Lift low bricks or pavers carefully and fill beneath them with sand; then reset them. Don't stand on the walk until you've filled the joints.

When you've finished a section, sweep fine, dry mason's sand into the joints, working across the surface of the path in all directions ❸. Wet thoroughly with a fine spray and let dry; then sweep in more sand if necessary. If you want a "living" walk, sweep a loam-sand mixture into the joints and plant small, tough, ground-hugging plants, such as thyme, in them.

Rare is the brick walk that can be laid without cutting something to fit. To cut brick, mark the line of the cut with a dark

Loose materials

Cover gravel base with water-permeable landscape fabric and add 2 to 3 in. of bark or wood chips.

Bricks and precast pavers

To turn square corners, align the edging board with a carpenter's square.

❶ Begin laying in a corner.

❷ Check the surface with a level or straightedge. Fill under low bricks; tamp down high ones. Use a plank to distribute your weight if you must work on the path.

❸ Sweep fine, dry sand into the joints to fix the bricks or pavers in place.

Cutting bricks

Wear safety glasses.

Scored line

Brickset chisel

pencil all around the brick. With the brick resting firmly on sand or soil, score the entire line by rapping a wide mason's chisel called a "brickset" with a heavy wooden mallet or a soft-headed steel hammer as shown on the facing page. Place the brickset in the scored line across one face and give it a sharp blow with the hammer to cut the brick.

If you have a lot of bricks to cut, or if you want greater accuracy, consider renting a masonry saw. Whether you work by hand or machine, always wear safety glasses.

Flagstones

Install cut stones of uniform thickness as described for bricks and pavers. Working out patterns beforehand is particularly important—stones are too heavy to move around more than necessary. To produce a level surface with cut or irregular stones of varying thickness, you'll need to add or remove sand for each stone. Set the stone carefully on sand; then move it back and forth to work it into place ❶. Lay a level or straightedge over three or four stones to check the surface's evenness ❷. When a section is complete, fill the joints with sand or with sand and loam as described for bricks and pavers.

You can cut flagstone with a technique similar to that used for bricks. Score the line of the cut on the top surface with a brickset and hammer. Prop the stone on a piece of scrap wood, positioning the line of cut slightly beyond the edge of the wood. Securing the bottom edge of the stone with your foot, place the brickset on the scored line and strike sharply to make the cut.

Cutting flagstones

Wear safety glasses.

Scored line

Wood batten

Brickset

❶ Set flagstones in place carefully to avoid disturbing the sand base.

Flagstones

❷ Extend a straightedge over several stones to check the surface for evenness. Tap high spots to level.

Steppingstones

A steppingstone walk set in turf creates a charming effect and is very simple to lay. You can use cut or irregular flagstones or fieldstone, which is irregular in thickness as well as in outline. Arrange the stones on the turf; then set them one by one. Cut into the turf around the stone with a sharp flat shovel or trowel, and remove the stone; then dig out the sod with the shovel. Placing stones at or below grade will keep them away from mower blades. Fill low spots beneath the stone with earth or sand so the stone doesn't move when stepped on.

Cut around steppingstone with shovel or trowel.

Remove sod and soil.

Set in place, filling with sand or soil to bed stone firmly.

Laying a Patio

You can make a simple patio using the same techniques and materials we have discussed for paths. To ensure good drainage, an even surface, and durability, lay hard surfaces such as brick, flagstone, and pavers on a well-prepared base of gravel, sand, and compacted soil. (Crushed-rock and gravel surfaces likewise benefit from a sound base.) Make sure the surface drains away from any adjacent structure (house or garage); a drop-off of 1/4 in. per foot is usu-ally adequate. If the patio isn't near a struc-ture, make it higher in the center to avoid puddles.

Establish the outline of the patio as described for paths; then excavate the area roughly to accommodate 4 in. of gravel, 2 in. of sand, and the thickness of the paving surface. (Check with a local nursery or landscape contractor to find out if local conditions require alterations in the type or amounts of base material.) Now grade the rough excavation to provide drainage, using a simple 4-ft. grid of wooden stakes as shown in the drawings.

Drive the first row of stakes next to the house (or in the center of a freestanding patio), leveling them with a 4-ft. builder's level or a smaller level resting on a straight 2x4. The tops of these stakes should be at the height of the top of the sand base (fin-ish grade of the patio less the thickness of the surface material) ❶. Working from this row of stakes, establish another row about 4 to 5 ft. from the first. Make the tops of these stakes 1 in. lower than those of the first row, using a level and spacer

48 in.

Level — Straightedge

6 in.

Slope = 1 in. in 48 in.

1 in.

6 in.

Attach a 1-in. block to straightedge for setting rows of stakes. — Final grade

Level the row of stakes next to the house. Place subsequent rows 4 to 5 ft. apart, each 1 in. lower.

1x2 stake

❶ Excavate roughly to depth. Then set a grid of stakes (4 to 5 ft. on center) to establish the grade at the height of the sand base.

❷ Using a tape measure and shovel, fine-tune the grade so the soil surface is 6 in. beneath the tops of all the stakes.

Laying a simple patio

block, as shown on the facing page. Continue adding rows of stakes, each 1 in. lower than the previous row, until the entire area is staked. Then, with a tape measure or ruler and a shovel, fine-tune the grading by removing or adding soil until the excavated surface is 6 in. (the thickness of the gravel-sand base) below the tops of all the stakes ❷.

When installing the sand-and-gravel base, you'll want to maintain the drainage grade you've just established and produce an even surface for the paving material. If you have a good eye or a very small patio, you can do this by sight. Otherwise, you can use the stakes to install a series of 1x3 or 1x4 "leveling boards," as shown in the drawing below. (Before adding gravel, you may want to cover the soil with water-permeable landscape fabric to keep perennial weeds from growing; just cut slits to accommodate the stakes.)

Add a few inches of gravel ❸. Then set leveling boards along each row of stakes, with the boards' top edges even with the top of the stakes ❹. Drive additional stakes to sandwich the boards in place (don't use nails). Distribute the remaining inch or so of gravel and compact it by hand or machine, then the 2 in. of sand. Dragging a straight 2x4 across two adjacent rows of leveling boards will produce a precise grade and an even surface ❺. Wet the sand and fill low spots that settle.

You can install the patio surface as previously described for paths, removing the leveling boards as the bricks or pavers reach them ❻. Disturbing the sand surface as little as possible, slide the boards out from between the stakes and drive the stakes an inch or so beneath the level of the sand. Cover the stakes and fill the gaps left by the boards with sand, tamped down carefully; then continue laying the surface. Finally, sweep fine sand into the joints.

❸ Add a few inches of gravel to the excavation.

❻ When you install the patio surface, remove leveling boards as you reach them.

Patio paving

Gravel subbase

Leveling board

Add another stake to sandwich the boards in place without nails.

❹ Set 1x3 leveling boards even with the top of the grade stakes. Then add sand.

For rectangular patios, equal diagonal measures will ensure square corners.

❺ Drag a straight 2x4 across the leveling boards to grade and smooth the sand base.

Work on plywood to avoid disturbing sand.

Leveling board

Drive stakes below the surface and fill gaps with sand.

Installing a Pond

It wasn't so long ago that a garden pond like the one in this book required yards of concrete, an expert mason, and deep pockets. Today's strong, lightweight, and long-lasting synthetic liners and rigid fiberglass shells have put garden pools in reach of every homeowner. Installation does require some hard labor, but little expertise: just dig a hole, spread the liner or seat the shell, install edging, and plant. We'll discuss installation of a linered pond in the main text; see below for installing a smaller, fiberglass pool.

Liner notes

More and more nurseries and garden centers are carrying flexible pond liners; you can also buy them from mail-order suppliers specializing in water gardens. Synthetic rubber liners are longer lasting but more expensive than PVC liners. (Both are much cheaper than rigid fiberglass shells.) Buy only liners specifically made for garden ponds—don't use ordinary plastic sheeting. Many people feel that black liners look best; blue liners tend to make the pond look like a swimming pool.

Before you dig

First, make sure you comply with any rules your town may have about water features. Then keep the following ideas in mind when locating your pond. Avoid trees whose shade keeps sun-loving water plants from thriving; whose roots make digging a chore; and whose flowers, leaves, and seeds clog the water, making it unsightly and inhospitable to plants or fish. Avoid the low spot on your property; otherwise your pond will be a catch basin for runoff. Select a level spot; the immediate vicinity of the pond must be level, and starting out that way saves a lot of work. (Use excavated soil to form the mound that borders the pond shown on pp. 64–65.)

Using graph paper, enlarge the outline of the pond provided on the site plan on p. 65, altering it as you wish. If you change the size or depth of the pond, or are interested in growing a wider variety of water plants or in adding fish, remember that a healthy pond must achieve a balance between the plants and fish and the volume, depth, and temperature of the water. Even if you're not altering size or pond plants and fish, it's a good idea to consult with a knowledgeable person at a nursery or pet store specializing in water-garden plants and animals.

Calculate the liner width by adding twice the maximum depth of the pool plus an additional 2 ft. to the width. Use the same formula to calculate the length. So, for a pond 2 ft. deep, 7 ft. wide, and 15 ft. long, the liner width would be 4 ft. plus 7 ft. plus 2 ft. (or 13 ft.). The length would be 4 ft. plus 15 ft. plus 2 ft. (or 21 ft.).

Small fiberglass pool

A fiberglass shell 2 to 3 ft. wide, 4 to 5 ft. long, and 2 to 3 ft. deep is ideal for the small pool on p. 66. Garden centers often stock pond shells in a variety of shapes.

Dig a hole about 6 in. wider on all sides than the shell; its depth should equal that of the shell plus 1 in. for a sand base, plus the thickness of the fieldstone edging. Compact the bottom of the hole and spread the sand; then lower the shell into place. Add temporary wedges or props if necessary to orient and level the shell. Slowly fill the shell with water, backfilling around it with sand or sifted soil, keeping pace with the rising water level. Excavate a wide relief for the edging stones, laying them on as firm a base as possible, slightly overhanging the rim of the shell.

Fiberglass pond shell

Flagstone edging

Sand base, 1 in. thick

Sand/soil backfill

Section through pond

15 ft.

2 ft.

12 to 16 in.

Slope in 6 to 8 in.

Slope bottom slightly to make draining the pond easier.

5 ft.

Slope in 3 to 4 in.

Slope in 3 to 4 in.

❷ Spread sand on horizontal surfaces; cushion walls with carpet underlayment.

Installing a linered pond

❶ Dig hole with sloping sides to correct depth. Make sure that perimeter of hole is level.

Excavate shallow relief for edging flagstones.

Excavation

If your soil isn't too compacted or rocky, a good-size pond can be excavated with a shovel or two in a weekend ❶. (Energetic teenagers are a marvelous pool-building resource.) If the site isn't level, you can grade it using a stake-and-level system like the one described on pp. 124–125 for grading the patio.

Outline the pond's shape with garden lime, establishing the curves freehand with a garden hose or by staking out a large grid and plotting from the graph-paper plan. The pond has two levels. The broad end, at 2 ft. deep, accommodates water lilies and other plants requiring deeper water as well as fish. Make the narrow end 12 to 16 in.

deep for plants requiring shallower submersion. (You can put plant pots on stacks of bricks or other platforms to vary heights as necessary.) The walls will be less likely to crumble as you dig and the liner will install more easily if you slope them in about 3 to 4 in. for each foot of depth. Make the walls smooth, removing roots, rocks, and other sharp protrusions.

Excavate a shallow relief about 1 ft. wide around the perimeter to contain the liner overlap and stone edging. (The depth of the relief should accommodate the thickness of the edging stones.) Somewhere along the perimeter, create an overflow channel to take runoff after a heavy rain. This can simply be a 1- to 2-in. depression

a foot or so wide spanned by one of the edging stones. Lengths of PVC pipe placed side by side beneath the stone (as shown in the drawing on p. 128) will keep the liner in place. The overflow channel can open onto a lower area of lawn or garden adjacent to the pond or to a rock-filled dry well.

Fitting the liner

When the hole is complete, cushion the surfaces to protect the liner ❷. Here we show an inch-thick layer of sand on the bottom surfaces and carpet underlayment on the sloping walls. Fiberglass batting insulation also works well, as do old blankets or even heavy landscaping fabric.

Elevation detail of pond overflow

Cover pipe with flagstone.

Flagstone edging, 12 in. or more wide

Pond liner

PVC pipe, 1- or 2-in.-dia., about 12 in. long

To overflow area

Garden bed or lawn

Carpet underlayment (walls)

1-in. layer of sand (horizontal surfaces)

Stretch the liner across the hole, letting it sag naturally to touch the walls and bottom but keeping it taut enough so it does not bunch up. Weight its edges with bricks or stones; then fill it with water ❸. The water's weight will push the liner against the walls; the stones will prevent it from blowing around. As it fills, tuck and smooth out as many creases as you can; the weight of the water makes this difficult to do after the pond is full. If you stand in the pond to do so, take care not to damage the liner. Don't be alarmed if you can't smooth all the creases. Stop filling when the water is 2 in. below the rim of the pond, and cut the liner to fit into the overlap relief ❹. Hold it in place with a few

❺ Fit and lay flagstone edging. Add sand beneath the liner or stones where necessary to create a firm bed. Brush sand into joints when edging is complete.

❸ Spread liner and begin to fill with water. As water rises, tuck and smooth out as many creases as possible. Fill with water to within 2 in. of pond rim.

To overflow area

❹ Trim liner to fit relief for flagstone edging. Fix liner in place with long nails or bent coat-hanger "staples."

Weigh down liner with stones.

long nails or large "staples" made from coat hangers while you install the edging.

Edging the pond

Finding and fitting flagstones so there aren't wide gaps between them is the most time-consuming part of this task. Cantilevering the stones an inch or two over the water will hide the liner somewhat.

The stones can be laid directly on the liner, as shown ❺. Add sand under the liner to level the surface where necessary so that the stones don't rock. Such treatment will withstand the occasional gingerly traffic of pond and plant maintenance but not the wear and tear of young children or large dogs regularly running across the edging. (The liner won't go long without damage if used as a wading pool.) If you anticipate heavier traffic, you can bed the stones in 2 to 3 in. of mortar. It's prudent to consult with a landscape contractor about whether your intended use and soil require some sort of footing for mortared stones.

Water work

Unless you are a very tidy builder, the water you used to fit the liner will be too dirty to leave in the pond. (Spilled mortar can also make the water too alkaline for plants or fish.) Siphon or pump out the water, clean the liner, and refill the pond. If you're adding fish to the pond, you'll need to let the water stand for a week or so to allow any chlorine (which is deadly to fish) to dissipate. Check with local pet stores to find out if your water contains chemicals that require commercial conditioners to make the water safe for fish.

Installing the pond and plants is only the first step in water gardening. It takes patience, experimentation, and usually some consultation with experienced water gardeners to achieve a balance between plants, fish, and waterborne oxygen, nutrients, and waste that will sustain all happily while keeping algae, diseases, insects, and predators at acceptable levels.

Growing pond plants

One water lily, a few upright-growing plants, and a bundle of submerged plants (which help keep the water clean) are enough for a medium-size pond. An increasing number of nurseries and garden centers stock water lilies and other water plants. For a larger selection, your nursery or garden center may be able to recommend a specialist supplier.

These plants are grown in containers filled with heavy garden soil (*not* potting soil, which contains ingredients that float). You can buy special containers designed for aquatic plants, or simply use plastic pails or dishpans. Line basket-like containers with burlap to keep the soil from leaking out the holes. A water lily needs at least 2 to 3 gal. of soil; the more, the better. Most other water plants, such as dwarf papyrus, need 1 to 2 gal. of soil.

After planting, add a layer of gravel on the surface to keep soil from clouding the water and to protect roots from marauding fish. Soak the plant and soil thoroughly; then set the container in the pond, positioning it so the water over the soil is 6 to 18 in. deep for water liles, 0 to 6 in. for most other plants.

For maximum bloom, push a tablet of special water-lily fertilizer into the pots once or twice a month throughout the summer. Most water plants are easy to grow and carefree, although many are tropicals that die after hard frost, so you'll have to replace them each spring.

Planting water plants

Set water plants in a container of heavy garden soil. Cover soil surface with gravel to keep soil from floating away.

Gravel

1- to 3-gal. dishpan or special container lined with burlap and filled with heavy garden soil

Building a Retaining Wall

Contours and sloping terrain can add considerable interest to a home landscape. But you can have too much of a good thing. Two designs in this book employ retaining walls to alter problem slopes. The wall shown on p. 44 eliminates a small but abrupt grade change, producing two almost level surfaces and the opportunity to install attractive plantings on them. On p. 80 a curving retaining wall helps turn a steep slope into a showpiece.

Retaining walls can be handsome landscape features in their own right. Made of cut stone, fieldstone, brick, landscape timbers, or concrete, they can complement the materials and style of your house or nearby structures. However, making a stable, long-lasting retaining wall of these materials can require tools and skills many homeowners do not possess.

For these reasons we've instead chosen retaining-wall systems made of precast concrete for designs in this book. Readily available in a range of sizes, surface finishes, and colors, these systems require few tools and no special skills to install. They have been engineered to resist the forces that soil, water, freezing, and thawing bring to bear on a retaining wall. Install these walls according to the manufacturer's specifications, and you can be confident that they will do their job for many years.

A number of systems are available in the region through nurseries, garden centers, and local contracting suppliers (check the Yellow Pages). But they all share basic design principles. Like traditional dry-stone walls, these systems rely largely on weight and friction to contain the weight of the soil. In many systems, interlocking blocks or pegs help align the courses and increase the wall's strength. In all systems, blocks must rest on a solid, level base. A freely draining backfill of crushed stone is essential to avoid buildup of water pressure (both liquid and frozen) in the retained soil, which can buckle even a heavy wall.

The construction steps shown here are typical of those recommended by most system manufacturers for retaining walls up to 3 to 4 ft. tall; be sure to follow the manufacturer's instructions for the system you choose. (Some installation guides are excellent; others are less helpful. Weigh the quality of instructions in your decision of which system to buy.) For higher walls, walls on loose soil or heavy clay soils, and walls retaining very steep slopes, it is prudent to consult with a landscape architect or contractor.

Building a wall

Installing a wall system is just about as simple as stacking up children's building blocks. The most important part of the job is establishing a firm, level base. Start by laying out the wall with string and hose (for curves) and excavating a base trench.

As the boxed drawing shows, the position of the wall in relation to the base of the slope determines the height of the

Original slope

New grade level

Excavate for wall; use to level surface behind wall.

New grade

Precast-system retaining wall
Drawing represents typical construction; dimensions and specifications will vary depending on the system.

Cap block

"Batter" wall by offsetting each course.

Topsoil, 6 to 8 in. deep

Backfill of clean crushed stone

Undisturbed soil

Set first course partially or completely below grade.

Base, 24-in. trench filled with 4 in. of $3/8$- to $3/4$-in. crushed stone wall, how much soil you move, and the leveling effect on the slope. Unless the wall is very long, it is a good idea to excavate along the entire length and fine-tune the line of the wall before beginning the base trench. Remember to excavate back far enough to accommodate the stone backfill. Systems vary, but a foot of crushed-stone backfill behind the blocks is typical.

Systems vary in the width and depth of trench and type of base material, but in all of them, the trench must be level across its width and along its length. We've shown a 4-in. layer of 3/8- to 3/4-in. crushed stone (blocks can slip sideways on rounded aggregate or pea gravel, which also don't compact as well). Depending on the system and the circumstances, a portion or all of the first course lies below grade, so the soil helps hold the blocks in place.

Add crushed stone to the trench, level it with a rake, and compact it with a hand tamper or mechanical compactor. Lay the first course of blocks carefully ❶. Check frequently to make sure the blocks are level across their width and along their length. Stagger vertical joints as you stack subsequent courses. Offset the faces of the blocks so the wall leans back into the retained soil. Some systems design this "batter" into their blocks; others allow you to choose from several possible setbacks.

As the wall rises, shovel backfill behind the blocks ❷. Clean crushed rock drains well; some systems suggest placing a barrier of landscaping fabric between the rock and the retained soil to keep soil from migrating into the fill and impeding drainage.

Thinner cap blocks finish the top of the wall ❸. Some wall systems recommend cementing these blocks in place with a weatherproof adhesive. The last 6 to 8 in.

Building a wall

❷ As you add subsequent courses, backfill behind blocks with clean crushed rock.

Stagger joints.

❸ Cap blocks complete the wall. Use topsoil for final 6 to 8 in. of backfill.

Offset courses so wall leans into retained soil.

Rock base

Level

❶ After digging and leveling the trench, spread, level, and compact the base materials; then lay the blocks. Check frequently to see that they are level across their width and length.

Wall parallel to a slope: Stepped base

Backfill so grade behind finishes level with top of wall.

Construct walls running parallel to a slope in "steps," each with a level base.

Crushed-stone base

Finish grade in front of wall

Wall parallel to a slope: Stepped cap

Sometimes the top of a wall needs to step up or down to accommodate grade changes in the slope behind.

Cap block

A "return" corner

Where you want the slope to extend beyond the end of the wall, make a corner that cuts into the slope.

Step wall below grade to provide solid foundation.

Line of finish grade outside wall

of the backfill should be topsoil, firmed into place and ready for planting.

If your site slopes along the wall's length, you'll need to "step" the bottom of the wall, as shown at top left. Create a length of level trench along the lowest portion of the site; then work up the slope, creating steps as necessary.

The top of the wall can also step if the slope dissipates at one end. Such slopes are common on sites such as the one shown on p. 80, which slopes away from the house and toward the driveway. Here the base of the wall will rest on level ground, but the slope behind the wall decreases along the wall's length. The design on p. 80 shows one solution to this dilemma—a wall of uniform height with a "return" corner at one end (see bottom left), backfilled to raise the grade behind to the top of the wall. Another solution, shown at center left, is to step the wall down as the slope decreases, which saves material, produces a different look, but still works with the planting design.

Curves and corners

Wall-system blocks are designed so that curves are no more difficult to lay than straight sections. Corners may require that you cut a few blocks or use specially designed blocks, but they are otherwise uncomplicated. If your wall must fit a prescribed length between corners, consider working from the corners toward the middle (after laying a base course). Masons use this technique, which also helps to avoid exposing cut blocks at the corners.

You can cut blocks with a mason's chisel and mallet or rent a mason's saw. Chiseling works well where the faces of the blocks are rough textured, so the cut faces blend right in. A saw is best for smooth-faced blocks and projects requiring lots of cutting.

Where the wall doesn't run the full length of the slope, the best-looking and most structurally sound termination is a corner constructed to cut back into the slope, as shown at bottom left.

Steps

Steps in a low retaining wall are not difficult to build, but they require forethought and careful layout. Systems differ on construction details. The drawing below shows a typical design where the blocks and stone base rest on "steps" cut into firm subsoil. If your soil is less stable or is recent fill, you should excavate the entire area beneath the steps to the same depth as the wall base and build a foundation of blocks, as shown in the boxed drawing.

These steps are independent of the adjacent "return" walls, which are vertical, not battered (stepped back). In some systems, steps and return walls are interlocked. To match a path, you can face the treads with the same stone, brick, or pavers, or you can use the system's cap blocks or special treads.

Solid foundation: Cross section

Cap block

Return wall

Slope path away from steps.

Slope treads ¼ in. per 12 in. toward front edge to promote runoff.

Stone base

In disturbed or problematic subsoil, make a solid foundation of blocks on a level gravel base.

"Stepped" foundation

Width and depth of treads will depend on size of system's block.

Surface steps with system-provided treads or stone, pavers, or brick, to match path. Set in mortar bed or weatherproof adhesive.

Increase width by adding full blocks.

Retaining wall

Return wall

Cap block

In firm, undisturbed or compacted subsoil, bed blocks on "steps" cut in the soil.

Path

Crushed-stone base

Wall block

Fences, Arbors, and Trellises

Novices who have no trouble tackling a simple flagstone path often get nervous when it comes time to erect a fence, an arbor, or even a trellis. While such projects can require more skill and resources than others in the landscape, the ones in this book have been designed with less-than-confident do-it-yourself builders in mind. The designs are simple, the materials are readily available, and the tools and skills will be familiar to anyone accustomed to ordinary home maintenance.

First we'll introduce you to the materials and tools needed for the projects. Then we'll present the small number of basic operations you'll employ when building them. Finally, we'll provide drawings and comments on each of the projects.

Materials

Of the materials offering strength, durability, and attractiveness in outdoor settings, wood is the easiest to work and affords the quickest results. While almost all commercially available lumber is strong enough for landscape structures, most decay quickly when in prolonged contact with soil and water. Cedar, cypress, and redwood, however, contain natural preservatives and are excellent for landscape use. Alternatively, a range of softwoods (such as pine, fir, and hemlock) are pressure-treated with preservatives and will last for many years. Parts of structures that do not come in contact with soil or are not continually wet can be made of ordinary construction-grade lumber, but unless they're regularly painted, they will not last as long as treated or naturally decay-resistant material.

In addition to dimension lumber, several of the designs incorporate lattice, which is thin wooden strips crisscrossed to form patterns of diamonds or squares. Premade lattice is widely available in sheets 4 ft. by 8 ft. and smaller. Lattice comes in decay-resistant woods as well as in treated and untreated softwoods. The strips are typically from $1/8$ to $3/8$ in. thick and about $1\frac{1}{2}$ in. wide, overlapped to form squares ranging from 1 to 3 in. or more on a side. Local supplies vary, and you may find lattice made of thicker or narrower material. Lattice can be tricky to cut; if you're uneasy about this task, many suppliers will cut it for you for a small fee.

Fasteners

For millennia, even basic structures such as these would have been assembled with complicated joints, the cutting and fitting of which required long training to master. Today, with simple nailed, bolted, or screwed joints, a few hours' practice swinging a hammer or wielding a cordless electric screwdriver is all the training necessary.

All these structures can be assembled entirely with nails. But screws are stronger and, if you have a cordless screwdriver, make assembly easier. Buy common or box nails (both have flat heads) hot-dipped galvanized to prevent rust. Self-tapping screws ("deck" screws) require no pilot holes. For rust resistance, buy galvanized screws or screws treated with zinc dichromate.

Galvanized metal connectors are available to reinforce the joints used in these projects. (See the joinery drawings on pp. 138–139.) For novice builders, connectors are a great help in aligning parts and making assembly easier. (Correctly fastened with nails or screws, the joints are strong enough without connectors.)

Finishes

Cedar, cypress, and redwood are handsome when left unfinished to weather, when treated with clear or colored stains, or when painted. Pressure-treated lumber is best painted or stained to mask the greenish cast of the preservatives; weathered it turns a rather unattractive gray-green.

Outdoor stains are becoming increasingly popular. Clear or lightly tinted stains can preserve or enhance the rich reddish browns of cedar, cypress, and redwood. Stains also come in a range of colors that can be used like paint. Because they penetrate the wood rather than forming a film, stains don't form an opaque surface—you'll still need paint to make a picket fence white. On the other hand, stains won't peel or chip like paint and are therefore easier to touch up and refinish.

When choosing a finish, take account of what plants are growing on or near the structure. It's a lot of work to remove yards of vines from a trellis or squeeze between a large shrub and a fence to repaint; consider an unfinished decay-resistant wood or an initial stain that you allow to weather.

Tools

Even the least-handy homeowner is likely to have most of the tools needed for these projects: claw hammer, crosscut handsaw, brace-and-bit or electric drill, adjustable wrench, combination square, tape measure, carpenter's level, and sawhorses. You may even have Grandpa's old posthole digger. Many will have a handheld power circular saw, which makes faster (though noisier) work of cutting parts to length. A cordless drill/screwdriver is invaluable if you're substituting screws for nails. If you have more than a few holes to dig, consider renting a gas-powered posthole digger. A 12-in.-diameter hole will serve for 4x4 posts; if possible, get a larger-diameter digger for 6x6 posts.

Setting posts

All the projects are anchored by firmly set, vertical posts. In general, the taller the structure, the deeper the post should be set. For the arbors and the tallest fences, posts should be at least 3 ft. deep. Posts for fences up to 4 ft. tall can be set 2 ft. deep. To avoid post movement caused in cold-winter areas by expansion and contraction of the soil during freeze-thaw cycles, set all arbor posts below the frost line. The colder the climate, the deeper the frost line; check with local building authorities.

The length of the posts you buy depends, of course, on the depth at which they are set and their finished heights. When calculating lengths of arbor posts, remember that the tops of the posts must be level. The easiest method of achieving this is to cut the posts to length after installation. For example, buy 12-ft. posts for an arbor finishing at 8 ft. above grade and set 3 ft. in the ground. The convenience is worth the expense of the foot or so you cut off. The site and personal preference can determine whether you cut fence posts to length after installation or buy them cut to length and add or remove fill from the bottom of the hole to position them at the correct heights.

Fence posts

Lay out and set the end or corner posts of a fence first; then add the intermediate posts. Dig the holes by hand or with a power digger ❶. To promote drainage, place several inches of gravel at the bottom of the hole for the post to rest on. Checking with a carpenter's level, plumb the post vertically and brace it with scrap lumber nailed to stakes ❷. Then add a few more inches of gravel around the post's base.

If your native soil compacts well, you can fix posts in place with tamped earth. Add the soil gradually, tamping it continuously with a heavy iron bar or 2x4. Check regularly with a level to see that the post doesn't get knocked out of plumb. This technique suits rustic or informal fences, where misalignments caused by shifting posts aren't noticeable or damaging.

For more formal fences, or where soils are loose or fence panels are buffeted by winds or snow, it's prudent to fix posts in concrete ❸. Mix enough concrete to set

Setting a fence post

Post

Slope top surface for drainage.

3 ft. (typical)

Concrete and rubble (shown), or tamped earth

Coarse gravel

1 ft. (typical)

❶ Position the end or corner posts; then dig holes for them.

❷ Plumb the post, checking on adjacent faces with a level. Hold it in position with stakes and braces.

❸ Fill the hole with concrete and rubble.

Fences, Arbors, and Trellises 135

④ Stretch a string between the tops of the two end posts. Then locate positions of intermediate posts with a plumb bob.

⑤ After digging the holes, stretch a string between the end posts to align intermediate posts. Use a level to plumb adjacent faces.

Fencing a slope

Whether you step the top of the fence or make it parallel to the slope, fence posts must be vertical.

the two end posts; as a rule of thumb, figure one 80-lb. bag of premixed concrete per post. As you shovel it in, prod the concrete with a stick to settle it, particularly if you've added rubble to extend the mix. Build the concrete slightly above grade and slope it away from the post to aid drainage.

Once the end posts are set, stretch a string between the posts. (The concrete should cure for 24 hours before you nail or screw rails and panels in place, but you can safely stretch string while the concrete is still wet.) Measure along the string to position the intermediate posts; drop a plumb bob from the string at each intermediate post position to gauge the center of the hole below ④. Once all the holes have been dug, again stretch a string between the end posts, near the top. Set the intermediate posts as described previously; align one face with the string and plumb adjacent faces with the carpenter's level ⑤. Check positions of intermediate posts a final time with a tape measure.

If the fence is placed along a slope, the top of the slats or panels can step down the slope or mirror it (as shown in the bottom drawing at left). Either way, make sure that the posts are plumb, rather than leaning with the slope.

Arbor posts

Arbor posts are installed just like fence posts, but you must take extra care when positioning them. The corners of the structure must be right angles, and the sides must be parallel. Locating the corners with batter boards and string is fussy but accurate. Make the batter boards by nailing 1x2 stakes to scraps of 1x3 or 1x4, and position them about 1 ft. from the approximate location of each post as shown in the boxed drawing on the facing page. Locate the exact post positions with string; adjust the string so the diagonal measurements are equal, which ensures that the corners of the structure will be at right angles.

At the intersections of the strings, locate the postholes by eye or with a plumb bob ❶. Remove the strings and dig the holes; then reattach the strings to position the posts exactly ❷. Plumb and brace the posts carefully. Check positions with the level and by measuring between adjacent posts and across diagonals. Diagonal braces between adjacent posts will stiffen them and help align their faces ❸. Then add concrete ❹ and let it cure for a day.

To establish the height of the posts, measure up from grade on one post; then use a level and straightedge to mark the heights of the other posts from the first one. Where joists will be bolted to the faces of the posts, you can install the joists and use their top edges as a handsaw guide for cutting the posts to length.

Batter boards

Set L-shaped batter boards at each corner and stretch string to position the posts exactly.

1x2 stakes and 1x3 boards

Taut string

Taut string

18 to 24 in.

For square or rectangular post layout, diagonal measurements should be equal.

Setting arbor posts

❶ Position the posts with batter boards, taut string, and a plumb bob.

Batter board

Plumb bob

❷ Remove the string to dig the holes; then reattach it and align the outer faces of the posts with the string while you plumb and brace them.

Taut string

❸ Check distances between posts at top. Add diagonal bracing between posts to fix positions.

❹ Cement posts in place.

Joints

The components of the fences, arbors, and trellises used in this book are attached to the posts and to each other with the simple joints shown below. Because all the parts are made of dimensioned lumber, the only cuts you'll need to make are to length. For strong joints, cut ends as square as you can, so the mating pieces make contact across their entire surfaces. If you have no confidence in your sawing, many lumberyards will cut pieces to length for a modest fee.

Beginners often find it difficult to keep two pieces correctly positioned while trying to drive a nail into them, particularly when the nail must be driven at an angle, called "toenailing". If you have this problem, predrill for nails, or use screws, which draw the pieces together, or metal connectors, which can be nailed or screwed in place on one piece and then attached to the mating piece.

For several designs, you need to attach lattice panels to posts. The panels are made by sandwiching store-bought lattice between frames of dimension lumber

Toenailed butt joints (use nails or screws)

Post

Rail

Post

Rail

Metal connectors for butt joints

Joist hanger: Nail through flanges to post and rail.

Angle clip

Rafter-to-joist joints

Rafter

Joist

Toenail

Rafter

Joist

Rafter tie

Joist

Rafter

(construction details are given on the following pages). While the assembled panels can be toenailed to the posts, novices may find that the job goes easier using one or more types of metal connector, as shown in the drawing at below right. Attach the angle clips or angle brackets to the post; then position the lattice panel and fix it to the connectors. For greatest strength and ease of assembly, attach connectors with self-tapping screws driven by an electric screwdriver.

In the following pages, we'll show and comment on construction details of the fences, arbors, and trellises presented in the Portfolio of Designs. (The page number indicates the design.) Where the basic joints discussed here can be used, we have shown the parts but left choice of fasteners to you. Typical fastenings are indicated for other joints. We have kept the constructions shown here simple and straightforward. They are not the only possibilities, and we encourage experienced builders to adapt and alter constructions as well as designs to suit differing situations and personal preferences.

Frame corner with metal connector

Nailing plate

Angled plate

Attaching framed lattice panels to posts

Post

Post

Lattice panel

Lattice panel

Toenail frame to post with nails or screws.

Angle clip

Fix angle brackets to post, then to top and bottom edges of frame.

Fix angle clips to post, then to panel frame.

Screen
(pp. 20–23)

This easy-to-build screen helps create a sense of intimacy and enclosure for greeting guests. At 7 ft. tall and wide, it forms a vine-covered extension of the small alcove that shelters the front door.

The screen is a snap to build. After setting the posts (see pp. 134–136), add the top and bottom rails. Trim the ends of the "pickets" at a 45° angle and fix them with a nail or screw into each rail. Position the pickets before fastening them to ensure even spacing. If you want a more solid-looking screen, offset the pickets so that those on one side fill the gaps left by those on the other. You can vary the size of the screen and the materials shown here. Keep in mind that the proportions are what make this simple design look good.

Plan view

4x4 post
2x2 picket
2x8 rail
2 in. (approximate)

4x4 post
2x8 top rail
2x2 picket
2x8 bottom rail

Front elevation

7 ft.
6 in.
2 in.
65 in.
2 in.
9 in.

Side elevation

Post cap (optional)
4x4 post
2x8 top rail
2x2 pickets
2x8 bottom rail
7 ft.

Picket fence
(pp. 28–31)

This fence, a modest embellishment of the traditional picket fence, adds a familiar touch to a formal design for a front yard. It is most convenient to build the fence in sections and then space the posts (pp. 134–136) accordingly. Sections are easier to handle if they are no longer than 8 ft.

Work will proceed quickly if you set up a small assembly line. Cut all the rails and pickets to length; then form the "arrow" ends on the pickets with two 45° saw cuts. Assemble the sections on a flat surface (a garage floor is ideal), fixing each picket with two nails or screws to each rail. The gate is just a short section of fence with a diagonal brace to keep it from sagging. Nail or screw the 2x4 rails of the assembled sections to the posts; then add a wide picket to cover the joint where the 2x4 rails butt together on a post.

Stylized pickets — This alternative uses 1x4s and 1x2s and requires a middle rail to support the tops of the shorter "pickets".

Gridwork fence — A more unconventional design incorporates a lightweight gridwork made of 1x2s. This fence is best made in 4- to 8-ft. panels, assembled on a flat surface, and then nailed or screwed to 4x4 posts. Proportion the fence to suit your situation. Here, the vertical members are spaced 8 in. apart. From bottom to top, the horizontal members are spaced 4 in., 6 in., and 12 in. apart.

Detail: Rail-to-post joint

2x4 rail

4x4 post

2x4 rail

1x4 picket

1x2 picket

Cover the ends of the rails with a 1x4 picket.

Plan view

Gate

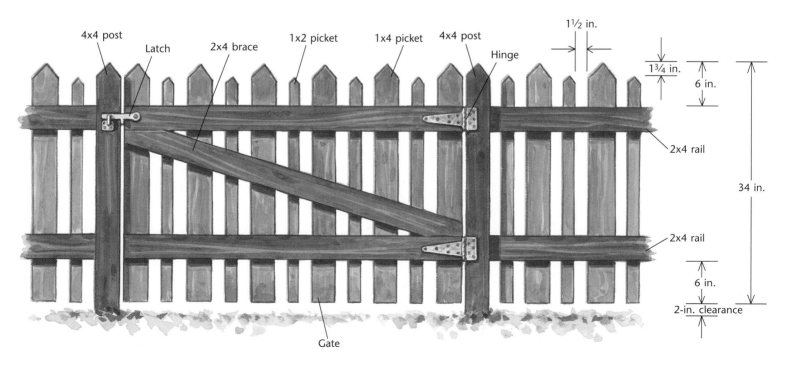

4x4 post

Latch

2x4 brace

1x2 picket

1x4 picket

4x4 post

Hinge

1½ in.

1¾ in.

6 in.

2x4 rail

34 in.

2x4 rail

6 in.

2-in. clearance

Gate

Planter
(pp. 32–35)

This planting box brings colorful annuals onto a small patio. Commercially made planters are available in a wide range of sizes, shapes, and materials. But a do-it-yourselfer can make this one in just an hour or so.

The design can be enlarged or reduced to suit your needs. For longevity, use cedar, cypress, redwood, or pressure-treated lumber. You can nail the box together, but the box will be stronger and the job easier if you use screws and an electric screwdriver. (Whether you opt for nails or screws, be sure to use fasteners treated against rust.)

Begin by assembling battens and boards to make the pair of long sides and the box bottom ❶. Note that the ends of the 1x2 battens on the box sides stop short of the two edges. Position the box bottom against the bottom ends of these battens ❷ and fix the sides to the bottom. (The top ends stop short so you can cover them with soil, which results in a neater appearance inside the box.) Complete the box by fastening the end boards to the edges of the battens on the ends of the sides and bottom ❸.

Bore $3/4$-in. drainage holes in the box bottom on a 6-in. grid. Cover the holes with pieces of window screen, fill the boxes with damp potting soil, and plant.

Arbor and fence
(pp. 50–51)

These structures work together to enhance the passage from driveway to back door. The fence separates the ball games and autos on the driveway from backyard activities, while the vine-covered arbor makes the journey a shady pleasure.

Build the arbor first. It is large, but uncomplicated. Position the posts to suit the dimensions of your property and set them in concrete as described on pp. 134–137. Cut the joists and crossties to length and fix them to the posts with galvanized carriage bolts. Tack the 2x8s in place with nails; then bore holes with a long electrician's auger bit. (Use crossties on all pairs of posts spanning the walk.) You can fix the rafters by toenailing or using metal rafter ties.

This fence is similar in construction to the one shown on p. 149. Note that the rails are fixed between the posts so that the faces of the pickets are flush with those of the posts. This fence, too, can be constructed by assembling sections, then positioning the posts to fit the sections. This ensures uniform spacing between the posts and adjacent pickets.

❶ Assemble sides and bottom by nailing or screwing battens to boards.

1½ in.

Basic box construction

Side

Intermediate batten

1x2 batten

2x10

2x10

End

1½ in.

❷ Fasten bottom to sides; position it against bottom ends of side battens.

Bottom

❸ Fix end boards to edges of battens.

Drainage hole

60 in.

24 in.

2x8 crosstie

2x6 rafter

Plan view

4x4 post

48 in.

2x8 joist

Extend arbor along walk, spacing posts 4 to 8 ft. on center.

12 in. o.c.

Center 8-ft.-long rafters across arbor width.

2x6 rafter

1½ in.

9 in.

20 in.

2x8 crosstie

1½ in.

9 in.

4x4 post

2x4 rail

2x4 rail

Position pickets 2 in. above ground.

2x8 joist

Extend arbor along walk, spacing posts 4 to 8 ft. apart.

80 in., joist to ground

1x4 picket

1x2 picket

6 in.

9 in.

2x4 rail

42 in.

6 in.

Homemade lattice trellis

(pp. 52–55)

The trellis shown here supports climbing plants to make a vertical garden of a blank wall. The design can be altered to fit walls of different sizes while keeping its pleasing proportions. The three 32-in.-wide modules are simpler to make than a single large trellis. Hung on L-hangers, they're easy to remove when you need to paint the wall behind. (If you're in a hurry for a trellis, you can just attach store-bought lattice to 2x2 frameworks of the same dimensions as shown here.)

Start by cutting all the pieces to length. (Here we'll call the horizontal members "rails" and the vertical members "stiles.") Working on a large flat surface, nail or screw the two outer stiles to the top and bottom rails, checking the corners with a framing square. The 2x2 rails provide ample material to house the L-hangers.

Carefully attach the three intermediate stiles, then the 1x2 rails. Cut a piece of scrap 6 in. long to use as a spacer. Fix the L-shaped hangers to 2x4 studs inside the wall. Buy hangers long enough to hold the trellis several inches away from the wall, allowing air to circulate behind the foliage.

32 in.

2x2 top rail

Make squares 6 in. by 6 in. (inside dimensions).

6 to 8 ft.

Outer stile

Intermediate stile

Unless otherwise noted, all parts are made of 1x2 stock.

Intermediate rail

2x2 bottom rail

Construction details

2x2 top rail

Hole for L-hanger

1x2 outer stile

1x2 intermediate stile

1x2 intermediate rail

Nail or screw each joint twice for rigidity.

Hole for L-hanger

Nail or screw through 1x2 stile into 2x2.

2x2 bottom rail

Trellis hanger

2x2 top rail

L-hanger

Hang trellis on wall for easy removal.

Stile

2x2 bottom rail

Hideaway arbor

(pp. 56–59)

This cozy enclosure shelters a bench and supports vines to shade the occupants. Once the posts are set in place, this project can be finished in a weekend.

Build the arbor before laying the pavers under it. After setting the posts (see pp. 134–137), attach the 2x10 joists with carriage bolts. (The sizes of posts and joists have been chosen for visual effect; 4x4 posts and 2x6 or 2x8 joists will work, too.) Tack the joists in place with nails; then bore holes for the bolts through post and both joists with a long electrician's auger bit. Fix the rafters by toenailing or using rust-protected metal rafter ties. Nail or screw the rafters at each end to the posts for added stability.

Sandwich store-bought lattice between 1x3s to make the trellis panels for the vines, and fix them to the posts with metal connectors. Offset the corner joints, as shown in the drawing, or reinforce them with metal brackets, or both.

Space rafters evenly

2x4 rafter, 7 ft. 6 in. long

Fix outer rafters to posts.

Lattice panel

1x3 frame

6 in. clearance

Bolt joists to post.

2x10 joist, 11 ft. 6 in. long

8 ft. o.c.

80 in. minimum from joist to ground.

6x6 post

4 ft. o.c.

Trellis-panel construction

Tack lattice to one set of 1x3s. Nail or screw 1x3s together.

Offset opposite corner joints.

1x3

Lattice

Post-to-joist detail

2x4 rafter

Washer

Hex nut

1/2x10 carriage bolt

6x6 post

2x10 joist

Patio screens
(pp. 60–61)

Made of vertical slats spaced a small distance apart, a pair of these 6-ft.-tall screens allow air circulation to plants and people near the patio while providing privacy. Be sure to check local codes about height and setback from property lines.

The slats are supported by three rails. The top and middle rails are 2x4s; a 2x6 bottom rail adds visual weight to the design. Set the posts (see pp. 134–136). Then cut and fix the rails to their back faces. Position the 1x6 slats with a spacer block $1^1/_2$ in. wide. (To ensure uniform spacing, position all the slats before assembly.) Alternatively, assemble the slats and rails on a flat surface first, and then set the posts at a distance determined by the assembly. Add the 1x6 cap piece to complete the screen.

1x6 cap

2x4 rail

2x4 rail

2x6 rail

1x6 slat

Front elevation

6 to 8 ft. o.c.

4x4 post $1^1/_2$ in.

1x6 cap   1x6 slat

8 in.

61 in.

6 ft.
8 in.

3 in.

8 in.

Side elevation

4x4 post
1x6 cap
2x4 rail
1x6 slat
2x4 rail
26 in.
2x6 rail

Scene-setting fence
(pp. 72–75)

This design provides privacy and an attractive backdrop for a perennial border. If the fence is used on a property line, be sure to check local codes for restrictions on placement and height.

This is a simple fence to construct. Assemble the panels on a flat surface, nailing or screwing the slats to the three 2x4 rails. You can lay out the arc at the top of each panel by "springing" a thin strip of wood, as shown on the facing page. Place the strip against a nail driven into a slat at the highest point of the arc in the center of the panel ❶. Enlist a couple of assistants to bend each end of the strip down to nails near each edge of the panel indicating the lowest points of the arc ❷. Pencil in the arc against the strip ❸; then cut to the line. (A handheld electric jigsaw does the job quickly, but the curve is gentle enough to cut with a handsaw.)

Set the posts (see pp. 134–136) according to the widths of the finished panels.

View from back of fence

1x4 slat

2x4 rail

2x4 rail

2x4 rail

The 6x6 posts shown here add an eye-pleasing heft to the fence, an effect emphasized by setting the face of the panel 1 in. back from the faces of the posts. (Posts made of 4x4s will work just as well.) Metal fasteners are the easiest means of attaching the completed panels to the posts. To allow yourself access to the rails when mounting the metal fasteners, leave the last slats at each end off when you assemble the panels. We've shown a spherical finial attached to the end of each post; you can buy finials of various types at home centers.

Springing an arc

❶ Position a thin strip of wood against nail driven into slat at top of arc.

❸ Scribe arc against bent strip.

Fence panel

❷ Pull ends of strip down to nails driven near low points of arc at panel edges.

Front elevation

Side elevation

6 ft. o.c.

Finial

6 in.

6x6 post

1x4 slat

6 ft.

6 in.

Finial

Finial

2x4 rail

6x6 post

20 in.

2x4 rail

20 in.

1x4 slat

12 in.

2x4 rail

Assemble rails and slats; then fix panel to posts.

Set slats back 1 in. behind face of post.

Lattice skirting for a deck
(pp. 92–95)

The wide lattice gridwork shown here gives the base of a tall deck an airy but substantial look and creates (with a planting of shrubs and trees) a sense of enclosure for a storage area beneath the deck.

The gridwork can be easily nailed or screwed together on a large flat area, then attached to the deck posts. If you want to assemble the gridwork on the deck posts, first fix the horizontal members. Then screw the vertical members to them using an electric screwdriver. (Nailing these unsupported pieces would be difficult.) To ensure equal spacing, lay out the vertical members before assembly.

We've shown a grid of 2x2s fixed to deck posts spaced 7 ft. apart. A lightweight grid made of 1x2s could be used for decks with posts spaced 4 to 6 ft. apart. Alter the size of the gridwork squares to ensure a uniform gridwork pattern between posts.

Note: Deck fascia and joists omitted for clarity.

Deck post

2x2 rail (horizontal member)

2x2 stile (vertical member)

Center stiles on deck posts.

Entry arbor and fence
(pp. 100–103)

This arbor makes an event of the passage from sidewalk to front door or from one part of your property to another. Two versions are shown in the Portfolio. One features the arbor and a holly hedge, the other replaces the hedge with a fence.

As with the other arbors in this book, once the posts are set (see pp. 134–137), assembly is easy. Nail the 2x6 joists to the posts or fix them with carriage bolts. (Clamp or tack the joists to the posts; then bore holes for the bolts with a long electrician's auger bit.) Short sections of fence attached between the posts on the sides of the arbor give young vines support. Heavier rafters attached to the arbor joists stabilize the structure and support the vines across the top of the arbor.

Elevation: Fence

4x4 post (fence or arbor)

1x4 slat

1x2 slat

2x4 rail

2x4 rail

2 in.

2 in.

2 in.

10 in.

The fence is easily made by nailing or screwing the slats to the rails. You can assemble sections of fence and space posts accordingly. If you'd rather set the posts first and build fence panels to fit, ensure uniform spacing by laying out and adjusting the position of the slats on the rails before fastening them in place.

Lattice attached to side of deck.

Front elevation

Deck fascia

2x2 lattice

12 in. on center

2x2 rafter

2x4 rafter

4x4 fence post,
48 in. above grade

2x6 joist

1x4 slat,
3 ft. long

1x2 slat,
3 ft. long

4x4
arbor
post

Fence
panel

Space fence posts
4 to 8 ft. apart.

6 ft. 8 in.
joist to
ground

3 ft.

4 ft.

Plan view: Arbor

2x4 end rafter,
62 in. long

2x2 rafter,
60 in. long

2x4 rafter,
60 in. long

Offset alternate center
rafters by 2 in.

Starting from center
of arbor, space all
but end rafters
about 2 in. apart.

2x6 joist

4x4 post

7 in.

Position rails on posts so
the faces of the slats and
posts are in alignment.

2x4 rail

Preparing the Soil for Planting

The better the soil, the better the plants. Soil quality affects how fast plants grow, how big they get, how good they look, and how long they live. But on many residential lots, the soil is shallow and infertile. Unless you're lucky enough to have a better-than-average site where the soil has been cared for and amended over the years, perhaps for use as a vegetable garden or flower bed, you should plan to improve your soil before planting in it.

If you were planting just a few trees or shrubs, you could prepare individual planting holes for them and leave the surrounding soil undisturbed. However, for nearly all the plantings in this book, digging individual holes is impractical, and it's much better for the plants if you prepare the soil throughout the entire area that will be planted. (The major exception is when you're planting under a tree, which we'll discuss on p. 152.)

For most of the situations shown in this book, you could prepare the soil with hand tools—a spade, digging fork, and rake. The job goes faster, though, if you use a rototiller, and a rototiller is better than hand tools for mixing amendments into the soil. Unless you grow vegetables, you probably won't use a rototiller often enough to justify buying one yourself, but you can easily borrow or rent a rototiller or hire someone with a tiller to come and prepare your site.

Loosen the soil

After you've removed any sod or other vegetation from the designated area (see pp. 116–117), the first step is digging or tilling to loosen the soil ❶. Do this on a day when the soil is moist—not so wet that it sticks to your tools or so dry that it makes dust. Start at one end of the bed and work back and forth until you reach the other end. Try to dig down at least 8 in., or deeper if possible. If the ground is very compacted, you'll need to make repeated passes with a tiller to reach 8 in. deep. Toss aside any large rocks, roots, or debris that you encounter. When you're working near a house or other buildings, be sure to locate buried wires, cables, and pipes. (This

Preparing the soil for planting

❶ Use a spade, digging fork, or tiller to dig at least 8 in. deep and break the soil into rough clods. Discard rocks, roots, and debris. Watch out for underground utilities.

❷ Spread a 2- to 3-in. layer of organic matter on top of the soil.

❸ Sprinkle measured amounts of fertilizer and mineral amendments evenly across the entire area, and mix thoroughly into the soil.

is required by law in some towns.) Most local governments have a number you can call to request help locating buried utilities.

After this initial digging, the ground will probably be very rough and lumpy. Whump the clods with the back of a digging fork or make another pass with the tiller. Continue until you've reduced all the clumps to the size of apples.

After loosening the existing soil and digging it as deeply as possible, you may need to add topsoil to fill in low spots, refine the grade, or raise the planting area above the surrounding grade for better drainage or to make it easier to see a favorite plant. Unless you need just a few bags of it, order topsoil by the cubic yard from a landscape contractor; make sure it has been screened to remove big lumps.

Add organic matter

Common dirt (and purchased topsoil, too) consists mainly of rock and mineral fragments of various sizes—which are mostly coarse and gritty in sandy soil, and dust-fine in clay soil. One of the best things you can do to improve any kind of soil for garden plants is to add some organic matter.

Sold in bags or in bulk at nurseries and garden centers, organic materials include all kinds of composted plant parts and animal manures. Whatever you choose, be sure that it has already been composted or stored in a pile for several months. Fresh, raw manure can "burn" plant roots. Fresh sawdust or chipped bark can "steal" nitrogen from the soil. Fresh hay can contain weed seeds.

How much organic matter should you use? Spread a layer 2 to 3 in. thick across the entire area you're working on ❷. At this thickness, a cubic yard (about one heaping pickup-truck load) of bulk material, or six bales of peat moss, will cover 100 to 150 sq. ft. If you're working on a large area and need several cubic yards of organic matter, have it delivered. Ask the driver to dump the pile as close to your project area as possible; it's worth allowing

the truck to drive across your lawn to get there. You can spread a big truckload of material in just a few hours if you don't have to cart it very far.

Add fertilizers and mineral amendments

Organic matter improves the soil's texture and helps it retain water and nutrients, but it doesn't actually supply many nutrients. To provide the nutrients that plants need, you need to use organic or synthetic fertilizers and powdered minerals. It's most helpful if you mix these materials into the soil before you do any planting, putting them down into the root zone as shown in the drawing ❸, but you can also sprinkle them on top of the soil in subsequent years to maintain a planting.

Getting a sample of soil tested (a service that's usually available free or at low cost through your County Extension Service) is the most accurate way to determine how much of which nutrients is needed. Less precise, but often adequate, is asking the advice of an experienced gardener in your neighborhood. Test results or a gardener's advice will point out any significant deficiencies in your soil, but these are uncommon. Most soil just needs a moderate, balanced dose of nutrients.

Most important is to avoid using too much of any fertilizer or mineral. Don't guess at this; measure and weigh carefully. Calculate your plot's area. Follow your soil-test results, instructions on a commercial product's package, or the general guidelines given in the chart above, and weigh out

Common fertilizers and soil amendments

The following materials serve different purposes. Follow soil-test recommendations or the advice of an experienced gardener in choosing which amendments would be best for your soil. If so recommended, you can apply two or three of these amendments at the same time, using the stated rate for each one.

Material	Description	Amount for 100 sq. ft.
Bagged steer manure	A weak all-purpose fertilizer.	6–8 lb.
Dried poultry manure	A high-nitrogen fertilizer.	2 lb.
5-5-5 all-purpose fertilizer	An inexpensive and popular synthetic fertilizer.	2 lb.
Superphosphate or rock phosphate	Supplies phosphorus. Work into the soil as deep as possible.	2–4 lb.
Greensand	Supplies potassium and many trace elements.	2–4 lb.
Regular or dolomitic limestone	Used primarily to sweeten acid soil.	5 lb.
Gypsum	Helps loosen clay soil. Also helps reduce salt buildup in roadside soil.	2 lb.
Wood ashes	Supply potassium, phosphorus, and lime.	2–4 lb.

the appropriate amount, using a kitchen or bathroom scale. Apply the material evenly across the plot with a spreader or by hand.

Mix and smooth the soil

Finally, use a digging fork or tiller and go back and forth across the bed again until the added materials are mixed thoroughly into the soil and everything is broken into nut-size or smaller lumps ❹. Then use a rake to smooth the surface ❺.

At this point, the soil level may look too high compared with adjacent pavement or lawn, but don't worry. It will settle a few inches over the next several weeks and end up close to its original level.

Working near trees

Plantings under the shade of stately old trees can be cool lovely oases, like the ones shown on pp. 84–87. But to establish the plants, you'll need to contend with the tree's roots. Contrary to popular belief,

most tree roots are in the top few inches of the soil, and they extend at least as far away from the trunk as the limbs do. If you dig anyplace in that area, you'll probably cut or bruise some of the tree's roots. When preparing for planting beneath a tree, therefore, it is important to disturb as few roots as possible.

It is natural for a tree's trunk to flare out at the bottom and for the roots near the trunk to be partly above ground. Don't bury them. However, if the soil has eroded away from roots farther out from the trunk, it's okay to add a layer of soil up to several inches deep and top the new soil with a thinner layer of mulch. Adding some soil like this makes it easier to start ground covers or other plants underneath a tree. (See p. 159 for planting instructions.) Just don't overdo it—covering roots with too much soil can starve them of oxygen, damaging or killing them, and piling soil close to the trunk can rot the bark.

❹ Use a tiller or digging fork to mix everything together, again working as deep as possible.

❺ Finish by smoothing the surface with a rake.

Making neat edges

All but the most informal landscapes look best if you define and maintain neat edges between the lawn and any adjacent plantings. There are several ways to do this, varying in appearance, effectiveness, cost, and convenience. For the Southeast region, the best edges are cut, brick or stone, and plastic strip. If you plan to install an edging, put it in after you prepare the soil but before you plant the bed.

Cut edge

Lay a hose or rope on the ground to mark the line where you want to cut. Then cut along the line with a sharp spade or edging tool. Lift away any grass that was growing into the bed (or any plants that were running out into the lawn). Use a rake or hoe to smooth out a shallow trench on the bed side of the cut. Keep the trench empty; don't let it fill up with mulch.

Pros and cons: Free. Good for straight or curved edges, level or sloped sites. You have to recut the edge every four to eight weeks during the growing season, but you can cut 50 to 100 ft. in an hour or so. Don't cut the trench too deep; if a mower wheel slips down into it, you scalp the lawn. Crabgrass and other weeds may sprout in the exposed soil; if this happens, hoe or pull them out.

Brick mowing strip

Dig a trench about 8 in. wide and 4 in. deep around the edge of the bed. Fill it halfway with sand; then lay bricks on top, setting them level with the soil on the lawn side. You'll need three bricks

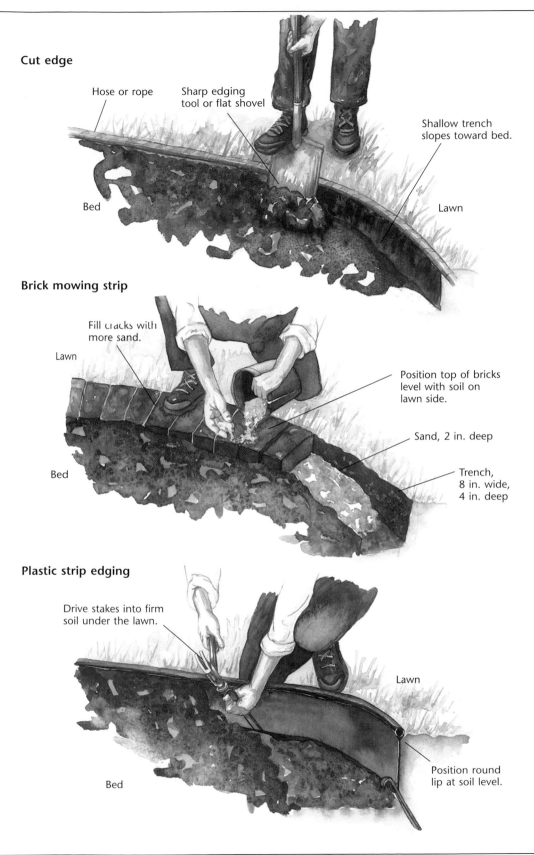

Cut edge

Hose or rope

Sharp edging tool or flat shovel

Shallow trench slopes toward bed.

Bed

Lawn

Brick mowing strip

Fill cracks with more sand.

Lawn

Position top of bricks level with soil on lawn side.

Sand, 2 in. deep

Bed

Trench, 8 in. wide, 4 in. deep

Plastic strip edging

Drive stakes into firm soil under the lawn.

Lawn

Bed

Position round lip at soil level.

per foot of edging. Sweep extra sand into any cracks between the bricks. In cold-winter areas, you'll probably need to reset a few frost-heaved bricks each spring. You can substitute cut stone blocks or concrete pavers for bricks.

Pros and cons: Good for straight or curved edges on level or gently sloped sites. Looks good in combination with brick walkways or brick house. Fairly easy to install and maintain. Some kinds of grass and plants will grow under, between, or over the bricks.

Plastic strip edging

Garden centers and home-improvement stores sell heavy-duty plastic edging in strips 5 or 6 in. wide and 20 or 50 ft. long. To install it, use a sharp tool to cut straight down through the sod around the edge of the bed. Hold the edging so the round lip sits right at soil level, and drive the stakes through the bottom of the edging and into the undisturbed soil under the lawn. Stakes, which are supplied with the edging, should be at least 8 in. long and set about 3 ft. apart.

Pros and cons: Good for straight or curved edges, but only on relatively level sites. Neat and carefree when well installed, but installation is a two- or three-person job. If the lip isn't set right on the ground, you're likely to hit it with the mower blade. Liable to shift or heave unless it's very securely staked. Hard to drive stakes in rocky soil. Some kinds of grass and ground covers can grow across the top of the edging.

Buying Plants

Once you have chosen and planned a landscape project, make a list of the plants you want and start thinking about where to get them. You'll need to locate the kinds of plants you're looking for, choose good-quality plants, and get enough of the plants to fill your design area.

Where and how to shop

You may already have a favorite place to shop for plants. If not, look in the Yellow Pages under Nursery Stock, Nurserymen, Garden Centers, and Landscape Contractors, and choose a few places to visit. Take your shopping list, find a salesperson, and ask for help. The plants in this book are commonly available in most parts of the Southeast region, but you may not find everything you want at one place. The salesperson may refer you to another nursery, offer to special-order plants, or recommend similar plants as substitutes.

If you're buying too many plants to carry in your car or truck, ask about delivery—it's usually available and sometimes free. Some nurseries offer to replace plants that fail within a limited guarantee period, so ask about that, too.

The staff at a good nursery or garden center will usually be able to answer most of the questions you have about which plants to buy and how to care for them. If you can, go shopping on a rainy weekday when business is slow so staff will have time to answer your questions.

Don't be lured by the low prices of plants for sale at supermarkets or discount stores unless you're sure you know exactly what you're looking for and what you're looking at. The salespeople at these stores rarely have the time or knowledge to offer you much help, and the plants are often disorganized, unlabeled, and stressed by poor care.

If you can't find a plant locally or have a retailer order it for you, you can always order it yourself from a mail-order nursery. Most mail-order nurseries produce good plants and pack them well, but if you haven't dealt with a business before, be smart and place a minimum order first. Judge the quality of the plants that arrive; then decide whether or not to order larger quantities from that firm.

Choosing particular plants

If you need, for example, five azaleas and the nursery or garden center has a whole block of them, how do you choose which five to buy? Because the sales staff may be too busy to help you decide, you may need to choose by yourself.

Most plants today are grown in containers, so it's possible to lift them one at a time and examine them from all sides. Following the guidelines shown in the drawings below, evaluate each plant's shape, size, health and vigor, and root system.

Trees and shrubs are sometimes sold "balled-and-burlapped," that is, with a ball

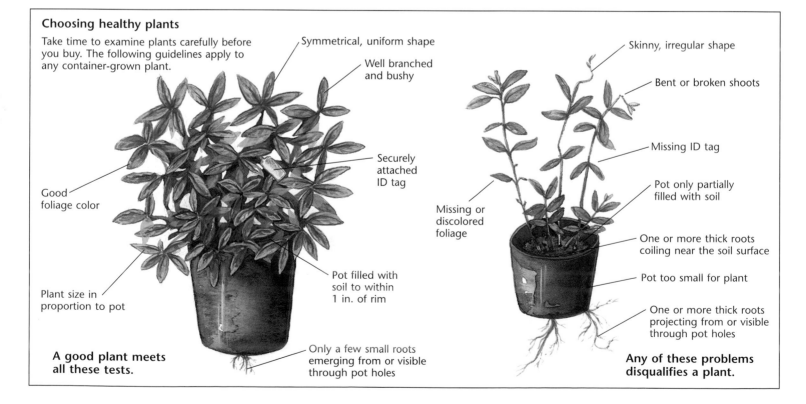

Choosing healthy plants

Take time to examine plants carefully before you buy. The following guidelines apply to any container-grown plant.

Symmetrical, uniform shape

Well branched and bushy

Securely attached ID tag

Good foliage color

Plant size in proportion to pot

Pot filled with soil to within 1 in. of rim

Only a few small roots emerging from or visible through pot holes

A good plant meets all these tests.

Skinny, irregular shape

Bent or broken shoots

Missing ID tag

Pot only partially filled with soil

Missing or discolored foliage

One or more thick roots coiling near the soil surface

Pot too small for plant

One or more thick roots projecting from or visible through pot holes

Any of these problems disqualifies a plant.

of soil and roots wrapped tightly in burlap. For these plants, look for strong limbs with no broken shoots, an attractive profile, and healthy foliage. Then press your hands against the burlap-covered root ball to make sure that it feels firm, solid, and damp, not loose or dry. (If the ball is buried within a bed of wood chips, carefully pull the chips aside; then push them back after inspecting the plant.)

To make the final choice when you're considering a group of plants, line them up side by side and select the ones that are most closely matched in height, bushiness, and foliage color. If your design includes a hedge or mass planting where uniformity is very important, it's a good idea to buy a few extra plants as potential replacements in case of damage or loss. It's easier to plan ahead than to find a match later. Plant the extras in a spare corner so you'll have them if you need them.

Sometimes a plant will be available in two or more sizes. Which is better? That depends on how patient you are. The main reason for buying bigger plants is to make a landscape look impressive right away. If you buy smaller plants and set them out at the same spacing, the planting will look sparse at first, but it will soon catch up. A year after planting, you can't tell if a perennial came from a quart- or gallon-size pot: they will look the same. For shrubs, the difference between one size pot and the next usually represents one year's growth.

Timing

It's a good idea to plan ahead and start shopping for plants before you're ready to put them in the ground. That way, if you can't find everything on your list, you'll have time to keep shopping around, place special orders, or choose substitutes. Most nurseries will let you "flag" an order for later pickup or delivery, and they'll take care of the plants in the meantime. Or you can bring the plants home; just remember to check the soil in the containers every day and water if needed.

The Planting Process

Throughout most of the Southeast region, summer is not a good season for starting a garden, because new plantings are very vulnerable to heat waves or droughts. It's better to plant during the cooler, moister weather of early spring or fall. Most nurseries have a wider selection of perennials and grasses in spring; shrubs and trees are available in spring and again in fall.

Although it's handy to plant a whole bed at once, you can divide the job, setting out some plants in fall and adding the rest in spring, or vice versa. If possible, do the actual planting on a cloudy day or evening when rain is forecast. Compared with preparing the soil, putting plants in the ground goes quite quickly. If you're well prepared, you can plant a whole bed in just an hour or two. On the following pages we'll give an overview of the process and discuss how to handle individual plants.

Try to stay off the soil

Throughout the planting process, do all you can by reaching in from outside the bed—don't step on the newly prepared soil if you can help it, because that compacts the soil and makes it harder to dig planting holes. Use short boards or scraps of plywood as temporary steppingstones if you do need to step on the soil. As soon as you can decide where to put them, lay permanent steppingstones for access to plants that need regular maintenance.

Check placement and spacing

The first step in planting is to mark the position of each plant. The simplest way to do this is to arrange the plants themselves on the bed. Use an empty pot or a stake to represent any plant that's too heavy to move easily. Follow the site plan for the design, use a yardstick to check the spacing, and set the plants in place.

Then step back and take a look. Walk around and look from all sides. Go into the house and look out the window. What do you think? Should any of the plants be adjusted a little—moved to the left or right, to the back or front, a little closer together or farther apart? Don't worry if the planting looks a little sparse now. It *should* look that way at first. Plants almost always grow faster and get bigger than you can imagine when you're first setting them out, and it's almost always better to allow space and wait a few years for them to fill in than to crowd them too close together at first and then need to keep pruning and thinning them later. (You might fill between them with low-growing annuals, as suggested in the box on page 156.)

Planting pointers When working on top of prepared soil, kneel on a piece of plywood to distribute your weight.

Use empty pots or stakes to mark positions of plants not yet purchased or too heavy to move frequently.

Moving through the job

When you're satisfied with the arrangement, mark the position of each plant with a stake or stone, and set the plants aside, out of the way, so you won't knock them over or step on them as you proceed. Start planting in order of size. Do the biggest plants first; then move on to the medium-size and smaller plants. If all the plants are about the same size, start at the back of the bed and work toward the front, or start in the center and work to the edges.

Using annuals as fillers

The plants in our designs have been spaced so they will not be crowded at maturity. Buying more plants and spacing them closer may fill things out faster, but in several years (for perennials; longer for shrubs) you'll need to remove plants or prune them frequently.

If you want something to fill the gaps between newly planted perennials, shrubs, or ground covers for that first year or two, use some annuals. The best annual fillers are compact plants that grow only 6 to 10 in. tall. These plants will hide the soil or mulch and make a colorful carpet. Avoid taller annuals, because they can shade or smother your permanent plantings.

The following annuals are all compact, easy to grow, readily available, and inexpensive. Seeds of those marked with a symbol (❀) can be sown directly in the garden. For the others, buy six-packs or flats of plants. Thin seedlings or space plants 8 to 12 in. apart.

❀ **Annual phlox:** Red, pink, or white flowers. Good for hot dry sites.

❀ **China pink:** Red, pink, white, or bicolor flowers. Blooms all summer.

Dusty miller: Silvery foliage, often lacy-textured. No flowers.

Edging lobelia: Dark blue, magenta, or white flowers. Likes afternoon shade.

Flossflower: Fluffy blue, lavender, or white flowers. Choose dwarf types.

Garden verbena: Bright red, pink, purple, or white flowers.

❀ **Globe candytuft:** Pink or white flowers. Best in cool weather.

❀ **Indian blanket:** Bright red-and-yellow flowers. Blooms all summer.

Moss rose: Bright flowers in many colors. Ideal for hot dry sites.

Pansy and viola: Multicolored flowers. Grow best in cool weather.

❀ **Sweet alyssum:** Fragrant white or lilac flowers. Blooms for months. Prefers cool weather.

Wax begonia: Rose, pink, or white flowers. Good for shady sites but takes sun if watered regularly.

Position trees and shrubs to show their best side

Most trees and shrubs are slightly asymmetric. There's usually enough irregularity in their branching or shape that one side looks a little fuller or more attractive than the other sides do. After you've set a tree or shrub into its hole, step back and take a look. Then turn it partway, or try tilting or tipping it a little to one side or the other. Once you've decided which side and position looks best, start filling in the hole with soil. Stop and check again before you firm the soil into place.

The fine points of spacing

When you're planting a group of the same kind of plants, such as perennials, bulbs, ferns, or ground covers, it normally looks best if you space them informally, in slightly curved or zigzag rows, with the plants in one row offset from those of the next row. Don't arrange plants in a straight row unless you want to emphasize a line, such as the edge of a bed. In that case, make the row perfectly straight by sighting down it and adjusting any plants that are out of line. (Stretch a string for long rows.) After planting, step back and evaluate the effect. If you want to adjust the placement or position of any plant, now is the time to do so.

Rake, water, and mulch

Use a garden rake to level out any high and low spots that remain after planting. Water enough to settle the soil into place around the roots. You can use a hose or watering can and water each plant individually, or you can set up a sprinkler to do the whole planting at once. Mulch the entire planting area with 1 to 3 in. of composted bark, wood chips, or other organic matter. Mulch is indispensable for controlling weeds and regulating the moisture and temperature of the soil. If you're running out of time, you don't have to spread the mulch right away, but try to get it done within the next week or so.

Planting Basics

Planting container-grown plants

❶ Dig a hole a little wider than the container but not as deep.

❷ Remove the plant from the container.

❸ Unwind any large, coiled roots and cut them off short. Cut vertical slits through masses of fine roots.

❹ Position the plant in the hole and fill around it with soil.

Most of the plants that you buy for a landscaping project today are grown and sold in individual plastic containers, but large shrubs and trees may be balled-and-burlapped. Mail-order plants may come bare-root. And ground covers are sometimes sold in flats. In any case, the basic concern is the same: Be careful what you do to a plant's roots. Spread them out; don't fold or coil them or cram them into a tight hole. Keep them covered; don't let the sun or air dry them out. And don't bury them too deep; set the top of the root ball level with the surrounding soil.

Planting container-grown plants

The steps are the same for any plant, no matter what size container it's growing in. Dig a hole that's a little wider than the container but not quite as deep **❶**. Check by setting the container into the hole—the top of the soil in the container should be slightly higher than the surrounding soil. Dig several holes at a time, at the positions that you've already marked out.

Remove the container **❷**. With one hand, grip the plant at the base of its stems or leaves, like pulling a ponytail, while you tug on the pot with the other hand. If the pot doesn't slide off easily, don't pull harder on the stems. Try whacking the pot with your trowel; if it still doesn't slide off, use a strong knife to cut or pry it off.

Examine the plant's roots **❸**. If there are any thick, coiled roots, unwind them and cut them off close to the root ball, leaving short stubs. If the root ball is a mass of fine, hairlike roots, use the knife to cut three or four slits from top to bottom, about 1 in. deep. Pry the slits apart and tease the cut roots to loosen them. This cutting or slitting may seem drastic, but it's actually good for the plant because it forces new roots to grow out into the surrounding soil. Work quickly. Once you've taken a plant out of its container, get it in the ground as soon as possible. If you want to prepare several plants at a time, cover them with an old sheet or tarp to keep the roots from drying out.

Set the root ball into the hole **❹**. Make sure that the plant is positioned right, with its best side facing out, and that the top of the root ball is level with or slightly higher than the surface of the bed. Then add enough soil to fill in the hole, and pat it down firmly.

Planting a balled-and-burlapped shrub or tree

Local nurseries often grow shrubs and trees in fields, then dig them with a ball of root-filled soil and wrap a layer of burlap snugly around the ball to keep it intact. The main drawback with this system is that even a

Balled-and-burlapped

The top of the ball should be level with the surrounding soil. Cut twine that wraps around the trunk. Fold down the burlap, but don't remove it.

Ground covers in flats

Remove a clump of little plants, tease their roots apart, and plant them quickly.

Bare-root plants

Dig a hole wide enough that you can spread out the roots. A stick helps position the plant at the correct depth as you fill the hole with soil.

Bulbs

Plant bulbs with the pointed end up, at a depth and spacing determined by the size of the bulb.

small ball of soil is very heavy. If the ball is more than a foot wide, moving the plant is usually a two-person job. If you're buying a tree with a ball bigger than that, ask the nursery to deliver and plant it. Here's how to proceed with plants that are small enough that you can handle them.

Dig a hole several inches wider than the root ball but not quite as deep as the root ball is high. Step in the bottom of the hole to firm the soil so the plant won't sink. Set the plant into the hole, and lay a stick across the top of the root ball to make sure it's at or a little higher than grade level.

Rotate the plant until its best side faces out. Be sure to cut or untie any twine that wraps around the trunk. Fold the burlap down around the sides of the ball, as shown in the drawing. Don't try to pull the burlap out altogether—roots can grow out through it, and it will eventually decompose. Fill soil all around the sides of the ball and pat it down firmly. Spread only an inch of soil over the top of the ball.

Planting bare-root plants

Mail-order nurseries sometimes dig perennials, roses, and other plants when the plants are dormant; cut back the tops; and wash all the soil off the roots, to save space and weight when storing and shipping them. If you receive a plant in bare-root condition, unwrap it, trim away any roots that are broken or damaged, and soak the roots in a pail of water for several hours.

To plant, dig a hole large enough that you can spread the roots across the bottom without folding them. Start covering the roots with soil, then lay a stick across the top of the hole and hold the plant against it to check the planting depth, as shown in the drawing. Raise or lower the plant if needed in order to bury just the roots, not the buds. Add more soil, firming it down around the roots, and continue until the hole is full.

Planting ground covers from flats

Sometimes ground covers are sold in flats of 25 or more rooted cuttings. Start at one corner, reach underneath the soil, and lift out a portion of the flat's contents. Working quickly, because the roots are exposed, tease the cuttings apart, trying not to break off any roots, and plant them individually. Then lift out the next portion and continue planting.

Planting bulbs

Plant daffodils, tulips, crocuses, and other spring-blooming bulbs in October and November, when fresh bulbs are available at local garden centers or delivered by catalog merchants. If the soil in the bed was well prepared, you can use a trowel to dig holes for planting individual bulbs; where you have room, you can dig a wider hole or trench for planting a group of bulbs all at once. The perennials, ground covers, shrubs, and trees you planted earlier in the fall or in the spring will still be small enough that planting bulbs among them won't unduly disturb their root systems. As a rule of thumb, plant small (grape- or cherry-size) bulbs about 2 in. deep and 3 to 5 in. apart, and large (walnut- or egg-size) bulbs 4 to 6 in. deep and 6 to 10 in. apart.

Planting under a tree

When planting beneath a mature tree, as for the designs on pp. 84–87, remember that most tree roots are in the top few inches of the soil, and they extend at least as far away from the trunk as the limbs do. For areas of ground cover and most container-grown perennials, you can add topsoil and organic amendments up to about 6 in. deep over the entire area; then set the plants out in the new soil. Larger plants need deeper holes. Whether you dig their planting holes in existing soil or through a layer of added topsoil, dig carefully, disturbing as few tree roots as possible. If you encounter a large root, move the planting hole rather than sever the root.

Basic Landscape Care

The landscape plantings in this book will grow increasingly carefree from year to year as the plants mature, but of course you'll always need to do some regular maintenance. Depending on the design you choose, this ongoing care may require as much as a few hours a week during the season or as little as a few hours a year. No matter what you plant, you'll have to control weeds, use mulch, water as needed, and do spring and fall cleanups. Trees, shrubs, and vines may need staking or training at first and occasional pruning or shearing afterward. Perennials, ground covers, and grasses may need to be cut back, staked, deadheaded, or divided. Performing these tasks, which are explained on the following pages, is sometimes hard work, but for many gardeners it is enjoyable labor, a chance to get outside in the fresh air. Also, spending time each week with your plants helps you identify and address problems before they become serious.

Mulches and fertilizers

Covering the soil in all planted areas with a layer of organic mulch does several jobs at once: it improves the appearance of your garden while you're waiting for the plants to grow, reduces the number of weeds that emerge, reduces water loss from the soil during dry spells, moderates soil temperatures, and adds nutrients to the soil as it decomposes. Inorganic mulches such as landscape fabric and gravel also provide some of these benefits, but their conspicuous appearance and the difficulty of removing them if you ever want to change the landscape are serious drawbacks.

Many materials are used as mulches; the box on p. 160 presents the most common, with comments on their advantages and disadvantages. Consider appearance, availability, cost, and convenience when you're comparing different products. Most garden centers have a few kinds of bagged mulch materials, but for mulching large areas, it's easier and cheaper to have a landscape contractor or other supplier deliver a truckload of bulk mulch. A landscape looks best if you see the same mulch throughout the entire planting area, rather than a patchwork of different mulches. You can achieve a uniform look by spreading a base layer of homemade compost, rotten hay, or other inexpensive material and topping that with a neater-looking material such as bark chips or shredded bark.

It takes at least a 1-in. layer of mulch to suppress weeds, but there's no need to spread it more than 3 in. deep. As you're spreading it, don't put any mulch against the stems of any plants, because that can lead to disease or insect problems. Put most of the mulch *between* plants, not right *around* them. Check the mulch each spring when you do an annual garden inspection and cleanup. Be sure it's pulled back away from the plant stems. Rake the surface of the mulch lightly to loosen it, and top it up with a fresh layer if the old material has decomposed.

Fertilizer

Decomposing mulch frequently supplies enough nutrients to grow healthy plants, but using fertilizer helps if you want to boost the plants—to make them grow faster, get larger, or produce more flowers. There are dozens of fertilizer products on the market—liquid and granular, fast-acting and slow-release, organic and synthetic. All give good results if applied as directed. And observe the following precautions: Don't overfertilize, don't fertilize when the soil is dry, and don't fertilize after midsummer, because plants need to slow down and finish the season's growth before cold weather comes.

Controlling weeds

Weeds are not much of a problem in established landscapes. Once the "good" plants have grown big enough to merge together, they tend to crowd or shade out all but the most persistent undesirable plants. But weeds can be troublesome in a new landscape unless you take steps to prevent and control them.

There are two main types of weeds: those that mostly sprout up as seedlings and those that keep coming back from perennial roots or runners. Try to identify and eliminate any perennial weeds before you start a landscaping project (see p. 116). Then you'll only have to deal with new seedlings later, which is a much easier job.

Annual and perennial weeds that commonly grow from seeds include crabgrass, chickweed, dandelions, plantain, purslane, and sorrel. Trees and shrubs such as cherry

---

Mulch materials

Bark products. Bark nuggets, chipped bark, shredded bark, and composted bark, usually from conifers, are available in bags or in bulk. All are attractive, long-lasting, medium-price mulches.

Chipped tree trimmings. The chips from utility companies and tree services are a mixture of wood, bark, twigs, and leaves. These chips cost less than pure bark products (you may be able to get a load for free), but they don't look as good and you have to replace them more often, because they decompose fast.

Sawdust and shavings. These are cheap or free at sawmills and woodshops. They make good path coverings, but they aren't ideal mulches, because they tend to pack down into a dense, water-resistant surface.

Hulls and shells. Cottonseed hulls, peanut shells, and nut shells are available for pickup at food-processing plants and are sometimes sold in bags or bulk at garden centers. They're all attractive, long-lasting mulches. Price varies from free to quite expensive, depending on where you get them.

Tree leaves. A few big trees may supply all the mulch you need, year after year. You can just rake the leaves onto a bed in fall, but they'll probably blow off it again. It's better to chop them up with the lawn mower, pile them in compost bins for the winter, and spread them where needed in late spring. If you have the space for two sets of compost bins, give leaves an extra year to decompose before spreading them. Pine needles make good mulch, too, especially for rhododendrons, mountain laurels, and other acid-loving shrubs. You can spread pine needles in fall, because they cling together and don't blow around.

Grass clippings. A 1- to 2-in. layer of dried grass clippings makes an acceptable mulch that decomposes within a single growing season. Don't pile clippings too thick, though. If you do, the top surface dries and packs into a water-resistant crust, and the bottom layer turns into nasty slime.

Hay and straw. Farmers sell hay that's moldy, old, or otherwise unsuitable for fodder as "mulch" hay. This hay is cheap, but it's likely to include weed seeds, particularly seeds of weedy grasses such as barnyard grass. Straw—the stems of grain crops such as wheat—is usually seed-free but more expensive. Both hay and straw are more suitable for mulching vegetable gardens than landscape plantings because they have to be renewed each year. They are bulky at first but decompose quickly. They also tend to attract rodents.

Gravel. A mulch of pea gravel or crushed rock, spread 1 to 2 in. thick, helps keep the soil cool and moist, and many plants grow very well with a gravel mulch. However, compared with organic materials such as bark or leaves, it's much more tiring to apply a gravel mulch in the first place; it's harder to remove leaves and litter that accumulate on the gravel or weeds that sprout up through it; it's annoying to dig through the gravel if you want to replace or add plants later; and it's extremely tedious to remove the gravel itself, should you ever change your mind about having it there.

Landscape fabrics. Various types of synthetic fabrics, usually sold in rolls 3 to 4 ft. wide and 20, 50, or 100 ft. long, can be spread over the ground as a weed barrier and topped with a layer of gravel, bark chips, or other mulch. Unlike plastic, these fabrics allow water and air to penetrate into the soil. It's useful to lay fabric under paths, but not in planted areas. In a bed, it's a two-person job to install the fabric in the first place, it's inconvenient trying to install plants through holes cut in the fabric, and it's hard to secure the fabric neatly and invisibly at the edges of the bed. The fabric lasts indefinitely, and removing it—if you change your mind—is a messy job.

Clear or black plastic. Don't even think about using any kind of plastic sheeting as a landscape mulch. The soil underneath a sheet of plastic gets bone-dry, while water accumulates on top. Any loose mulch you spread on plastic slips or floats around and won't stay in an even layer. No matter how you try to secure them, the edges of plastic sheeting always pull loose, appear at the surface, degrade in the sun, and shred into tatters.

laurel, Chinese tallow tree, chokeberry, privet, mimosa, cottonwood, and honeysuckle produce weedy seedlings, too. For any of these weeds that grow from seeds, the strategy is twofold: try to keep the weed seeds from sprouting, and eliminate any seedlings that do sprout as soon as you see them, while they are still small.

Almost any patch of soil includes weed seeds that are ready to sprout whenever that soil is disturbed. You have to disturb the soil to prepare it before planting, and that will probably cause an initial flush of weeds, but you'll never see that many weeds again if you leave the soil undisturbed in subsequent years. You don't have to hoe, rake, or cultivate around perennial plantings. Leave the soil alone, and fewer weeds will appear. Using mulch helps even more; by shading the soil, it prevents weed seeds from sprouting. And if weed seeds blow in and land on top of the mulch, they'll be less likely to germinate there than they would on bare soil.

Pull or cut off any weeds that appear while they're young and small, just a few inches tall. Don't let them mature and go to seed. Most weed seedlings emerge in late spring and early summer, but if you get rid of them then, you won't see many more seedlings for the rest of the growing season.

Using herbicides

Two kinds of herbicides can be very useful and effective in maintaining home landscapes, but only if used correctly. You have to choose the right product for the job and follow the directions on the label regarding dosage and timing of application exactly.

Preemergent herbicides. Usually sold in granular form, these herbicides are designed to prevent weed seeds, particularly crabgrass and other annual weeds, from sprouting. Make the first application in early spring, at the time when forsythias bloom. Depending on your climate, you'll probably need to make a second or third application later in the growing season.

Weeds that sprout from seeds
Simple root systems can be easily pulled while still small.

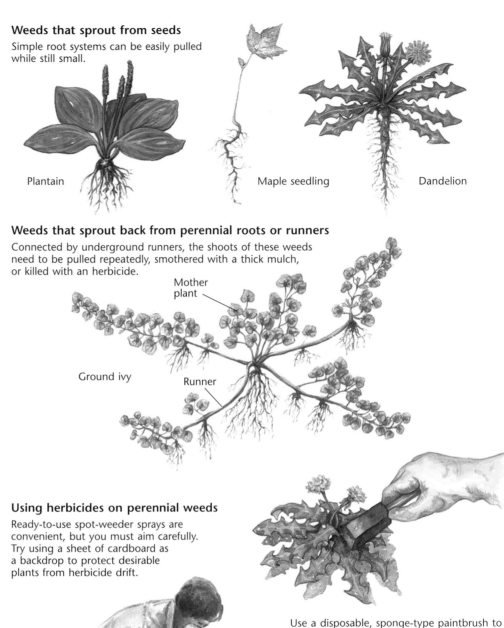

Plantain

Maple seedling

Dandelion

Weeds that sprout back from perennial roots or runners
Connected by underground runners, the shoots of these weeds need to be pulled repeatedly, smothered with a thick mulch, or killed with an herbicide.

Mother plant

Ground ivy

Runner

Using herbicides on perennial weeds
Ready-to-use spot-weeder sprays are convenient, but you must aim carefully. Try using a sheet of cardboard as a backdrop to protect desirable plants from herbicide drift.

Use a disposable, sponge-type paintbrush to apply the herbicide selectively, painting only the weeds. Prepare the solution as directed for spray application. Use only enough to wet the leaves, so none drips off.

Follow package directions to determine how long to wait between applications.

Read the label carefully, and make sure the herbicide you buy is registered for use around the kinds of ground covers, perennials, shrubs, or other plants you have. Measure the area of your bed, weigh out the appropriate amount of granules, and sprinkle them as evenly as possible across the soil. Wear heavy rubber gloves that are rated for use with farm chemicals, not common household rubber gloves, and follow the safety precautions on the product label.

Postemergent herbicides. These chemicals are used to kill plants. Some kinds kill only the aboveground parts of a plant; other kinds are absorbed into the plant and kill it, roots and all. Postemergent herbicides are typically applied as sprays, which you can buy ready-to-use or prepare by mixing a concentrate with water. Look for those that break down quickly, and read the label carefully for registered applications, specific directions, and safety instructions.

Postemergent herbicides work best if applied when the weeds are growing vigorously. You usually have to apply enough to thoroughly wet the plant's leaves, and do it during a spell of dry weather. Applying an herbicide is an effective way to get rid of a perennial weed that you can't dig or pull up, but it's really better to do this before you plant a bed, as it's hard to spray herbicides in an established planting without getting some on your good plants. Aim carefully, shielding nearby plants as shown in the drawing on p. 161, and don't spray on windy days. Brushing or sponging the herbicide on the leaves is slower than spraying, but you're sure to avoid damaging adjacent plants.

Using postemergent herbicides in an established planting is a painstaking job, but it may be the only way to get rid of a persistent perennial weed. For young weed seedlings, it's usually easier and faster to pull them by hand than to spray them.

Watering

Watering is less of a concern for gardeners in the Southeast region than in other parts of the country, but even here there are dry spells and droughts when plants could use some extra water. New plantings, in particular, almost always need water more often than rain provides it.

Deciding if water is needed

Usually only experienced gardeners can judge whether plants need water simply by looking at their leaves. The appearance of the leaves can be misleading. Moreover, you can't go by your own feelings about the weather. One of the ironies of the region's climate is that the air can be very humid, making us humans feel all wet, even though at the same time the soil is so dry that the plants around us are suffering from drought.

Fortunately, there are two very reliable ways of deciding whether you should water. One is to check the soil. Get a paint stirrer or similar piece of unfinished, light-colored wood and use it like a dipstick.

Push it down through the mulch and a few inches into the soil, leave it there for an hour or so, and pull it out to see if moisture has discolored the wood. If so, the soil is moist enough for plants. If not, it's time to water. Let the stick dry out before you use it again; it's handy to have several of these sticks around the garden shed.

The other method is to make a habit of monitoring rainfall by having your own rain gauge or listening to the weather reports, and marking a calendar to keep track of rainfall amounts. In the Southeast region, most landscape plants thrive if they get 3 to 4 in. of rain a month. You should make every effort to water new plantings if there's been less than 1 in. of rain in two weeks. In subsequent years, after the plants have had time to put down roots, they can endure three or more weeks with no rain at all; even so, you should water them if you can. In this region, established plants rarely die from drought, but they do show many signs of stress—wilting leaves, premature leaf drop, failure to bloom or to set fruit, and

Checking soil moisture
Stick a paint stirrer or similar piece of light-colored, unfinished wood down through the mulch and into the soil. Pull it up after an hour. If the bottom of the stick looks and feels damp, the soil is moist enough for plants.

Monitoring a sprinkler
Set several tuna-fish cans throughout the area, and let the sprinkler run until about 1 in. of water has collected in each can.

increased susceptibility to insect and disease attacks.

Pay attention to soil moisture or rainfall amounts all year round, because plants can suffer from dryness in any season, not just in the heat of summer, and water whenever the soil is dry. As for time of day, you can water whenever the plants need it and you get the chance—morning, afternoon, evening, or night. Gardening books sometimes warn against watering plants late in the day, saying that plants are more vulnerable to fungal infections if the leaves stay wet at night. That's true, but in this region plants get wet with dew most nights anyway, whether you water or not.

How much to water

It's easy to overwater a houseplant but hard to overwater a plant that is growing in the ground. Outdoors, you're much more likely to water too little than too much. You could spend an hour with hose in hand, watering the plants in a flower bed, and supply the equivalent of $1/4$ in. of rain or less. Holding a hose or carrying a bucket is practical for watering new plantings only where the plants are few, small, or relatively widely spaced. To thoroughly water an area that's filled with plants, you need a system that allows you to turn on the water, walk away, and come back later. An oscillating sprinkler on the end of a hose works fine, or you can weave a soaker hose through the bed.

No matter how you water, you should monitor how much water you have applied and how evenly it was distributed. If you're hand-watering or using a soaker hose, the watering pattern may be quite uneven. Put several wooden "dipsticks" in different parts of the bed to make sure that all areas have received enough water to moisten the sticks. Monitor the output of a sprinkler by setting tuna-fish cans around the bed and checking to see how much water they catch, like measuring rainfall. Let the sprinkler run until there's about an inch of water in each can.

Caring for Woody Plants

A well-chosen garden tree, such as the ones recommended in this book, grows naturally into a pleasing shape, won't get too large for its site, is resistant to pests and diseases, and doesn't drop messy pods or other litter. Once established, these trees need very little care from year to year.

Regular watering is the most important concern in getting a tree off to a good start. Don't let it suffer from drought for the first few years. To reduce competition, don't plant ground covers or other plants within 2 ft. of the tree's trunk. Just spread a thin layer of mulch there.

Arborists now dismiss other care ideas that once were common practice. According to current thinking, you don't need to fertilize a tree when you plant it (in fact, most landscape trees never need fertilizing). Keep pruning to a minimum at planting time; remove only dead or damaged twigs, not healthy shoots. Finally, if a tree is small enough that one or two people can carry and plant it, it doesn't need staking and the trunk will grow stronger if unstaked. Larger trees that are planted by a nursery may need staking, especially on windy sites, but the stakes should be removed within a year.

Shaping young trees

As a tree grows, you can direct its shape by pruning once a year, in winter or summer. (See the box below.) Take it easy, though. Don't prune just for the sake of pruning; that does more harm than good. If you

---

Pruning to direct growth

Pruning shapes plants not only by removing stems, branches, and leaves but also by inducing and directing new growth. All plants have a bud at the base of every leaf. New shoots grow from these buds. Cutting off the end of a stem encourages the lower buds to shoot out and produces a bushier plant. This type of pruning makes a hedge fill out and gives an otherwise lanky perennial or shrub a better rounded shape.

The same response to pruning also allows you to steer the growth of a plant. The bud immediately below the cut will produce a shoot that extends in the direction the bud was pointing. To direct a branch or stem, cut it back to a bud pointing in the direction you want to encourage growth. This technique is useful for shaping young trees and shrubs and for keeping their centers open to light and air.

Bushier growth
Cut off the end of a stem to induce growth from lower buds.

Directing growth
Make an angled cut above a bud facing the direction you want the shoot to grow.

Pruning roses

Roses are vigorous, fast-growing shrubs that need regular pruning to keep them shapely and attractive. Most of this pruning is done in early spring, just as the buds start to swell but before the new leaves start to unfold. Always use sharp pruning shears and cut back to a healthy bud, leaving no stub. Right after pruning is a good time to add fresh mulch around the plant.

Prune hybrid tea roses to keep them neat, compact, and shapely. Remove any extremely skinny or weak stems plus a few of the oldest stems (you can tell by looking at their bark, which is tan or gray instead of green) by cutting them off at the ground. Prune off any shoots that got frozen or broken during the winter, remove old or weak shoots and crossing or crowded stems, and trim back any asymmetric or unbalanced shoots. Don't be afraid of cutting back too hard; it's better to leave just a few strong shoots than a lot of weak ones. If you cut old stems off at ground level, new ones will grow to replace them. Cut damaged or asymmetric stems back partway and they will branch out.

Hybrid tea roses bloom on new growth, so if you prune in spring you aren't cutting off any flower buds. During the growing season, make a habit of removing the flowers as soon as they fade. This keeps the plant neat and makes it bloom more abundantly and over a longer season. At least once a week, locate each faded flower, follow down its stem to the first or second five-leaflet leaf, and prune just above one of those leaves. (Follow the same steps to cut roses for a bouquet.)

Climbing roses don't need as much spring pruning as hybrid tea roses do. Remove any weak, dead, or damaged shoots by cutting them back to the ground or to healthy wood. You may need to untie and untangle the canes in order to do this spring pruning.

Climbing roses need regular attention throughout the summer, because their stems or canes can grow a foot or more in a month. Check regularly and tie this new growth to the trellis while it's still supple and manageable. When the canes grow long enough to reach the top of the trellis or arbor, cut off their tips and they will send out side shoots, which are where the flowers form. Remove the individual roses or clusters of roses as the petals fade by cutting the stems back to the nearest healthy five-leaflet leaf.

Pruning a hybrid tea rose

Every spring, remove old, weak, or damaged shoots; stems that are crossing or crowded; and stems that stick out too far and look asymmetric. Don't be afraid to cut a lot away.

Removing flowers

Roses can look messy as they fade. Cut off by pruning the stem back to the first healthy five-leaflet leaf.

Cut blackened winter-damaged shoots back to healthy, green tissue.

Old

Weak, crossing

Before

After

Five-leaflet leaf

(Continued from p. 163)

don't have a good reason for making a cut, don't do it. Follow these guidelines:

• *Use sharp pruning* shears, loppers, or saws, which make clean cuts without tearing the wood or bark.

• *Cut branches back* to a healthy shoot, leaf, or bud, or cut back to the branch collar at the base of the branch, as shown at right. Don't leave any stubs; they're ugly and prone to decay.

• *Remove any dead* or damaged branches and any twigs or limbs that are very spindly or weak.

• *Where two limbs* cross over or rub against each other, save one limb—usually the thicker, stronger one—and prune off the other one.

• *Prune or widen* narrow crotches. Places where a branch and trunk or two branches form a narrow V are weak spots, liable to split apart as the tree grows. Where the trunk of a young tree exhibits such a crotch or where either of two shoots could continue the growth of a branch, prune off the weaker of the two. Where you wish to keep the branch, insert a piece of wood as a spacer to widen the angle, as shown in the drawings below. Leave the spacer in place for a year or so.

One trunk or several?

If you want a young tree to have a single trunk, identify the leader or central shoot and let it grow straight up, unpruned. The

Where to cut

When removing the end of a branch, cut back to a healthy leaf, bud, or side shoot. Don't leave a stub. Use sharp pruning shears to make a neat cut that slices the stem rather than tears it.

trunk will grow thicker faster if you leave the lower limbs in place for the first few years, but if they're in the way, you can remove them. At whatever height you choose—usually about 8 ft. off the ground if you want to walk or see under the tree—select the shoots that will become the main limbs of the tree. Be sure they are evenly spaced around the trunk, pointing outward at wide angles. Remove any lower or weaker shoots. As the tree matures, the only further pruning required will be an annual checkup to remove dead, damaged, or crossing shoots.

Several of the trees in this book, including crape myrtle, fringe tree, redbud, Japanese ligustrum, river birch, and sweet

When removing an entire branch, cut just outside the slightly thickened area, called the branch collar, where the branch grows into the trunk.

bay magnolia, are often grown with multiple (usually two to four) trunks, for a graceful, clumplike appearance. When buying a multiple-trunk tree, choose one with trunks that diverge at the base. The more space between them, the better, so they can grow without squeezing each other. Prune multiple-trunk trees as previously described for single-trunk trees. Remove some of the branches that are growing toward the center of the clump, so the center doesn't get too dense and tangled.

Pruning shrubs

Shrubs are generally carefree plants, but they almost always look better if you do some pruning at least once a year. As a

Avoiding narrow crotches

A tree's limbs should spread wide, like outstretched arms. If limbs angle too close to the trunk or to each other, there isn't room for them to grow properly and they may split apart after a few years, ruining the tree.

Single-trunk trees: Correct narrow crotches on a young tree by removing the less desired limb or by widening the angle with a wooden spacer block. Choose well-spaced shoots to become the main limbs of a shade tree.

Multiple-trunk trees: Whether the stems of a multiple-trunk tree emerge from the ground or from a single trunk near the ground, widen angles if necessary to keep the trunks from touching.

Selective pruning

Remove weak, spindly, bent, or broken shoots (red). Where two branches rub on each other, remove the weakest or the one that's pointing inward (orange). Cut back long shoots to a healthy, outward-facing bud (blue).

Severe pruning

In late winter or early spring, before new growth starts, cut all the stems back close to the ground.

Shearing

Trim with hedge clippers to a neat profile.

minimum, remove dead twigs from time to time, and if any branches are broken by storms or accidents, remove them as soon as convenient, cutting back to a healthy bud or to the plant's crown. Also, unless the shrub produces attractive seedpods or berries, it's a good idea to trim off the flowers after they fade.

Beyond this routine pruning, some shrubs require more attention. (The entries in Plant Profiles, pp. 174–197, give more information on when and how to prune particular shrubs.) Basically, shrub pruning falls into three categories: selective pruning, severe pruning, and shearing.

Selective pruning means using pruning shears to remove or cut back individual shoots, in order to refine the shape of the bush and maintain its vigor, as well as limit its size. (See the drawing at left.) This job takes time but produces a very graceful and natural-looking bush. Cut away weak or spindly twigs and any limbs that cross or rub against each other, and cut all the longest shoots back to a healthy, outward-facing bud or to a pair of buds. You can do selective pruning on any shrub, deciduous or evergreen, at any time of year.

Severe pruning means using pruning shears or loppers to cut away most of a shrub's top growth, leaving just short stubs or a gnarly trunk. This kind of cutting back is usually done once a year in late winter or early spring. Although it seems drastic, severe pruning is appropriate in several situations.

It makes certain fast-growing shrubs such as bluebeard and butterfly bush flower more profusely. It keeps others, such as spirea and 'Powis Castle' artemisia, compact and bushy, and it stimulates smoke tree to make bold, unbranched stems with larger-than-average leaves.

One or two severe prunings done when a shrub is young can make it branch out at the base, producing a bushier specimen or a fuller hedge plant. Nurseries often do this pruning as part of producing a good plant,

and if you buy a shrub that's already bushy, you don't need to cut it back yourself.

Older shrubs that have gotten tall and straggly sometimes respond to a severe pruning by sprouting out with renewed vigor, sending up lots of new shoots that bear plenty of foliage and flowers. This strategy doesn't work for all shrubs, though—sometimes severe pruning kills a plant. Don't try it unless you know it will work (check with a knowledgeable person at a nursery) or are willing to take a chance.

Shearing means using hedge shears or an electric hedge trimmer to trim the surface of a shrub, hedge, or tree to a neat, uniform profile, producing a solid mass of greenery. Both deciduous and evergreen shrubs and trees can be sheared; those with small, closely spaced leaves and a naturally compact growth habit usually look best. A good time for shearing most shrubs is early summer, after the new shoots have elongated but before the wood has hardened, but you can shear at other times of year, and you may have to shear some plants more than once a year.

If you're planning to shear a plant, start when it is young and establish the shape — cone, pyramid, flat-topped hedge, or whatever. Looking at the profile, always make the shrub wider at the bottom than on top, otherwise the lower limbs will be shaded and won't be as leafy. Shear off as little as needed to maintain the shape as the shrub grows. Once it gets as big as you want it, shear as much as you have to to keep it that size.

Making a hedge

To make a hedge that's dense enough that you can't see through it, choose shrubs that have many shoots at the base. If you can only find skinny shrubs, prune them severely the first spring after planting to stimulate bushier growth.

Hedge plants are set in the ground as described on pp. 157–158 but are spaced closer together than they would be if planted as individual specimens. We took that into account in creating the designs and plant lists for this book; just follow the spacings recommended in the designs. If you're impatient for the hedge to fill in, you can space the plants closer together, but don't put them farther apart.

A hedge can be sheared, pruned selectively, or left alone, depending on how you want it to look. Slow-growing, small-leaved plants such as boxwood and Japanese holly make rounded but natural-looking hedges with no pruning at all, or you can shear them into any profile you choose and make them perfectly neat and uniform. (Be sure to keep them narrower at the top.) Choose one style and stick with it. Once a hedge is established, you can neither start nor stop shearing it without an awkward transition that may last a few years before the hedge looks good again.

Getting a vine off to a good start

Nurseries often sell Carolina jasmine, clematis, honeysuckle, wisteria, and other vines as young plants with a single stem fastened to a stake. To plant them, remove the stake and cut off the stem right above the lowest pair of healthy leaves, usually about 4 to 6 in. above the soil ❶. This forces the vine to send out new shoots low to the ground. As soon as those new shoots have begun to develop (a month or so after planting), cut them back to their first pairs of leaves ❷. After this second pruning, the plant will become bushy at the base. Now, as new shoots form, use sticks or strings to direct them toward the base of the support they are to climb ❸.

Once they're started, twining vines such as the ones named at left can scramble up a lattice trellis, although it helps if you tuck in any stray ends. The plants can't climb a smooth surface, however. To help them cover a fence with wide vertical slats or a porch post, you have to provide something the vine can wrap around. Screw a few eyebolts to the top and bottom of such a support and stretch wire, nylon cord, or polypropylene rope between them. (The wires or cords should be a few inches out from the fence, not flush against it.)

Clinging vines such as Confederate jasmine and English ivy are both slow starters, but once under way, they can climb any surface by means of their adhesive rootlets and need no further assistance or care.

So-called climbing roses don't really climb at all by themselves—you have to fasten them to a support. Twist-ties are handy for this job. Roses grow fast, so you'll have to tie in the new shoots every few weeks from spring to fall.

After the first year, most vines need annual spring pruning to remove any dead, damaged, or straggly stems. If vines grow too long, you can cut them back anytime, and they will branch out from below the cut.

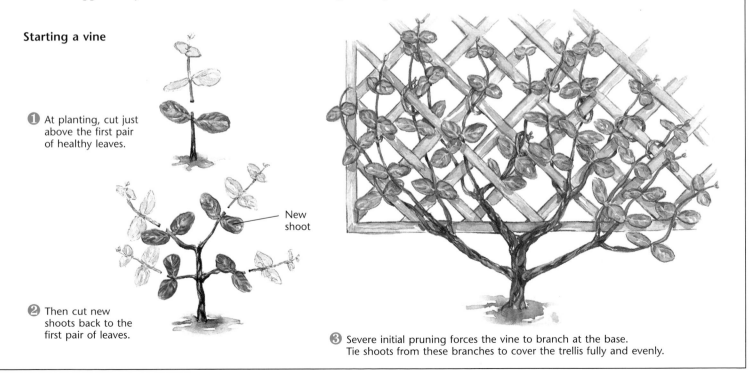

Starting a vine

❶ At planting, cut just above the first pair of healthy leaves.

New shoot

❷ Then cut new shoots back to the first pair of leaves.

❸ Severe initial pruning forces the vine to branch at the base. Tie shoots from these branches to cover the trellis fully and evenly.

Caring for Perennials

Perennials are simply plants that send up new growth year after year. A large group, perennials include flowering plants such as daylilies and astilbes as well as grasses, ferns, and hardy bulbs. Although some perennials need special conditions and care, most of the ones in this book are adaptable and easygoing. Get them off to a good start by planting them in well-prepared soil, adding a layer of mulch, watering as often as needed throughout the first year, and keeping weeds away. After that, keeping perennials attractive and healthy typically requires just a few minutes per plant each year.

Routine annual care

Some of the perennials that are used as ground covers, such as ajuga, cast-iron plant, lilyturf, mondo grass, moneywort, and vinca, need virtually no care. On a suitable site, they'll thrive for decades even if you pay them no attention at all.

Most garden perennials, though, look and grow better if you clean away the old leaves and stems at least once a year. When to do this depends on the plant. Perennials such as canna, daylily, dwarf fountain grass, hosta, cinnamon fern, and Siberian iris have leaves and stalks that turn tan or brown after they're frosted in fall. Cut these down to the ground in late fall or early spring; either time is okay.

Perennials such as 'Becky' Shasta daisy, bigroot geranium, blue fescue grass, Japanese autumn fern, dianthus, foamflower, Lenten rose, and moss phlox have foliage that is more or less evergreen, depending on the severity of the winter. For those plants, wait until early spring; then cut back any leaves or stems that are discolored or shabby-looking. Don't leave cuttings lying on the soil, because they may contain disease spores. Do not compost diseased stems or leaves.

Right after you've cleared away the dead material is a good time to renew the mulch on the bed. Use a fork, rake, or cultivator to loosen the existing mulch, and add some fresh mulch if needed. Also, if you want to sprinkle some granular fertilizer on the bed, do that now, when it's easy to avoid getting any on the plants' leaves. Fertilizing perennials is optional, but it does make them grow bigger and bloom more than they would otherwise.

Pruning and shearing perennials

Some perennials that bloom in summer or fall respond well to being pruned earlier in the growing season. Boltonia, chrysanthemum, garden phlox, and 'Autumn Joy' sedum all form tall clumps of stems topped with lots of little flowers. Unfortunately, tall stems are liable to flop over in stormy

Pruning a perennial

Prune to create neater, bushier clumps of some summer- and fall-blooming perennials such as garden phlox, chrysanthemums, 'Autumn Joy' sedum, and boltonia. When the stalks are about 1 ft. tall, cut them all back by one-third. Remove the weakest stalks at ground level.

weather, and even if they don't, too-tall clumps can look leggy or top-heavy. To prevent floppiness, prune these plants when the stems are about 1 ft. tall. Remove the weakest stems from each clump by cutting them off at the ground, then cut all the remaining, strong stems back by about one-third. Pruning in this way keeps these plants shorter, stronger, and bushier, so you don't have to bother with stakes to keep them upright.

Germander and 'Powis Castle' artemisia are grown more for their foliage than for their flowers. You can use hedge shears to keep them neat, compact, and bushy, shearing off the tops of the stems once or twice in spring and summer.

Remove faded flowers

Removing flowers as they fade (called "deadheading") makes the garden look neater, prevents unwanted self-sown seedlings, and often stimulates a plant to continue blooming longer than it would if you left it alone, or to bloom a second time later in the season. (This is true for shrubs and annuals as well as for perennials.)

Pick large flowers such as daisies, daylilies, irises, and lilies one at a time, snapping them off by hand. Use pruning shears on perennials such as astilbe, hosta, phlox, veronica, and yarrow that produce tall stalks crowded with lots of small flowers, cutting the stalks back to the height of the foliage. Use hedge shears on bushy plants that are covered with lots of small flowers on short stalks, such as autumn sage, 'Moonbeam' coreopsis, dianthus, evergreen candytuft, and 'Homestead Purple' verbena, cutting the stems back by about one-half.

Instead of removing them, you may want to let the flowers remain on coneflower, purple coneflower, Siberian iris, 'Autumn Joy' sedum, and the various grasses. These plants all bear conspicuous seedpods or seed heads on stiff stalks that remain standing and look interesting throughout the fall and winter.

Dividing perennials

Most perennials send up more stems each year, forming denser clumps or wider patches. Dividing is the process of cutting or breaking apart these clumps or patches. This is an easy way to make more plants to expand your garden, to control a plant that might otherwise spread out of bounds, or to renew an old specimen that doesn't look good or bloom well anymore.

Most perennials can be divided as often as every year or two if you're in a hurry to make more plants, or they can go for several years if you don't have any reason to disturb them. You can divide them in early spring, just as new growth is starting, or in late summer and fall, up until a month before hard frost.

There are two main approaches to dividing perennials, as shown in the drawings at right. You can leave the plant in the ground and use a sharp shovel to cut it apart, like slicing a pie, then lift out one chunk at a time. Or you can dig around and underneath the plant and lift it out all at once, shake off the extra soil, and lay the plant on the ground or a tarp where you can work with it.

Some plants, such as boltonia, yarrow, and most ferns, are easy to divide. They almost fall apart when you dig them up. Others, such as astilbe, daylily, and most grasses, have very tough or tangled roots and you'll have to wrestle with them, chop them with a sharp butcher knife, pry them apart with a strong screwdriver or garden fork, or even cut through the roots with a hatchet or pruning saw. However you approach the job, before you insert any tool, take a close look at the plant right at ground level, and be careful to divide *between*, not *through*, the biggest and healthiest buds or shoots. Using a hose to wash loose mulch and soil away makes it easier to see what you're doing.

Don't make the divisions too small; they should be the size of a plant that you'd want to buy, not just little scraps. If you have more divisions than you need or want, choose just the best-looking ones to replant and discard or give away the others. Replant new divisions as soon as possible in freshly prepared soil. Water them right away, and water again whenever the soil dries out over the next few weeks or months, until the plants are growing again.

Divide hardy bulbs such as daffodils and crocuses every few years by digging up the clumps after they have finished blooming but before the foliage turns yellow. Shake the soil off the roots, pull the bulbs apart, and replant them promptly, setting them as deep as they were buried before.

Dividing perennials

You can divide a clump or patch of perennials by cutting down into the patch with a sharp spade, like slicing a pie or a pan of brownies, then lifting out the separate chunks.

Or you can dig up the whole clump, shake the extra soil off the roots, then pull or pry it apart into separate plantlets.

Problem Solving

Some plants are much more susceptible than others to damage by severe weather, pests, or diseases. In this book, we've recommended plants that are generally trouble-free, especially after they have had a few years to get established in your garden. But even these plants are subject to various mishaps and problems. The challenge is learning how to distinguish which problems are really serious and which are just cosmetic, and deciding how to solve— or, better yet, prevent—those problems that are serious.

Identify, then treat

Don't jump to conclusions and start spraying chemicals on a supposedly sick plant before you know what (if anything) is actually wrong with it. That's wasteful and irresponsible, and you're likely to do the plant as much harm as good. Pinpointing the exact cause of a problem is difficult for even experienced gardeners, so save yourself frustration and seek out expert help from the beginning.

If it seems that there's something wrong with one of your plants—for example, if the leaves are discolored, have holes in them, or have spots or marks on them— cut off a sample branch, wrap it in damp paper towels, and put it in a plastic bag (so it won't wilt). Take the sample to the nursery or garden center where you bought the plant, and ask for help. If the nursery can't help, contact the nearest office of your state's Cooperative Extension Service or a public garden in your area and ask if they have a staff member who can diagnose plant problems.

Meanwhile, look around your property and around the neighborhood, too, to see if any other plants (of the same or different kinds) show similar symptoms. If a problem is widespread, you shouldn't have much trouble finding someone who can

identify it and tell you what, if anything, to do. If only one plant is affected, it's often harder to diagnose the problem, and you may just have to wait and see what happens to it. Keep an eye on the plant, continue with watering and other regular maintenance, and see if the problem gets worse or goes away. If nothing more has happened after a few weeks, stop worrying. If the problem continues, intensify your search for expert advice.

Plant problems stem from a number of causes: insect and animal pests, diseases, and poor care, particularly in winter. Remember that plant problems are often caused by a combination of these; all the more reason to consult with experts about their diagnosis and treatment.

Pests, large and small

Deer, rabbits, and woodchucks are liable to be a problem if your property is surrounded by or adjacent to fields or woods. You may not see them, but you can't miss the damage they do—they bite the tops off or eat whole plants of hostas, daylilies, and many other perennials. Deer also eat the leaves and stems of maples, azaleas, and many other trees and shrubs. Commercial or homemade repellents that you spray on the foliage may be helpful if the animals aren't too hungry. (See the box at right for plants that deer seem to avoid.) But in the long run, the only solution is to fence out deer and to trap and remove smaller animals.

Chipmunks and squirrels are cute but naughty. They normally don't eat much foliage, but they do eat some kinds of flowers and several kinds of bulbs. They also dig up new transplants, and they plant nuts in your flower beds and lawns. Meadow voles and field mice can kill trees and shrubs by stripping the bark off the trunk, usually near the ground. Pine voles eat the roots of

shrubs and perennials, too. Moles don't eat plants, but their digging makes a mess of a lawn or flower bed. Persistent trapping is the most effective way to control all of these little critters.

Aphids, beetles, bugs, caterpillars, grubs, grasshoppers, spider mites, scale insects, slugs, snails, weevils, and countless other pests can cause minor or devastating damage in a home landscape. Most plants can afford to lose part of their foliage or sap without suffering much of a setback, so don't panic if you see a few holes chewed in a leaf. However, whenever you suspect that insects are attacking one of your plants, try to catch one of them in a glass jar and get it identified, so you can decide what to do.

There are several new kinds of insecticides that are quite effective but much safer to use than the older products. For example, insecticidal soap, a special kind of detergent, quickly kills aphids and other soft-bodied insects, but it's nontoxic to

---

Deer-resistant plants

Deer may nibble these plants, but they're unlikely to strip them bare. If you live in an area where deer populations are high, consider substituting some of these plants for others that are specified in a design.

Trees and shrubs

Barberry	Forsythia	Pine
Boxwood	Holly	Spirea
Daphne	Lilac	Sweet olive
Dogwood	Magnolia	Wax myrtle

Perennials

Astilbe	Geranium	Lenten rose
Bee balm	Grasses	Peony
Blazing star	Heuchera	Russian sage
Bluebeard	Iris	Sage
Daffodil	Lamb's ears	Veronica
Ferns	Lavender	Yarrow

Deer have been known to jump very tall fences, so a wide fence is one of the best ways to protect your landscape plants from deer. This fence is suitable for a larger property. It is about 6 ft. wide and 5 ft. high, and consists of angled poles fixed to posts spaced about 10 ft. apart. Attach electric wires at 12 in. intervals to the poles. For advice on deer fences that work best in your area, consult your Cooperative Extension agent.

mammals and birds and breaks down quickly, leaving no harmful residue. Horticultural oil, a highly refined mineral oil, is a good control for scale insects, which frequently infest gardenias, camellias, and other broad-leaved evergreens. Most garden centers stock these and other relatively safe insecticides.

Before using any insecticide, study the fine print on the label to make sure that the product is registered to control your particular pest. Carefully follow the directions for how to apply the product, or it may not work.

Diseases

Several types of fungal, bacterial, and viral diseases can attack garden plants, causing a wide range of symptoms such as disfigured or discolored leaves or petals, powdery or moldy-looking films or spots, mushy or rotten stems or roots, and overall wilting. As with insect problems, if you suspect that a plant is infected with a disease, gather a sample of the plant and show it to someone who can identify the problem before you do any spraying.

In general, plant diseases are hard to treat, so it's important to take steps to prevent problems. These steps include choosing plants adapted to your area, choosing disease-resistant plants, spacing plants far enough apart so that air can circulate between them, and removing dead stems and litter from the garden.

Perennials that would otherwise be healthy are prone to fungal infections during spells of hot humid weather, especially if the plants are crowded together or if they have flopped over and are lying on top of each other or on the ground. If your garden has turned into a jungle, look closely for moldy foliage, and if you find any, prune it off and discard (don't compost) it. It's better to cut the plants back severely than to let the disease spread. Plan to avoid repeated problems by dividing the perennials, replanting them farther apart, and pruning them early in the season so they don't grow so tall and floppy again. Crowded shrubs are also subject to fungal problems in the summer and should be pruned so that air can flow around them.

Winter damage

More plants are damaged or killed in the winter than in any other season. Shrubs, trees, and woody vines may get broken by heavy, wet snows or ice storms. When this happens, prune off the broken limbs, cut-ting them back to a main trunk or branch, sometime before new growth starts in spring. Severe cold spells or a sudden change from mild to freezing weather can kill the tops of woody plants. In this case, wait until early spring to assess the severity of the damage; then prune off any limbs that are definitely brown and dead. In most cases, new growth will sprout out from the surviving stems; if no buds appear by late spring, replace the plant.

Even in midwinter, evergreen trees, shrubs, vines, and perennials lose moisture through their leaves on warm, sunny, breezy days. Normally, rain wets the soil enough to meet these plants' water needs, but you should give them a deep watering if there's a long dry spell. Deciduous plants rarely need watering in winter.

In mountainous regions or the upper Southeast, any small or medium-size perennial or shrub that is planted in the fall is liable to be pushed up out of the ground, or frost-heaved, as the soil repeatedly freezes and thaws, and that means its roots get dried out. To prevent this, cover the ground around these plants with a loose mulch such as evergreen boughs as soon as the soil has frozen hard, and don't remove the covering until midspring.

Plant Profiles

Plants are the heart of the designs in this book. In this section you'll find descriptions of all the plants used in the designs, along with information on planting and maintaining them. These trees, shrubs, perennials, grasses, bulbs, and vines have all proven themselves as dependable performers in the region. They offer a wide spectrum of lovely flowers and fruits, handsome foliage, and striking forms. Most contribute something of note in at least two seasons. You can use this section as an aid when installing the designs in this book and as a reference guide to desirable plants for other home landscaping projects.

Using the plant profiles —

All of these plants are proven performers in many of the soils, climates, and other conditions commonly found in the Southeast region. But they will perform best if planted and cared for as described in the Guide to Installation. In these descriptions and recommendations, the term "garden soil" means soil that has been prepared for planting by digging or tilling and adding some organic matter, so that it's loose enough for roots and water to penetrate easily. Here also, "full sun" means a site that gets at least eight hours a day of direct sun throughout the growing season. "Partial sun" and "partial shade" both refer to sites that get direct sun for part of the day but are shaded the rest of the time by a building, fence, or tree. "Full shade" means sites that don't receive direct sunlight.

The plants are organized here alphabetically by their scientific name. If you're browsing, page references direct you to the designs in which the plants appear. Those in **bold italic** type indicate the page where a photo of the plant can be found.

Abelia

Abelia

ABELIA. Evergreen shrubs that bear countless small flowers over a very long season from early summer until frost and attract many butterflies. Lustrous pointed leaves are dark green in summer, purple-bronze in winter. Chinese abelia, *A. chinensis* (p. 36), has sweet-scented white flowers. 'Edward Goucher' abelia (p. 109) has rosy purple flowers. Glossy abelia, *A. × grandiflora* (pp. 96, 111), has pale pink flowers. All need full or partial sun and grow 3 to 6 ft. tall and wide, with arching limbs. Prune annually in early spring to keep the plants compact and neat.

Acer palmatum

JAPANESE MAPLE. Neat, small deciduous trees with delicate-looking leaves that have jagged edges. There are many kinds, growing 10 to 25 ft. tall and wide, with foliage that is green, bronze, or red in summer and red or scarlet in fall. They need shade from the midday sun and rich, moist soil covered with a layer of mulch. Water deeply once a week during dry weather. These maples grow slowly, so buy the biggest tree you can afford. Prune only to remove weak, damaged, or crossing limbs. Pages: 20, 26, 33, 34, *35*, 49, 65, 94.

Acer palmatum 'Sango Kaku'

CORAL BARK MAPLE. A small deciduous tree, reaching 15 ft. or taller, with twigs that turn bright coral-red in winter and early spring. Lobed leaves are light green in summer, scarlet in fall. Needs full or partial sun and rich, moist soil covered with a layer of mulch. Pages: 96, 99, *99*.

Acer rubrum

RED MAPLE. An adaptable native that makes a good shade tree. Grows fast and reaches 40 ft. or taller. Deciduous leaves with three pointed lobes turn bright red in the fall. Clusters of small red flowers dangle from the bare twigs in early spring. Needs full sun. Native to swampy sites but adapts to drier soil. Pages: 92, *94*.

Achillea

YARROW. Long-blooming perennials with flat clusters of small flowers on stiff stalks 2 to 3 ft. tall and finely divided gray-green leaves that have a pungent aroma. 'Appleblossom' (pp. 104, *107*) has pink flowers. 'Coronation Gold' (pp. 72, 75, *75*) bears bright yellow-gold flowers. 'Moonshine' (p. 59) has lemon yellow flowers. All need full sun. Cut off old flower stalks when the blossoms fade. Divide every few years in spring or fall.

Ajuga reptans

AJUGA. A low, mat-forming perennial used as a ground cover. Erect 6-in. spikes densely packed with blue flowers are very showy for a few weeks in spring. Glossy evergreen foliage is typically green, but 'Burgundy Glow' (pp. *42,* 70) has multicolored purple, green, and white leaves, and other cultivars have dark purple-bronze leaves. Prefers partial shade but tolerates full sun in sites with moist soil. After flowers fade, cut them off with a string trimmer, lawn mower, or hedge shears. Spreads quickly and will invade a lawn unless you keep cutting along the edge or install a mowing strip. Pages: 43, 74.

Annuals

Gardeners in the Southeast use annuals generously to provide bright patches of colorful flowers throughout the year. You can buy inexpensive six-packs or flats of the most popular annuals at any garden center or nursery. They're fast-growing plants that bloom abundantly for months, and when they're finished, it's easy to uproot them and replace them with something else. One of the fun things about growing annuals is that you can try different kinds from year to year, choosing varieties with small or large flowers in a wide range of colors, on plants ranging from 6 to 30 in. tall.

Most annuals can be divided into two groups. Cool-season annuals are planted when the weather starts to cool off in fall. They live through the winter, perhaps blooming off and on, and put on a good show in spring, before hot weather starts. This group includes pansies, snapdragons, foxgloves, Iceland poppy, dianthus, and dusty miller. Hot-season annuals are planted after the last frost in spring. They grow and bloom throughout the heat of summer, usually continuing until the first hard frost in fall. This group includes coleus, pentas, lantana, salvia, gomphrena, impatiens, vincas, ageratum, and begonias. (See pages 27, 29, 33, 34, 39, 74.)

Some kinds of annual wildflowers, such as Indian blanket (*Gaillardia pulchella*) and annual phlox (*Phlox drummondii*), are easily grown from seed (pp. 77, 79). Prepare the soil for planting and sow the seeds in late fall or early spring. Water as needed to keep the seeds and little seedlings from drying out. They will grow quickly in the spring, bloom in early summer, then set seed and die in late summer or fall. Once established, they self-sow and bloom

Achillea 'Moonshine'
YARROW

year after year, as in the roadside plantings that are so popular throughout the Southeast.

Aronia arbutifolia

CHOKEBERRY. A deciduous native shrub that grows erect to about 10 ft. tall and 8 ft. wide, with white flowers in late spring, crimson fall foliage, and small red berries that last all winter. Grows in sun or shade, in almost any soil. Carefree. Pages: 77, *78,* 79.

Artemisia 'Powis Castle'

'POWIS CASTLE' ARTEMISIA. A shrubby perennial that forms a dome-shaped mound 2 to 3 ft. tall and 4 to 5 ft. wide. The finely divided gray-green leaves have a pleasant aroma and are evergreen in mild winters. Needs full sun. Tolerates dry sites. Prune hard every spring, cutting stems back by about one-half. Pages: 57, 104, 106, *107.*

Aspidistra elatior

CAST-IRON PLANT. An unusual perennial with stiff, dark evergreen leaves about 24 in. tall and 4 in. wide. Flowers are inconspicuous. Spreads slowly to form a dense, weed-proof patch. Grows well in full or partial shade. Substitute hostas in Zone 6. Carefree. Pages: 84, *86.*

Astilbe

ASTILBE. Among the best perennials for shady or partly shady sites, with fluffy plumes of tiny flowers in summer and healthy, glossy, compound leaves all season. There are many kinds of hybrid astilbes that

Astilbe

maroon all summer, turning crimson in late fall. Needs full sun (foliage turns green if it doesn't get enough sun) and well-drained soil. Pruning is not needed, but you can shape it by shearing if you want to. Pages: 38, 41, *42,* 59.

Betula nigra

RIVER BIRCH. A deciduous tree with very attractive beige, tan, or coppery bark that peels loose and curls back like the pages of a book that's gotten wet. The leaves are glossy green all summer and turn tan or gold in fall. Grows 1 to 2 ft. a year, reaching 60 ft. tall and almost that wide when mature. Needs full sun. Prefers moist soil but adapts to drier sites. Subject to various diseases and insects, but usually the damage is minor. Train young trees to eliminate narrow crotches, which often break apart in ice storms. Pages: 20, 81, *83.*

Boltonia asteroides 'Snowbank'

'SNOWBANK' BOLTONIA. A perennial wildflower that blooms for many weeks in fall, bearing thousands of small white asterlike blossoms. Forms an erect clump of many stems. Grows 3 to 4 ft. tall, 2 to 4 ft. wide. Foliage is pale green and stays healthy all summer. Needs full or partial sun. Cut stems back partway in late spring to reduce height of clump, if desired. Cut to the ground in winter. Divide every few years in early spring. Pages: 45, *47.*

Buddleia davidii

BUTTERFLY BUSH. A fast-growing deciduous shrub that blooms from midsummer through fall. Arching shoots form a vase-shaped clump. Spikes of small white, pink, lilac, blue, or purple flowers form at the end of each stem. The flowers have a sweet fragrance and really do attract butterflies. 'Black Knight' (pp. 51, 77, 79, 111), with dark blue-purple flowers, and 'White Profusion' (pp. 36, 57, 70, *71*), with pure white flowers, grow 6 to 8 ft. tall and wide and have dark green foliage. 'Nanho Blue' (pp. 72, 74) has medium blue flowers and gray-green foliage and grows only 4 to 5 ft. tall and wide. All kinds need full sun and well-drained soil. Cut old stems down to 1-ft. stubs in early spring to promote vigorous growth and maximum flowering.

Bulbs

The bulbs recommended in this book are perennials that come up year after year and bloom in late winter or spring. After they flower, their leaves continue growing until sometime in summer, when they

grow from 18 to 42 in. tall and have white, pale pink, rose, or red flowers in early to midsummer (pp. 88, *90,* 91, 95, 101). A related plant, the dwarf Chinese astilbe, *A. chinensis* var. *pumila* (pp. 87, *94,* 95), grows only 1 ft. tall and has mauve flowers in August.

All astilbes prefer rich, moist, well-drained soil. They definitely need shade from the midday sun and tolerate full shade. Cut off flower stalks when the blooms turn brown (or leave them in place, if you like the looks of the dried flowers). Cut foliage to the ground in late fall or early spring. Divide every three to five years in spring or late summer, using a sharp spade, ax, or old pruning saw to cut the tough woody rootstock into a few large chunks.

Aucuba japonica 'Variegata'

GOLD-DUST AUCUBA. An evergreen shrub with thick, erect stems. Grows 6 to 10 ft. tall, at least 5 ft. wide. Large, toothed, leathery leaves are dark green speckled with yellow dots. Female plants bear cherry red berries, if there's a male plant nearby. One of the best shrubs for dark shady sites. Prune in late winter, if desired. Pages: 84, 88, *90,* 91.

Berberis thunbergii 'Crimson Pygmy'

'CRIMSON PYGMY' JAPANESE BARBERRY. A deciduous shrub that grows naturally into a broad, low, cushionlike mound about 2 ft. tall and 3 to 5 ft. wide. Valued for its shape and its foliage, which is dark

Buddleia davidii 'Black Knight' BUTTERFLY BUSH

Recommended bulbs

***Chionodoxa luciliae*,
Glory-of-the-snow**
Sprays of starlike blue, white, or pink flowers on 6-in. stalks in February. Plant bulbs 3 in. deep, 3 in. apart. Pages: 33, 39.

***Crocus*, Crocus**
Cup-shaped flowers on 4-in. stalks in February. Available in white, yellow, lilac, and purple. Plant bulbs 4 in. deep, 4 in. apart. Pages: 33, 39, 82.

***Muscari armeniacum*, Grape hyacinth**
Grapelike clusters of sweet-scented purple flowers last for several weeks in midspring. Plant bulbs 3 in. deep, 3 in. apart. Grassy foliage appears in fall, dies down in late spring. Pages: 33, 39, 82.

***Narcissus*, Daffodil, jonquil,
and narcissus**
Bright yellow, white, or bicolor flowers, often fragrant, on stalks 6 to 18 in. tall. Different kinds bloom in sequence from January through early April. Plant bulbs 4 to 6 in. deep, 4 to 6 in. apart, depending on their size. Miniature daffodils (pp. *38*, 39) such as yellow 'Baby Moon' have flowers about 2 in. wide and short leaves that are inconspicuous after the flowers fade. Full-size daffodils such as white 'Ice Follies' (pp. 39, 74) have flowers 3 to 4 in. wide and long floppy leaves.

***Scilla siberica*, Squill**
Loose clusters of bell-shaped flowers on 5-in. stalks in March. 'Spring Beauty', the most popular cultivar, has clear blue flowers. Plant bulbs 3 in. deep, 3 in. apart. Pages: 33, 82.

***Tulipa*, Tulip**
Large flowers in bright or pastel shades of all colors but blue, held on stalks 6 to 20 in. tall. Different kinds bloom between February and April. Plant bulbs 4 to 6 in. deep, 4 to 6 in. apart. Pages: 33, *35*.

Narcissus
DAFFODIL

gradually turn yellow and die down to the ground. To get started, you must buy bulbs from a garden center or catalog as soon as the weather starts to cool off in fall (usually in October or November). Plant them promptly in a bed with well-prepared soil. In subsequent years, all you have to do is pick off the faded flowers in spring and remove (or ignore, if you choose) the old leaves after they turn brown in summer. Most bulbs can be divided every few years if you want to make more. Dig them up as the foliage is turning yellow, shake or pull them apart, and replant them right away. For more information on specific bulbs, see box above.

Buxus
BOXWOOD. Very popular and highly prized shrubs that form a dense mass of neat, small, glossy evergreen leaves. The leaves, and also the small flowers in spring, have a distinct fragrance. Boxwood forms soft mounded shapes if left alone or can be sheared into formal globes, cones, hedges, or topiary. There are many kinds of boxwood, differing in rate of growth, size of leaf, and natural habit (upright or spreading). Most cultivars of littleleaf boxwood, *B. microphylla* (pp. 24, 30, 109, 111, *111*), have small, bright green leaves and form compact globes up to 4 ft. tall. English boxwood, *B. sempervirens* (p. 23), has larger, darker green leaves and can grow quite large, up to 20 ft. tall. Boxwoods grow slowly, so buy the largest plants you can afford. They need well-drained soil covered with a layer of mulch. Shear in early summer, if desired.

Buxus sempervirens
ENGLISH BOXWOOD

Camellia sasanqua
'Jean May'

Camellia

CAMELLIA. Evergreen shrubs with glossy foliage and lovely white, pink, or rose flowers. There are hundreds of cultivars, differing mostly in flower color, size, and form (single or double) as well as in overall plant habit, mature size, and hardiness. 'Magnoliaeflora' Japanese camellia, *C. japonica* (pp. 96, 99), is a compact plant about 6 ft. tall, hardy to Zone 7, with large lustrous leaves and pale pink semidouble flowers off and on throughout the winter and spring. 'Jean May' sasanqua camellia, *C. sasanqua* (pp. 88, 91, 99), grows about 6 ft. tall, is hardy to Zone 8, and has smaller leaves and large pink double flowers that bloom throughout the late fall. Camellias need moist, well-drained, acid soil with a layer of mulch, and a site that is shaded from midday sun. Prune immediately after flowering, if desired. Camellias are not recommended for colder regions of Zone 6 or 7, because freezing temperatures kill the flowers and buds. In cold areas, plant rhododendrons instead. Page: 103.

Campsis radicans

TRUMPET CREEPER. A vigorous vine with a stout woody trunk and thick stems, large compound leaves, and very showy clusters of coral-red flowers throughout the summer. Needs full sun. Once started, it can climb and cover a trellis with no further assistance or care. Grows at least 10 ft. tall; can reach 30 to 40 ft. Prune in early spring to control size, if desired. Pages: 102, *102*.

Canna

CANNA. Big, bold perennials with smooth oval leaves up to 1 ft. wide and 2 ft. long and loose clusters of large red, orange, salmon, pink, or yellow flowers on stalks 3 to 6 ft. tall. The foliage can be either green or bronze (pp. 59, 60, *62*). 'Pretoria', often called the Bengal tiger canna (pp. 68, *71*, 72, 75), has bright yellow-and-green-striped leaves and orange flowers. Cannas need full sun. They spread by rhizomes to form a patch; divide every few years in early spring. In Zone 6, dig rhizomes in fall and store in a cool dry place; then replant in spring.

Carex morrowii 'Aureo-variegata'

VARIEGATED JAPANESE SEDGE. An evergreen perennial that looks like a windswept tuft of grass with slender green-and-gold leaves. Flowers are inconspicuous. Grows about 1 ft. tall, 1 to 2 ft. wide. Needs partial shade and moist, fertile soil. Trim off any tattered foliage in early spring. Divide every few years to make more plants. Pages: 66, 84, 93, *94*.

Caryopteris × clandonensis 'Longwood Blue'

'LONGWOOD BLUE' BLUEBEARD. A small deciduous shrub with soft gray foliage. Bears fluffy clusters of medium blue flowers for weeks in late summer and attracts many butterflies. Needs full sun and well-drained soil. Thrives in a warm dry spot. Cut it down close to the ground each spring for compact growth and maximum bloom. Grows about 3 ft. tall and wide by fall. Pages: *38*, 39, 47, 111.

Cephalotaxus harringtonia 'Prostrata'

PROSTRATE JAPANESE PLUM YEW. An evergreen conifer with shiny dark green needles. Spreads to form a low mound 2 to 3 ft. tall and wide. Grows slowly and needs little pruning. Adapts to sun or shade. An excellent conifer for the South, as it's very tolerant of hot weather, but it's not commonly grown, so you may have to ask your local nursery to order one for you. Pages: 84, *86,* 87.

Ceratostigma plumbaginoides

DWARF PLUMBAGO. A perennial ground cover with indigo blue flowers in summer and fall. Deciduous foliage is late to appear in spring, turns from dark green to maroon or crimson in fall. Needs full or partial sun. Cut old stems to the ground in early spring. Stays under 1 ft. tall, spreads 2 to 3 ft. wide. Pages: 65, 66, *67*.

Cercis canadensis

REDBUD. A small deciduous tree. Clusters of tiny bright pink-purple flowers line the bare branches in early spring. May reach 20 to 25 ft. tall and wide. Heart-shaped leaves are medium green all summer and turn gold in fall. Needs partial shade and well-drained soil. Available with single or multiple trunks. Grows quickly, so it's reasonable to start with a small plant. Prune every summer, removing limbs that hang too low and dead twigs that accumulate inside the crown. Pages: *42*, 43.

Chasmanthium latifolium

NORTHERN SEA OATS. A native grass that forms erect leafy clumps about 3 ft. tall, topped with loose clusters of flat seed heads that dance in the breeze from midsummer through winter. All parts are green in summer, russet or tan in winter. Grows in sun or shade and adapts to almost any soil. Cut to the ground in spring. Divide every few years, if you want more plants. Spreads by seed but isn't weedy. Pages: 66, 77, *78*, 79.

Chionanthus virginicus

FRINGE TREE, GRANCY GRAY-BEARD. A deciduous small tree or large shrub with multiple trunks and a rounded or domed crown. Blooms in May, with loose clusters of fragrant white flowers dangling from every branch. Leaves are medium to dark green in summer and may turn an attractive yellow in fall. Needs full or partial sun. Nurseries usually sell it in small sizes, since larger plants don't transplant well. Grows slowly, so use low-growing perennials, bulbs, or annuals to fill the space around it for the first few years. Eventually it will reach 20 ft. tall and wide. Pages: 96, *99*.

Chrysanthemum × superbum 'Becky'

'BECKY' SHASTA DAISY. A popular cultivar of this favorite perennial, named for Atlanta garden designer Becky Stewart, who contributed several of the designs in this book. Blooms all summer despite heat and humidity, with large daisy blossoms on stalks 3 ft. tall. Forms a low mat of glossy foliage in winter. Needs full sun. Divide every year or two in early spring. Pages: 45, 47, *47*, 72, 75.

Caryopteris × *clandonensis* 'Longwood Blue'
BLUEBEARD

Clematis

CLEMATIS. Popular vines that climb or sprawl, forming a tangle of leafy stems adorned with masses of flowers, which can be tiny or large. All clematis need full or partial sun and good garden soil. If your soil is acid, add a cup or so of ground limestone to the planting area and mix it into the soil. Plant clematis in spring. Unlike for most plants, dig the hole deep enough to cover the root ball and base of the stem with about 2 in. of soil. Cut the stem back to the lowest set of healthy leaves to encourage the plant to branch out near the base. Guide the new stems into position and use twist-ties to secure them as soon as they have grown long enough to reach the trellis, wire, or other support.

Evergreen clematis, *C. armandii* (pp. 50, 72, 74, *75*), has glossy evergreen leaves, climbs 15 to 20 ft. tall, and bears fragrant white flowers in spring. Prune after it flowers to control its size, if desired.

Pink anemone clematis, *C. montana* 'Rubens' (pp. 58, *58*), has deciduous leaves, climbs 20 ft. or taller, and bears fragrant pink flowers in late spring that resemble dogwood blossoms. Prune after it flowers to control its size, if desired.

Jackman clematis, *C.* × *jackmanii* (pp. 21, *22*, 27), has deciduous leaves, climbs about 10 ft. tall, and bears large violet-purple flowers in summer. Prune all stems down to 1 ft. tall in spring, just as the buds start to swell.

Clethra alnifolia
'Hummingbird'
SUMMERSWEET

Cornus florida
DOGWOOD

Clethra alnifolia 'Hummingbird'

'HUMMINGBIRD' SUMMERSWEET. A compact form of this popular native shrub, growing only 4 ft. tall instead of the normal 6 to 8 ft. Very sweet-scented white flowers bloom for weeks in midsummer. Deciduous leaves are glossy green in summer, golden yellow in fall. Very adaptable—tolerates sun or shade and damp soil. Prune each year in early spring, cutting some of the older stems to ground level and cutting new stems back by one-third. Sends up suckers around the base and gradually forms a patch. Page: 96.

Coreopsis verticillata 'Moonbeam'

'MOONBEAM' COREOPSIS. A long-blooming perennial that bears hundreds of small, daisylike, lemon yellow blossoms, starting in June and repeating until September if you shear off the old flowers from time to time. The dark green leaves are short and threadlike. Grows about 18 in. tall and wide. Spreads by underground runners but isn't invasive. Needs full sun. Pages: 45, 47, *47*, 66.

Cornus florida

DOGWOOD. A very popular native deciduous tree with showy flowers in spring, red berries that attract birds in fall, and crimson autumn foliage. Grows up to 25 ft. tall and wide, with a rounded crown. Typically has white flowers but can have pink flowers instead (p. 70). Adapts to full sun or partial shade. Small sizes transplant better than large specimens do. Plant when dormant in early spring or late fall, not in the heat of summer. Prune in early summer, right after it blooms, only to remove weak, crossing, or lower limbs. Pages: 22, 62, 82.

Cotinus coggygria 'Royal Purple'

'ROYAL PURPLE' SMOKE TREE. A deciduous shrub with rounded leaves that open red, turn dark purple for the summer, then turn gold or orange in fall. Fluffy pink flower plumes are showy for many weeks in summer and fall. Grows about 10 ft. tall and wide if unpruned, or you can prune it hard every year to have a smaller shrub with larger leaves; this makes a very dramatic specimen. Needs full sun for good color; it will turn green if shaded. Pages: 52, *55*, 57, 102.

Cotoneaster salicifolius 'Repens'

CREEPING WILLOWLEAF COTONEASTER. A shrub often used as a ground cover, with glossy evergreen leaves that turn purple in cold weather, white flowers in spring, and red berries in fall. Grows about 1 ft. tall and spreads up to 6 ft. wide. Prune anytime. Needs full sun. If 'Repens' is unavailable, 'Scarlet Leader' is a good substitute. Pages: 21, 81, **83**.

Cryptomeria japonica 'Yoshino'

'YOSHINO' JAPANESE CEDAR. A fast-growing conifer that forms a neat cone-shaped tree with needlelike foliage that is bright green in summer, bronzy in winter. Grows to 30 ft. or taller. Needs full sun. Requires no care at all. Pages: 29, **31**, 70.

Daphne odora 'Aureomarginata'

VARIEGATED WINTER DAPHNE. A compact, slow-growing shrub that reaches about 4 to 5 ft. tall and wide, with glossy evergreen leaves that have a thin gold stripe around the edge. Crimson buds open into small white flowers that have a powerful sweet fragrance. Blooms mostly in spring, but sometimes scattered flowers appear in fall. Needs full or partial sun and well-drained soil. Prune only to remove damaged shoots. In Zone 6, substitute *Daphne* × *burkwoodii* 'Carol Mackie', a similar-looking, but hardier, plant. Pages: 30, 84, **86**, 87.

Dendranthema

HARDY CHRYSANTHEMUM, DAISY. Popular perennials that bloom for several weeks in fall. Soft, gray-green, aromatic foliage is quietly attractive throughout the summer. The following cultivars all have single or semidouble daisylike flowers and are widely available in the Southeast. *D. rubellum* 'Clara Curtis' (pink flowers) and 'Mary Stoker' (yellow) bloom in September. *D.* × *grandiflorum* 'Sheffield' and 'Venus' both have pink flowers and bloom in October and November. All form rounded clumps about 2 to 3 ft. tall and wide; you can cut them back partway in early summer to make them bushier and more compact. Full sun. Divide every few years in early spring. (Nurseries often sell these plants under the name *Chrysanthemum*.) Pages: 66, **67**, 71.

Dianthus

DIANTHUS, PINK. Low-growing perennials with very fragrant flowers like small carnations, held on supple stalks 8 to 12 in. tall. 'Bath's Pink' (pp. 31, 104, **107**), with clear pink flowers in late spring, and 'It-saul White' (pp. 34, 52), with white flowers in early summer, are unusually tolerant of the hot humid summers typical in the Southeast. They need full sun and well-drained soil. After they bloom, shear off the flower stalks and cut the leaves back halfway.

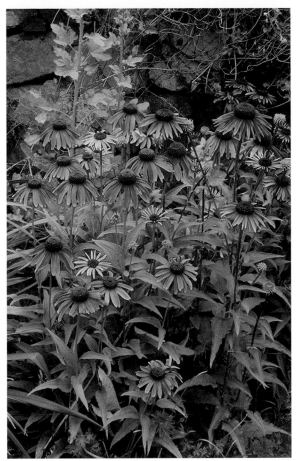

Echinacea purpurea
PURPLE CONEFLOWER

Fresh new foliage will soon develop and form a grassy blue-green mat 1 to 2 ft. wide. Divide every few years in early spring.

Echinacea purpurea

PURPLE CONEFLOWER. A prairie wildflower that thrives in gardens and blooms for several weeks in midsummer. Large pink daisylike blossoms are held on stiff branching stalks about 3 ft. tall, above a mound of dark green basal foliage about 2 ft. wide. Needs full sun. Cut back flower stalks if you choose, or let the seed heads ripen for winter interest. May self-sow but isn't weedy. Older plants can be divided in early spring. Pages: 45, 47, **47**, 71, 72, 75, 77, 79, 111.

Ferns

Ferns are carefree, long-lived perennials for shady sites. Despite their delicate appearance, they're among the most durable and trouble-free plants you can grow. Almost all ferns need shade from the midday and afternoon sun. They grow best in soil

Recommended ferns

***Athyrium goeringianum* 'Pictum',**
Japanese painted fern
A colorful fern that forms rosettes of finely cut fronds marked in shades of green, silver, and maroon. They look almost iridescent. Deciduous. Grows about 1 ft. tall, 2 ft. wide. Pages: *22,* 23, 87, 88.

***Cyrtomium falcatum*,**
Holly fern
A showy evergreen fern with fronds divided into large, glossy, hollylike leaflets. Forms clumps about 2 ft. tall and 3 ft. wide. Hardy only to Zone 8; in colder regions, substitute another fern. Pages: *90,* 91.

***Dryopteris erythrosora*,**
Japanese autumn fern
A beautiful fern with glossy fronds that start out coppery-colored, then turn dark green. Evergreen in mild winters but may freeze to the ground in cold years. Forms erect clumps about 2 to 3 ft. tall, 1 ft. wide. Pages: 86, *86*.

***Osmunda cinnamomea*,**
Cinnamon fern
A native fern that forms erect clumps of finely divided deciduous fronds. Grows 2 to 3 ft. tall and spreads to form a patch. Needs moist soil. In drier conditions, substitute the similar-looking interrupted fern, *O. claytoniana*. Pages: 82, *83*.

***Polystichum polyblepharum*,**
Tassel fern
An evergreen fern with stiff, glossy, finely divided fronds. Needs moist soil. Forms a clump about 2 ft. tall, 3 to 4 ft. wide. Pages: 86, 95.

Polystichum polyblepharum
TASSEL FERN

that's been amended with extra organic matter. You can divide them every few years in early spring if you want more plants, or leave them alone for decades. They need no routine care. See box above for more information on specific ferns.

Festuca ovina var. *glauca*
BLUE FESCUE GRASS. A neat compact grass that forms a dense tuft, about 1 ft. tall and wide, of hair-thin, blue-green leaves. Slender flower spikes appear in early summer and soon turn tan. Needs full sun and well-drained soil. Cut old foliage to the ground in late winter. Divide every few years in early spring. Pages: *58,* 59.

Forsythia × intermedia

Forsythia × intermedia
FORSYTHIA. A large, fast-growing deciduous shrub whose arching limbs are covered with bright yellow flowers for a few weeks in early spring, followed in summer by soft green foliage that turns purple before dropping in late fall. Typically grows 6 to 8 ft. tall, 8 to 10 ft. wide; prune immediately after it flowers if you want to keep it smaller. Needs full or partial sun. Page: 81.

Gardenia jasminoides
GARDENIA. An evergreen shrub with intensely fragrant white flowers in summer. 'August Beauty' and 'Mystery' (pp. 26, 49, *50,* 111) are popular cultivars with double flowers up to 4 in. wide and an upright or rounded habit, reaching 5 ft. or taller and 3 to 5 ft. wide. 'Radicans' (pp. 60, *62*) has 1-in. flowers and grows about 1 ft. tall and 2 to 3 ft. wide. All need full or partial sun and acid soil. Prune in winter to control size and shape. Subject to many insect pests, but most can be controlled by a few applications of horticultural oil spray. Not hardy in Zone 6; substitute azaleas there (see *Rhododendron*).

Gelsemium sempervirens
CAROLINA JASMINE. An evergreen vine native to the Southeast and beloved throughout the region for its showy display of fragrant yellow bell-shaped flowers in early spring. The neat small leaves are dark green all summer, maroon in winter. Can climb trees but is usually trained against a fence, trellis, or post and pruned annually (right after it blooms) to keep it under 10 ft. tall. Can also be used as a ground cover; prune annually to keep it within bounds. Needs full

or partial sun. Not hardy in Zone 6; substitute clematis. Pages: 21, 23, 39, 57, 103.

Geranium macrorrhizum

BIGROOT GERANIUM. A short, compact perennial that forms bushy clumps, about 12 in. tall and 18 to 24 in. wide, of fragrant semievergreen foliage. The large lobed leaves are medium green in summer, turning shades of red and purple in winter. Clusters of magenta or pink flowers last for a few weeks in late spring. Makes a good ground cover for partial shade and dry soil. Divide every few years in spring or early fall. Pages: 60, *62*.

Hamamelis

WITCH HAZEL. Deciduous small trees or large shrubs, often grown with multiple trunks. *H.* × *intermedia* 'Arnold Promise' (pp. 98, *99*) grows up to 20 ft. tall and wide and bears clusters of sweet-scented yellow flowers for several weeks in early spring. The vernal, or Ozark, witch hazel, *H. vernalis* (p. 26), reaches only about 10 ft. tall and wide and has smaller but equally fragrant reddish or gold flowers a few weeks earlier, in late winter. Both bloom before the leaf buds swell. The large rounded leaves are dull green in summer, bright gold in fall. Witch hazels prefer partial shade and moist soil and grow fairly slowly, so buy a big plant to start with. Prune in early summer.

Hedera helix

ENGLISH IVY. A vigorous vine with large, lobed evergreen leaves and woody stems that send out roots and cling to any surface they touch. Spreads fast as a ground cover or climbs to cover a fence, wall, or tree trunk. There are slower-growing, fancy kinds with fine-cut or variegated leaves as well as the regular plain green kinds. Grows in sun or shade. Takes a year or two to get established, then lasts forever. Mow or prune it back whenever it grows too far. Pages: *42*, 43, 82.

Helleborus orientalis

LENTEN ROSE. A carefree, long-lived perennial with evergreen foliage and cup-shaped round flowers that bloom for many weeks in early spring. The flowers can be pink, rosy, white, or greenish. The leaves are large and deeply lobed. Forms a clump about 18 in. tall, 18 to 24 in. wide. Needs partial shade and rich, well-drained soil. Looks its best when you groom it once a year by cutting off any dead leaves when the flower buds appear. Pages: 23, 68, 84, 87.

Gelsemium sempervirens
CAROLINA JASMINE

Helleborus orientalis
LENTEN ROSE

Left:
Hemerocallis
DAYLILY

Right:
Hemerocallis 'Stella d'Oro'
DAYLILY

Hemerocallis

DAYLILY. Among the most reliable and popular perennials, with large lilylike flowers in summer, held above dense clumps of grassy arching leaves. Each clump produces several flower stalks 2 to 4 ft. tall, bearing up to a dozen or more flowers apiece. Hundreds of cultivars produce flowers in shades of orange, gold, yellow, cream, pink, red, or purple (pp. 29, 37, 45, 47, 60, 81, *83*), each blooming for a few weeks or more during June or July. 'Stella d'Oro' (pp. 21, 29, 41, 49, 59, 73, 75, *75,* 111) is especially popular because it blooms almost continuously from late spring until hard frost, with golden yellow flowers on stalks about 2 ft. tall. Daylilies prefer full sun. Cut off flower stalks after blooming is finished. Divide every few years in late summer.

Hibiscus syriacus 'Diana'

'DIANA' ROSE-OF-SHARON. A deciduous shrub with large, pure white, hollyhock-like flowers from July through September. Grows 8 to 10 ft. tall, 6 to 8 ft. wide. Needs full sun. Prune in early spring by cutting some of the oldest stems down to the ground. Japanese beetles may chew on the flowers; their damage looks ugly but doesn't really hurt the plant, and there isn't much you can do to deter them. Pages: 49, *50,* 96.

Hosta

HOSTA. Long-lived, carefree perennials with beautiful leaves in a wide variety of colors and sizes. The plants form dome-shaped clumps or spreading patches of foliage that looks good from spring to fall and dies down in winter. Stalks of lavender, purple, or white flowers appear in mid- to late summer. A few hostas tolerate full sun, but most grow better in partial or full shade. All need fertile, moist, well-drained garden soil. Cut off flower stalks before seedpods ripen. Clumps can be divided in early spring if you want to make more plants; otherwise, leave them alone. See box on facing page for more information on specific hostas.

Hydrangea macrophylla

HYDRANGEA. A bushy, rounded deciduous shrub with showy clusters of papery-textured flowers that look fresh and bright for several weeks in midsummer and smooth, glossy, heart-shaped leaves. 'Blue

Wave' (pp. 54, *55*) grows about 6 ft. tall and wide and has flat, lacy flower clusters about 8 in. wide. The flowers are blue if the plant is growing in acid soil, pink if growing in alkaline soil. The variegated lacecap hydrangea, 'Mariesii Variegata' (pp. 86, *86*), has similar but smaller flowers and is a smaller plant, growing only 4 to 5 ft. tall and wide, with leaves that are edged with irregular white stripes. 'Nikko Blue' (pp. 30, *31*, 51, 99) has puffy, spherical, blue or pink flower heads and grows about 6 ft. tall and wide. Hydrangeas prefer partial shade and need well-drained soil. Flower color varies with soil pH, as noted above. Prune every year in early spring, removing stalks that flowered the previous summer by cutting them off at the ground. Trouble-free.

Hydrangea quercifolia

OAKLEAF HYDRANGEA. A deciduous shrub native to the Southeast and well adapted to hot humid weather. Large lobed leaves emerge pale green in spring, turn dark in summer, and display winelike shades of red and purple in fall. Grows fairly quickly, reaching at least 8 ft. tall and wide. The stems have peeling, cinnamon-colored bark that's attractive in winter. Clusters of papery white flowers top the stems in late spring, then turn beige or pink-tan and last through the summer and fall. 'Snow Queen' has larger-than-average flowers, and 'Snowflake' has double flowers. Adapts to sun or shade. Water regularly during long dry spells. Needs no other care. Pages: 62, 77, 79, 82, 93, *94*, 96, 99.

Recommended hostas

'Antioch' hosta
Large leaves are medium green edged with a wide creamy white stripe. Lavender flowers. Forms a clump about 2 ft. tall, 3 ft. wide. Pages: 54, *94*, 95.

'Frances Williams' hosta
Very large, puckered leaves are iridescent blue-green in the center, gold around the edge. White flowers. Grows slowly but forms giant clumps over 2 ft. tall and 4 ft. wide. Pages: 84, 87.

'Halcyon' hosta
Leaves are solid-colored powder blue in spring, darker blue-green in summer. Forms low mounds, about 1 ft. tall and 2 ft. wide. Lilac flowers. Pages: 54, 68, 91.

Hosta sieboldiana 'Elegans'
Large, round, puckered leaves have a lovely blue-gray color and waxy texture. White flowers. Forms a very impressive clump, 2 to 3 ft. tall, up to 8 ft. wide. Pages: *22*, 23, 43, 87, 95.

'Piedmont Gold' hosta
Bright yellow-gold leaves are large and puckered, with wavy edges. White flowers. Grows about 2 ft. tall, 3 to 4 ft. wide. Page: 60.

'Royal Standard' hosta
Forms large clump of sizable medium green leaves. Large white flowers with a very sweet fragrance bloom in August. Forms a mound under 2 ft. tall, about 3 ft. wide. Pages: 54, *55*, 87.

Hosta 'Frances Williams'

Hosta 'Halcyon'

Recommended evergreen hollies

Ilex × attenuata
A slim, columnar or conical tree, growing about 25 ft. tall and 10 to 15 ft. wide, with shiny leaves and lots of red berries. 'Foster #2' (pp. 30, 33, 34, 109, 111, *111*) is a popular cultivar with slender leaves. 'Savannah' (pp. 81, 82) is similar but has larger leaves and berries.

I. cornuta
A large, dense, bushy shrub with glossy foliage. 'Burfordii', or Burford holly (pp. 20, 77, *78*, 79), grows 15 to 20 ft. tall, has large leaves with few spines, and bears abundant crops of red berries. 'Needlepoint' (pp. 49, 109, 111, *111*) can reach 10 ft. tall and wide but is often kept smaller by shearing. It has lobed leaves with very sharp spines, and bright red-orange berries.

I. crenata, Japanese holly
A dense twiggy shrub with small dark green leaves and inconspicuous dark berries. 'Compacta' (pp. 24, 30, 50, 101) grows about 6 ft. tall and wide, with glossier-than-average leaves. 'Helleri' (pp. 21, 24, 30, 65) reaches only 4 ft. tall and wide and has dull leaves. Both are often sheared, but they don't need it, as their natural growth habit is very neat and compact. Japanese hollies need acid soil; where the soil is alkaline, plant dwarf yaupon holly instead.

I. 'Nellie R. Stevens'
A slim, columnar or conical tree with narrow shiny leaves and lots of red berries. Grows quickly, reaching 25 to 30 ft. tall, 10 to 15 ft. wide, but can be kept smaller. Pages: 57, *58*, 79.

I. opaca, American holly
A conical tree, native to the Southeast, with broad leaves that have a few spines. Foliage is typically olive green, but selected cultivars have bright green leaves. Berries are dark red. Can reach 50 ft. tall, 30 ft. wide. Page: 79.

I. vomitoria, Yaupon holly
A native tree with small, shiny, spineless leaves. Bears huge crops of juicy red berries. Grows about 15 to 20 ft. tall, usually with multiple trunks, and is easily trained and pruned into a picturesque specimen (pp. 101, *102*). Dwarf yaupon holly, 'Nana' (pp. 26, 31, *31*, 49), is a low, compact, shrubby form that grows 3 to 5 ft. tall and wide. It has attractive leaves but bears few berries. Yaupon hollies are very tough, adaptable, and easy to grow.

Ilex crenata 'Compacta'
JAPANESE HOLLY

Iberis sempervirens
EVERGREEN CANDYTUFT. A bushy perennial that forms a low or sprawling mound, about 1 ft. tall and 2 to 3 ft. wide, of slender, glossy evergreen foliage, topped for several weeks in March or April with clusters of bright white flowers. Needs full or partial sun, well-drained soil. Shear off the top half of the plants after they bloom. Needs no other care. Don't try to divide it; buy new plants if you want more. Pages: 33, 34, *35*, 45, 47, 71.

Ilex, Evergreen hollies
A versatile group of evergreen shrubs and trees used for foundation plantings, hedges, and specimens. The stiff-textured leaves can be small or large, smooth or spiny, dull or glossy. Holly plants are either male or female. Females typically bear heavy crops of small round berries that ripen in fall and last through the next spring. See box above for more information on specific hollies. All tolerate sun or shade. Prune or shear at any season to keep them at the desired size.

Ilex decidua
POSSUMHAW. Also known as winterberry holly. A native small tree or large shrub that grows fairly quickly, reaching 15 to 20 ft. tall. Usually trained with multiple trunks and a rounded crown. Small spineless leaves are deciduous and don't have much fall color, but the large red or orange berries look wonderful all fall and winter. Only females produce berries, and there has to be a male within a few hundred yards. A local nursery can advise whether there's likely to be a male growing wild in your vicinity or if you should plant your own. Needs full or partial sun. Pages: 24, *27*.

Ilex verticillata

WINTERBERRY HOLLY. A native deciduous shrub with many twiggy stems and soft spineless leaves that turn yellow in fall. Grows about 8 to 12 ft. tall, 6 to 8 ft. wide. Female cultivars such as 'Sparkleberry' and 'Winter Red' bear tremendous crops of small bright red berries, if there's a wild male or a male cultivar such as 'Apollo' or 'Southern Gentleman' growing within a few hundred yards. Slow-growing, so start with the largest, fullest plants you can find and prune only to remove dead or damaged shoots. Needs full or partial sun. Pages: 77, *78*, 79, 98.

Iris

GERMAN OR BEARDED IRIS. Popular perennials that bloom in midspring, with large elegant flowers in shades of blue, purple, pink, yellow, or white, on stalks 1 to 3 ft. tall. Irises form patches of stiff, bladelike, gray-green leaves about 1 ft. tall. They need full sun and well-drained soil. Divide every few years in late summer, cutting the thick finger-like rhizomes into sections with three or four buds

Ilex verticillata
WINTERBERRY HOLLY

or fans of foliage each. When planting, lay the rhizome horizontally right at the surface of the soil. Pages: 24, 52, 106, *107*.

Iris sibirica

SIBERIAN IRIS. A carefree perennial that forms a large, vase-shaped clump of slender green leaves up to 2 ft. long and bears scores of showy flowers in late spring on stalks 2 to 3 ft. tall. 'Caesar's Brother' (pp. 45, 65, *67*, 68) is a popular cultivar with very dark blue-purple flowers. 'White Swirl' (pp. 72, 75) has clear white flowers. Other cultivars have indigo, sky blue, or yellow flowers. Let the seedpods develop if you choose; they look interesting from summer through winter, and setting seed doesn't seem to reduce the next year's display of flowers. Needs full or partial sun. Divide clumps after several years, in early fall. Pages: 24, 93, 109.

Itea virginica 'Henry's Garnet'

'HENRY'S GARNET' VIRGINIA SWEETSPIRE. A native deciduous shrub that forms a clump of erect or arching stems 6 to 8 ft. tall, topped with clusters of fragrant white flowers in early summer. Smooth leaves are glossy green in summer, rich wine red or burgundy throughout the fall. Adapts to sun or shade. Prefers moist soil. Pages: 98, *99.*

Juniperus chinensis 'Torulosa'

HOLLYWOOD JUNIPER. A small evergreen tree with an interesting irregular profile and bright green, fine-textured foliage. Grows 15 to 20 ft. tall, 4 to 8 ft. wide. Needs full sun. Prune only if needed to remove damaged shoots. Carefree. Pages: 29, 52, *55.*

Iris sibirica 'White Swirl'
SIBERIAN IRIS

Juniperus conferta 'Blue Pacific'

'BLUE PACIFIC' SHORE JUNIPER. An evergreen shrub that makes a good ground cover, staying under 1 ft. tall and spreading several feet wide, with short soft blue-green needles. Needs full sun. Prune only if needed to control its spread. Carefree. Pages: 41, *42*.

Juniperus davurica 'Expansa'

PARSON'S JUNIPER. A low evergreen shrub with gray-green foliage. Grows about 2 ft. tall and can spread several feet wide but is often pruned to keep it narrower. One of the best shrubby junipers for southeastern gardens. Needs full sun. Pages: 29, *31*.

Kalimeris pinnatifida

DOUBLE JAPANESE ASTER. An easy-to-grow perennial that forms an upright clump about 3 ft. tall, with small neat leaves and masses of daisylike flowers. Blooms in the heat of summer; cut it back afterward and it will rebloom in fall. Needs full or partial sun. Pages: 68, *71*.

Lagerstroemia indica 'Natchez'

'NATCHEZ' CRAPE MYRTLE. A deciduous small tree, 20 to 25 ft. tall, usually grown with multiple trunks. Blooms all summer, with large clusters of papery-textured white flowers atop each stem. Leaves turn bright red, orange, or purplish in fall. Flaking cinnamon-colored trunk bark is attractive in winter. Needs full sun and well-drained soil. Prune in spring, removing weak, broken, or frozen shoots. May freeze back in severe winters but soon recovers. Unlike old-fashioned crape myrtles, 'Natchez' is resistant to powdery mildew and its foliage looks nice all summer. Pages: 28, *31,* 38, 91.

Leucothoe

LEUCOTHOE. Evergreen shrubs with arching stems, glossy leaves, and clusters of fragrant white flowers in spring. Drooping leucothoe, *L. fontanesiana* (pp. 63, 82, *83*), grows up to 6 ft. tall and wide. It needs full or partial shade and moist soil and suffers in hot dry weather. Florida leucothoe, *L. populifolia,* sometimes listed as *Agarista populifolia* (pp. *62*, 63), grows up to 16 ft. tall but can be pruned if you need to control its size. It tolerates hot summers and adapts to sunny or shady sites.

Liatris spicata

BLAZING STAR. A perennial prairie wildflower that blooms in midsummer, with dense spikes of small purple flowers on stiff stalks 3 to 4 ft. tall, arising

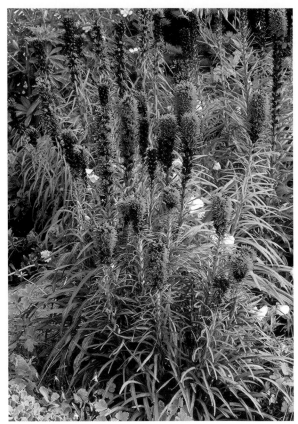

Liatris spicata
BLAZING STAR

from a basal tuft of grassy dark green foliage. Attracts butterflies. Needs full sun. Cut off the flower stalks after it blooms. Needs no other care. 'Kobold' is a smaller cultivar that grows only 2 to 3 ft. tall. Pages: 47, 77, 79, 109.

Ligustrum japonicum

JAPANESE OR WAX-LEAF LIGUSTRUM. A fast-growing evergreen shrub or small tree with very glossy bright green leaves, clusters of heavy-scented white flowers in early summer, and dark blue-black berries in fall and winter. Develops a graceful shape if you leave it alone and can reach 15 to 20 ft. tall, or you can prune it however (and whenever) you choose. Needs full or partial sun and well-drained soil. Not hardy in Zone 6; substitute sweet bay magnolia there. Pages: 41, 88.

Lilium

HYBRID LILY. There are hundreds of wonderful lily cultivars, all with large flowers on leafy stalks. Flower colors include white, yellow, gold, orange, pink, red, and magenta. Different kinds bloom in sequence from May through August. The so-called Asiatic hybrids (pp. 37, *38*) typically have scentless flowers on stalks 2 to 4 ft. tall and bloom in early summer. Most Oriental hybrids such as 'Casablanca' (white flowers) and 'Stargazer' (pink) have sweet-scented flowers in late summer on stalks 3 to 5 ft. tall (pp. 72, 75, *75*). All lilies prefer full sun and deep, fertile, well-drained soil. Plant bulbs when they are available in late fall or early spring, burying them about 6 in. deep. Lilies multiply slowly and can remain in the same place for years (unless they get eaten by rodents). Sprinkle some bulb fertilizer on the soil each fall.

Liriope muscari

LILYTURF. A perennial that forms clumps about 1 to 2 ft. tall and wide of grasslike evergreen leaves. Bears spikes of small violet, purple, or white flowers in late summer, followed by pea-size black berries. Often used as a ground cover. The leaves are typically dark green, but 'Silvery Sunproof' (p. 54) and 'Variegata' (pp. 49, *50*) have leaves edged with narrow golden-yellow stripes that fade to creamy white. Prefers partial sun or shade. Mow or shear off old foliage in early spring. Can be divided every few years to make more plants. Pages: 27, 51, 109, *111*.

Liriope spicata

CREEPING LILYTURF. Resembles regular lilyturf but spreads fast by underground runners to form a dense patch, not just clumps. It also has narrower leaves and the flowers are less conspicuous. The grassy-looking foliage stays dark green all year. Makes a good ground cover for shady sites but can spread into a lawn. Mow or shear off old foliage in early spring. Can be divided every few years to make more plants. Pages: 21, *22*, 66.

Lonicera

HONEYSUCKLE. Fast-growing vines with woody stems that twine around a support, climbing 10 to 15 ft. or higher. The smooth oval leaves are evergreen or nearly so and are arranged in neat pairs on the stems. The native trumpet honeysuckle, *L. sempervirens* (pp. 58, 60), has coral, red, or sometimes yellow flowers that are scentless but are very attractive to hummingbirds. Blooms heavily in early summer and continues off and on until fall. Songbirds eat the bright red berries. Goldflame honeysuckle, *L. × heckrottii* (pp. 37, *38*, 54, 57), is similar but has fragrant pink-and-yellow flowers. Unlike Japanese honeysuckle, *L. japonica*, which is not recom-

Ligustrum japonicum JAPANESE OR WAX-LEAF LIGUSTRUM

Loropetalum chinense

mended for the Southeast, these two species are not aggressive or invasive. Both need full or partial sun in order to bloom well. Prune in winter, thinning out some of the older stems.

Loropetalum chinense

LOROPETALUM. A small shrub with lustrous oval evergreen leaves and fluffy clusters of lovely white flowers. Blooms mostly in spring but occasionally in summer and fall. Grows about 5 ft. tall, up to 8 ft. wide, with arching limbs. Prefers partial shade and acid soil. Needs minimal pruning. Trouble-free. In Zone 6, substitute 'Delaware Valley White' azalea. Pages: 24, 96.

Lysimachia nummularia

MONEYWORT. A creeping, clinging perennial that forms a carpet of round coin-size leaves. Cheerful yellow flowers last for a month or so in summer. Tolerates full sun if the soil is moist, but also does well in full shade. Buy one to start and divide it later if you want more plants. Spreads fast, up to 1 ft. per year. Normally has medium green leaves, but 'Aurea' (pp. 45, 84) has golden yellow leaves. Pages: 65, *67*.

Magnolia

MAGNOLIA. Popular trees with showy flowers in spring or summer. Saucer magnolia or tulip tree, M. × soulangiana (pp. 57, *58*, 65, 68), blooms in early spring, with upright, cup-shaped flowers in shades of pink, purple, or white. Its large oblong leaves are deciduous. It can grow 30 ft. tall and wide. Star magnolia, M. stellata (pp. 24, *27*), also blooms in early spring, with fresh white flowers that have floppy petals. It is deciduous, with leaves smaller than those of other magnolias. It grows slowly but eventually reaches 15 to 20 ft. tall. Sweet bay magnolia, M. virginiana (pp. 88, *90,* 96), has fragrant round white flowers in early summer and glossy leaves with silver bottoms that flash in the breeze. Its leaves hang on partway through winter and sometimes year-round. It grows fairly quickly and reaches 30 ft. or taller. Magnolias prefer full or partial sun. Plant in spring, being careful not to break the roots, which are rather brittle. If you don't prune them, magnolias retain their lower limbs and form impressive specimens that are bushy all the way to the ground. If you want to shape them into a tree with a trunk and open up the space underneath the boughs, prune in midsummer.

Mahonia bealei

LEATHERLEAF MAHONIA. An evergreen shrub whose large compound leaves with hollylike leaflets radiate from a clump of stout, erect, usually unbranched stems. Dense clusters of fragrant golden yellow flowers in early spring are followed by grapelike clusters of blue berries that birds enjoy. Grows upright, 8 to 10 ft. tall and 3 to 4 ft. wide. Prefers partial shade and well-drained soil. Groom in early spring, removing tattered or discolored leaves. To prune, remove old, weak, or broken stems at ground level. Pages: 22, *22,* 54, 84, 98.

Miscanthus sinensis

JAPANESE SILVER GRASS, MISCANTHUS. A showy grass that forms vase-shaped or rounded clumps of long arching leaves. Blooms in late summer or fall, and fluffy seed heads last through the winter. 'Morning Light' (pp. 37, 59, 72, 74, *75*) and 'Sarabande' (p. 71) both have very slender, white-striped leaves that look silvery from a distance. Both form a clump of foliage 4 to 5 ft. tall, with flower stalks about 6 ft. tall. 'Variegatus' (pp. 65, 66, *67*) has broader leaves with distinct green and white stripes; its foliage is up to 7 ft. tall and it produces taller flower stalks. All cultivars need full sun. Cut old leaves and stalks close to the ground in late winter or early spring. Divide clumps in early spring every few years.

Myrica cerifera

WAX MYRTLE. An evergreen native shrub that grows upright and bushy, with slender twigs and glossy leaves that have a delicious spicy aroma. Clusters of small gray berries line the stems of female plants in fall and winter. Needs full or partial sun. Grows quickly and can reach 30 ft. tall; prune in winter if you want to keep it smaller or control its shape. Pages: 30, 68, 81, *83*, 91, 94.

Nandina domestica

HEAVENLY BAMBOO. An evergreen shrub that forms a clump of slender erect stems. Fine-textured compound leaves change color with the seasons, from gold to green to red. Common nandina (pp. 20, 24, 33, 34, 49, *50,* 51, 60) grows 4 to 6 ft. tall, 2 to 3 ft. wide, and bears fluffy clusters of white flowers in summer followed by long-lasting red berries. 'Harbour Dwarf' (pp. 50, 68, 71, *71,* 106) and 'Moon Bay' (p. 106) are nonflowering dwarf forms that make bushy mounds 18 to 24 in. tall and wide, with fine-textured foliage that turns bright crimson in winter. All need full or partial sun. Prune in spring, removing old, weak, or winter-damaged stems.

Ophiopogon japonicus

MONDO GRASS. A perennial ground cover with shiny dark green leaves about 1/8 in. wide and up to 1 ft. long. Looks like unmown grass. The flowers are inconspicuous. Grows best in full or partial shade; foliage burns in the sun. A patch fills in better if you start with several small plants instead of a few large ones. Mow or shear off the top of the old foliage in early spring. Fresh new growth will look neat the rest of the year. Pages: 39, 65, *67,* 88, 91, 106.

Ophiopogon planiscapus 'Ebony Knight'

BLACK MONDO GRASS. A small, slow-growing perennial with grassy evergreen foliage in an unusual shade of purple-black. Spreads gradually to form a patch, under 1 ft. tall and 1 to 2 ft. wide. Prefers partial sun and moist, well-drained soil. Cut the leaves back partway in early spring to remove any damaged tips. Needs no other care. Pages: 33, 34, *35,* 65, 66.

Osmanthus × *fortunei*

SWEET OLIVE. An evergreen shrub with hollylike leaves and white flowers that are tiny but very sweet-scented. Blooms in late summer and fall. The habit is dense and compact. Grows at least 6 ft. tall and wide. Adapts to sun or shade. Needs minimal pruning. Pages: 93, 98, 109, 111, *111.*

Pennisetum alopecuroides 'Hameln'

DWARF FOUNTAIN GRASS. A grass that forms a hassocklike clump of arching leaves, green in summer and gold or tan in fall. Grows 2 ft. tall, 3 ft. wide. Blooms over a long season from midsummer to fall, with fluffy spikes on arching stalks. Needs full sun, garden soil. Cut old leaves to the ground in late winter, or sooner if storms knock them down. Can go many years without being divided. Pages: 37, 41, *42,* 47, 57, 65, 109.

Phlox paniculata 'David'

'DAVID' GARDEN PHLOX. A perennial with clusters of fragrant white flowers in late summer. Forms a clump or patch 3 to 4 ft. tall, 2 to 3 ft. wide. Unlike most cultivars of garden phlox, 'David' is resistant to powdery mildew and does well in heat and humidity, with foliage that stays green and healthy-looking all summer. Needs full or partial sun. Cut off flowers after they fade. Divide clumps every few years in spring. Pages: 45, 49, *50.*

Phlox stolonifera

CREEPING PHLOX. A low perennial with creeping stems, small evergreen leaves, and clusters of fragrant flowers in spring. 'Bruce's White' has white flowers. 'Blue Ridge' bears blue flowers. Other cultivars are good, too. Grows only a few inches tall but can spread 1 to 2 ft. in a year. Makes a good ground cover for sites with partial or full shade and fertile, moist, well-drained soil. Pages: 63, 68, *71.*

Phlox subulata

MOSS PHLOX. A low perennial that forms dense mats of prickly-textured evergreen foliage. Pink, magenta, lilac-blue, or white flowers completely cover the foliage for a few weeks in spring. Grows about 6 in. tall and spreads to form a patch 2 to 3

Pennisetum alopecuroides 'Hameln'
DWARF FOUNTAIN GRASS

ft. wide. Needs full or partial sun. Tolerates dry sites. Shear the plants back halfway after they bloom to promote neat, compact growth. Divide every few years in fall or early spring. Pages: 49, *50,* 101, 104.

Pinus

PINE. Several pines are native to the Southeast. All have evergreen needles and woody cones and grow upright with a thick central trunk and spreading limbs. Loblolly pine, *P. taeda* (p. *78*), has green or yellow-green needles 6 to 9 in. long and thrives in warmer regions. Eastern white pine, *P. strobus*, has green or blue-green needles 2 to 4 in. long and prefers cooler regions. Both grow quickly (1 to 1½ ft. per year) and soon provide shade and screening. Longleaf pine, *P. palustris*, has needles up to 18 in. long. Seedlings grow very slowly at first but mature into beautiful specimens with a tall trunk and open crown. (Buy plants with at least two lateral branches—this ensures that they are past the slowest stage of growth.) All pines need full sun. Young trees retain their lower limbs, but you can remove these when the trees reach 15 to 20 ft. or taller, to expose the trunk and to create a shady space for growing other plants. Pages: 77, 79.

Pittosporum tobira

PITTOSPORUM. An evergreen shrub with tufts of glossy leaves, fragrant white flowers in early summer, and a rounded bushy habit. The most popular

Pittosporum tobira 'Wheeleri'
DWARF PITTOSPORUM

and typically turn yellow in fall. Full sun. These trees grow quickly but are subject to several pests and diseases and may be short-lived. Prune and train to avoid narrow crotches, which are liable to split apart.

Prunus laurocerasus

CHERRY LAUREL. An adaptable evergreen shrub, often used for foundation plantings. Leathery leaves are glossy dark green. Spikes of heavy-scented white flowers stick up like birthday candles in late spring. Adapts to sun or shade. Prefers moist, well-drained soil but tolerates dry sites. 'Otto Luyken' (pp. 21, 26, 33, 34, *35,* 57, 93) is the most popular cultivar. If unpruned, it grows 3 to 4 ft. tall, 6 to 8 ft. wide. 'Zabelliana' (p. 81) grows a little taller and wider and has narrower leaves. Both stay compact even if you don't prune them and look fine if you leave them alone, but can be pruned at any time if you prefer a tidy, formal look.

Rhaphiolepis indica

INDIAN HAWTHORN. A low, spreading evergreen shrub with thick-textured dull green leaves, small pink or white flowers in spring, and blue berries that last through the summer and fall. Grows 2 to 4 ft. tall, 3 to 6 ft. wide. There are many fine cultivars. Needs full sun. Requires minimal pruning or care. Hardy only to Zone 8; substitute 'Crimson Pygmy' Japanese barberry (*Berberis thunbergii*) in colder areas. Pages: 29, *31.*

Rhododendron

RHODODENDRON AND AZALEA. An especially diverse and popular group of shrubs with very showy flowers in spring or summer. The leaves can be small or large, deciduous or evergreen. The plants can be short, medium, or tall, with spreading, mounded, or erect habits. All rhododendrons and azaleas do best with partial shade and need fertile, moist, well-drained soil. Mix a 3-in. layer of peat moss into the soil to prepare a bed for these plants.

Plant rhododendrons and azaleas in spring or early fall. Be sure not to plant them too deep—the top of the root ball should be level with, or a little higher than, the surrounding soil. Azaleas are usually sold in containers. When planting them it's very important that you make a few deep cuts down the root ball and tease apart some of the roots; otherwise, azaleas typically do not root well into the surrounding soil. Treat container-grown rhododendrons the same way. Large rhododendron plants are

cultivars are 'Variegata', variegated pittosporum (pp. 24, *27*), which has gray-green leaves with white edging and grows about 6 ft. tall and wide; and 'Wheeleri', dwarf pittosporum (pp. 29, 60), which has bright green leaves and grows only 3 to 4 ft. tall and wide. Both adapt to sun or shade and need only minimal pruning. Hardy only to Zone 8; in colder regions substitute cherry laurel (*Prunus laurocerasus*) there.

Polygonatum odoratum 'Variegatum'

VARIEGATED SOLOMON'S SEAL. A perennial that forms a patch of upright or arching stems 2 to 3 ft. tall, with lovely green-and-white leaves and fragrant white flowers that dangle below the leaves in late spring. Needs full or partial shade; grows well under trees. Trouble-free. Can grow for years without needing division or other care. Pages: 27, *27.*

Prunus

FLOWERING CHERRY. Small deciduous trees. The autumn cherry or twice-blooming cherry, *P. subhirtella* 'Autumnalis' (pp. 96, *99*), bears delicate pale pink flowers in late fall and again in early spring and grows upright, 20 to 30 ft. tall, with a slender, vase-shaped habit. The Yoshino cherry, *P. × yedoensis* (pp. 60, *62*), has fragrant flowers in early spring; they can be single or double, pink or white. There are many cultivars. Most form a rounded or weeping crown and grow to 25 ft. or taller. Cherry leaves are medium green in summer

Recommended azaleas and rhododendrons

'Amagasa' Satsuki azalea
A spreading shrub, 3 to 4 ft. tall, with small evergreen leaves and large, rosy pink flowers in late spring. Page: 95.

'Delaware Valley White' azalea
An upright shrub, 4 to 6 ft. tall, with medium-size evergreen leaves and masses of single white flowers in midspring. Pages: *90*, 91, 96.

'Fiedlers White' azalea
A vigorous evergreen shrub, 7 to 8 ft. tall, with lovely single white flowers in midspring. Hardy to Zone 8; in colder regions substitute 'Delaware Valley White'. Page: 94.

'George Lindley Taber' azalea
A vigorous evergreen shrub, 7 to 8 ft. tall, with beautiful pale pink flowers in midspring. Hardy to Zone 8; in colder regions substitute a pink Glen Dale azalea. Pages: 88, 94, *94*.

Glen Dale azaleas
A group of azaleas that grow about 3 to 6 ft. tall, with evergreen foliage and large white, pink, red, or orange flowers in midspring. Unusually cold-hardy, they are especially valuable in Zones 7 and 6, where other evergreen azaleas might freeze. Page: 49.

Gumpo azaleas
Low, spreading shrubs, 2 to 3 ft. tall and wide, with small evergreen leaves and large pink or white flowers in late spring. Pages: 23, 43, 63, 66, 95, 101.

Pink Gumpo evergreen azalea (left); white evergreen azalea (right)

Rhododendron canescens, Piedmont azalea
A deciduous native azalea with clove-scented white or pink flowers in midspring. Grows 10 to 15 ft. tall and spreads to form a colony. Pages: 98, *99*.

R. prunifolium, Plumleaf azalea
A deciduous native azalea that bears its orange-red flowers in midsummer, long after other azaleas have finished blooming. Grows 8 to 10 ft. tall and wide. Pages: 88, *90*.

'Roseum Elegans' rhododendron
A fast-growing shrub with large glossy evergreen leaves and rounded clusters of pink or pink-purple flowers in late spring. Grows about 6 ft. tall and wide. Pages: 22, 62, 82.

Rhododendron 'Roseum Elegans'

(Continued from p. 192)

often sold balled-and-burlapped. In that case, the roots were cut when the plants were dug and need no further attention. They will grow out through the burlap in time.

Use a layer of mulch to keep the soil cool and damp around your azaleas and rhododendrons, and water the plants during any dry spell for the first few years. Prune or shear off the flower stalks as soon as the petals fade, to prevent seed formation and to neaten the plants. Prune or shear to control plant size and shape at the same time (in early summer). See box on p. 193 for more information on specific varieties.

Rohdea japonica

JAPANESE SACRED LILY, LILY OF CHINA. An evergreen perennial with broad, arching, straplike leaves about 2 ft. long, 3 in. wide. Spreads slowly to form a patch with many clumps of foliage. The short-stalked yellow flowers are insignificant, but the red berries that follow look nice. Needs full or partial shade and rich, moist soil. Carefree. In Zone 6, substitute a hosta. Pages: 84, *86*.

Rosa

ROSE. Vigorous shrubs with thorny woody stems and deciduous compound leaves. Hybrid tea roses (pp. 109, *111*), the most popular group of cultivars, typically have stiff upright stems 3 to 6 ft. tall. They bear exquisite long-stalked red, orange, pink, yellow, or white flowers from late spring until hard frost. The plants need regular fertilizing, spraying, and pruning; ask local rose enthusiasts for advice.

So-called climbing roses are really shrubs, not vines, and they don't climb without assistance—you have to fasten them to a trellis, fence, or other support. 'Blaze' (pp. 29, 52, *55*) is an old favorite with semidouble red flowers, starting in June and continuing through the summer. Its canes grow about 12 ft. long. Lady Bank's rose, *R. × banksiae* (pp. 102, *102*), has long flexible canes that are almost thornless, small leaves that are almost evergreen, and puffy clusters of double yellow flowers in spring.

All roses grow best in full sun and fertile, well-drained soil topped with a few inches of mulch. Prune them every in spring, before new growth starts. (See p. 164 for rose-pruning instructions.)

Rosmarinus officinalis 'Arp'

'ARP' ROSEMARY. An evergreen shrub with gray-green needlelike leaves that combine a lovely fragrance with a tasty flavor. Small blue, lilac, or white flowers bloom in late winter and early spring. Grows upright and bushy, 3 to 4 ft. tall. 'Arp' is the hardiest cultivar of this popular herb and survives outdoors throughout the Southeast; other cultivars are hardy only to Zone 8. Needs full sun and well-drained soil. Prune or shear in spring or summer. Pages: 51, 72, 74, *75*.

Rudbeckia fulgida 'Goldsturm'

'GOLDSTURM' CONEFLOWER. An improved form of a popular perennial wildflower. Bears hundreds of gold-and-brown flowers, which are often called black-eyed Susans, for several weeks in late summer. Forms a robust clump about 3 ft. tall and wide, with large dark green leaves at the base and stiff branching flower stalks. Needs full or partial sun. Cut down the flower stalks in fall or spring, as you choose. Divide every few years in early spring. Pages: 37, 77, 79, 103, 104, *107*.

Salvia coccinea

SCARLET SAGE. A perennial Texas wildflower that grows about 2 ft. tall and wide, with a bushy habit, heart-shaped green leaves, and flower stalks at the top of every stem. Blooms for months throughout the summer and fall. 'Lady in Red' is a popular cultivar with bright red flowers; although sold as a bedding plant, it often overwinters in the Southeast. Needs full sun. Carefree. Page: 109.

Salvia farinacea

MEALY BLUE SAGE. Another perennial Texas wildflower. Grows 2 to 3 ft. tall and wide, with a bushy habit and slender, glossy green leaves. Blooms all summer and fall, with dense spikes of violet, blue, or white flowers on slender stiff stalks. Often sold as a bedding plant but frequently overwinters in the Southeast. Cut down old stalks in fall or spring. Needs full sun. Carefree. Pages: 52, *55*, 57.

Salvia greggii

AUTUMN SAGE. A shrubby perennial with small semievergreen leaves. Grows about 2 to 3 ft. tall and wide. Blooms throughout the summer and fall. Flowers are typically bright red, but they can be pink, salmon, or white. 'Cherry Chief' (pp. 104, 106, *107*) has cherry red flowers. Needs full sun. In spring, prune or shear off any weak, damaged, or frozen stems. In Zone 6, substitute scarlet sage (*Salvia coccinea*). Pages: 29, 31, 45, 52, 65.

Salvia greggii 'Cherry Chief'
AUTUMN SAGE

Salvia coccinea
SCARLET SAGE

Sarcococca hookeriana 'Humilis'

SWEET BOX. A slow-growing evergreen shrub with small, leathery, pointed leaves that are glossy green all year. Grows 12 to 18 in. tall and spreads 2 to 3 ft. wide. Can be used as a ground cover. Blooms in February or March, with small white flowers that are very sweet-scented. Needs full or partial shade. Care-free. Pages: 54, *55*.

Scabiosa columbaria 'Butterfly Blue'

'BUTTERFLY BLUE' PINCUSHION FLOWER. A compact perennial that forms a neat clump of bright green foliage. It will bloom continuously from May to hard frost if you keep picking off the old flowers. The round, sky blue flowers really do attract butterflies, and they make good cut flowers, too. Grows about 1 ft. tall and wide. Needs full sun and well-drained soil. Divide every few years in early spring. Pages: 47, 68, *71*, 73.

Sedum

SEDUM. Perennials that form clumps of succulent foliage on thick stems topped with flat clusters of flowers. 'Autumn Joy' (pp. 34, *35,* 59, 71, 104, 106) grows 2 to 3 ft. tall, with erect stems, gray-green foliage, and flowers that change color from pale to deep salmon-pink to rusty red over a span of many weeks in late summer and fall as they open, mature, and go to seed. 'Vera Jameson' (pp. 47, *47*) grows about 1 ft. tall, with floppy stems, rounded leaves in an unusual shade of purple-gray, and pink flowers in August. Sedums need full sun. Cut down old stalks in winter or spring. Divide clumps every few years in early spring.

Spiraea japonica

JAPANESE SPIREA. A deciduous shrub that forms a low mound of thin, graceful, arching stems, with small toothed leaves and round flat clusters of tiny flowers in summer. 'Goldflame' (pp. 58, *58*) has bright gold leaves that are tinged with orange in spring and turn red in fall, and pink-red flowers. This cultivar is sometimes listed under the species *S.* × *bumalda*. 'Little Princess' (pp. 33, 34, *35,* 41) has dark green leaves and rosy pink flowers. Both grow about 2 to 3 ft. tall and wide and need full or partial sun. Prune every year in spring, removing some of the older stems at ground level and cutting others back partway. In summer, shear off faded flowers to promote reblooming. Trouble-free.

Spiraea nipponica 'Snowmound'

'SNOWMOUND' SPIREA. A deciduous shrub that forms a dense rounded clump of arching branches covered with fine-textured, dark blue-green foliage. Grows about 4 ft. tall and wide. Clusters of pure white flowers line the stems in spring. Needs full or partial sun. Prune right after it flowers, cutting off some of the stems at ground level and shearing the rest back partway. Pages: 38, *38,* 68.

Stokesia laevis

STOKE'S ASTER. A native perennial wildflower that blooms from June until frost, with flowers like large flat bachelor's buttons; they make excellent long-lasting cut flowers. 'Blue Danube' has sky blue flowers on stalks 12 to 18 in. tall. The basal foliage is evergreen. Adapts to full sun or partial shade. Needs well-drained soil. Pick the flowers regularly to promote continuous bloom. Divide every few years in spring or fall. Pages: 104, *107.*

Ternstroemia gymnanthera

CLEYERA. A neat, compact evergreen shrub with glossy leaves in changeable colors; they can be red, gold, green, or purple, depending on stage of growth, season, and light level. Large red berries that ripen in fall are attractive, too. Grows about 4 ft. tall and 3 ft. wide. Prefers full or partial shade and acid soil. Needs minimal pruning. Trouble-free. Not hardy in Zone 6; substitute 'Roseum Elegans' rhododendron there. Pages: 58, *58.*

Teucrium chamaedrys

GERMANDER. A low, mounded shrub with small, glossy, dark evergreen leaves and pink-purple flowers in late summer. Grows about 1 ft. tall and 2 ft. wide. Needs full or partial sun and well-drained soil. Shear stems back partway every spring to keep it compact and bushy. Pages: 37, *38,* 66.

Trachelospermum jasminoides

CONFEDERATE JASMINE. An evergreen vine. The woody twining stems are lined with pairs of small leathery oval leaves. Bears dangling clusters of cream-colored, sweet-scented flowers in early summer. Climbs 10 to 15 ft. tall. Prefers partial shade. Prune at least once a year, cutting out older stems and cutting new ones back partway. Normally hardy only to Zone 8, but 'Madison' is hardy in Zone 7. In Zone 6, substitute a clematis. Pages: 24, 27, *27,* 102.

Verbena bonariensis

PURPLE VERBENA. A perennial that thrives in hot weather and blooms from June or July until frost. Forms a low mound of basal foliage topped by a thicket of stiff, erect, much-branched but almost leafless flower stalks, 3 to 4 ft. tall. Bears countless small clusters of small purple flowers that butterflies love. Needs full sun. Carefree; simply cut down old stalks in winter or spring. May self-sow but isn't weedy. Pages: 29, 101, *102,* 103.

Verbena canadensis 'Homestead Purple'

'HOMESTEAD PURPLE' VERBENA. A perennial with sprawling stems, evergreen leaves, and round clusters of purple flowers. Blooms nonstop from late spring until hard frost if regularly deadheaded. Grows about 1 ft. tall, spreads 3 ft. or wider. Needs full sun. Prune any damaged or frosted shoots in early spring. Pages: 45, 47, *47,* 71, 72.

Veronica 'Sunny Border Blue'

'SUNNY BORDER BLUE' VERONICA. A perennial that blooms from early summer until frost if regularly deadheaded, with spikes of blue-purple flowers on stalks 18 to 24 in. tall. The leaves are green and glossy, with a crisp texture. Needs full sun. Divide every few years, in spring or fall. Pages: 45, 71.

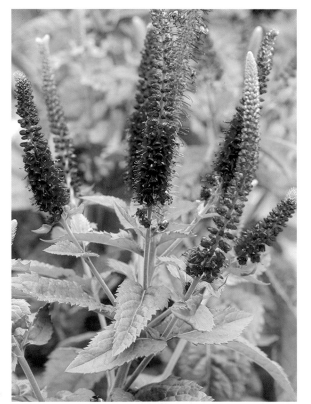

Veronica 'Sunny Border Blue'

Vinca minor

VINCA. An evergreen ground cover that spreads by long runners to form dense patches. Planted 1 ft. apart, soon forms a solid mass. The small leathery leaves are shiny green. Round blue-purple flowers bloom for a few weeks in spring. Adapts to most soils, in partial sun or shade. Once established, needs absolutely no care. If you want something special, look for the lovely variegated or white-flowered forms of this plant. They are just as easy to grow as the common type. Pages: *22*, 23, 63, 103.

Water plants

Most big garden centers have a small collection of water plants. Mail-order water-garden specialists offer several dozen kinds. Most water plants are fast-growing, even weedy, so you need only one of each kind to start with.

There are two main groups of water lilies (*Nymphaea*). Hardy water lilies survive outdoors from year to year and bloom in midsummer. Tropical water lilies bloom from summer through fall, but in most of the Southeast they need to be stored indoors in winter or treated as annuals. Both hardy and tropical water lilies are available in dwarf-size plants, suitable for small pools, with fragrant or scentless flowers in shades of white, yellow, and pink; tropicals also come in shades of blue and purple. All water lilies need full sun. Plant in a container of heavy, rich garden soil, and set it in the pool so about 6 in. of water covers the soil. (See p. 129 for more on planting water plants.)

Lotuses (*Nelumbo*) grow like water lilies but hold their leaves and flowers above the water. They have fragrant yellow, pink, or white flowers and interesting seedpods. Most kinds are hardy, but only dwarf cultivars are suitable for small ponds. Full-size lotuses get to be huge plants.

Marginal or emergent water plants grow well in containers covered with 2 in. or more of water; their leaves and flower stalks stick up into the air. For example, dwarf papyrus (*Cyperus haspan*) is a popular marginal with leaves that branch out like umbrella spokes; it grows 18 in. tall. Floating plants have leaves that rest on the water and roots that dangle down into it. Water lettuce (*Pistia stratiotes*) is a floater that forms saucer-size rosettes of iridescent pale green leaves. Oxygenating or submerged plants grow underwater; they help keep the water clear and provide oxygen, food, and shelter for fish. Anacharis (*Elodea canadensis*) is a popular oxygenator with tiny dark green leaves. Pages: 65, *67*.

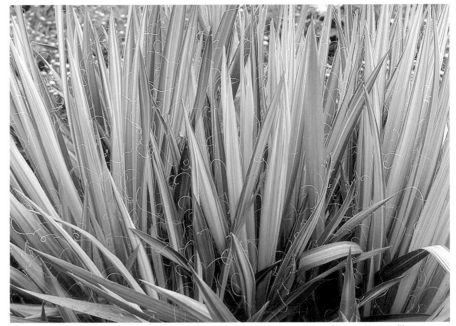

Yucca filamentosa
'Golden Sword'

Wisteria sinensis

CHINESE WISTERIA. A very vigorous vine with woody stems that twine around any support, deciduous compound leaves, and long drooping clusters of very fragrant blue-purple, lilac, or white flowers in late spring. Sometimes reblooms a little in summer. Needs full sun. Provide a very sturdy trellis or support. Wisteria can climb to 40 ft., and you will need to prune it hard once or twice every summer to keep it smaller. It's worth spending extra to buy a named cultivar; these bloom at an early age. With inexpensive seed-raised plants, you may wait years before seeing a flower. Pages: 101, *102*.

Yucca filamentosa 'Golden Sword'

'GOLDEN SWORD' YUCCA. An unusual shrub or perennial with evergreen daggerlike leaves, 2 ft. long, that stick out in all directions from a short thick trunk. Leaves have a broad yellow stripe down the middle and green edges; although lovely, this cultivar does grow more slowly than the common all-green form. Blooms in June, with large creamy white flowers on stiff branching stalks 4 to 6 ft. tall. The woody seedpods are decorative, too. Needs full or partial sun. Cut down the old flower stalks whenever you choose, and peel dead leaves from around the base of the plant in spring. Once established, it lives for decades and can't be moved, although you can dig up the baby plants that form around the base and transplant them. Pages: 37, 104, 106.

Glossary

Amendments. Organic materials or minerals used to improve the soil. Peat moss, perlite, and compost are commonly used.

Annual. A plant that grows from seed, flowers, produces new seeds, and dies during a single growing season; a perennial plant treated like an annual in that it is grown for only a single season's display and then removed.

Balled-and-burlapped. Describes a tree or shrub dug out of the ground with a ball of soil intact around the roots, the ball then wrapped in burlap and tied for transport.

Bare-root. Describes a plant dug out of the ground and then shaken or washed to remove the soil from the roots.

Balled-and-burlapped

Bare-root

Compound leaf. A leaf consisting of two or more leaflets branching from the same stalk.

Container-grown. Describes a plant raised in a pot that is removed before planting.

Crown. That part of a plant where the roots and stem meet, usually at soil level.

Cultivar. A cultivated variety of a plant, often bred or selected for some special trait such as double flowers, compact growth, cold hardiness, or disease resistance.

Deadheading. Removing spent flowers during the growing season to improve a plant's appearance, prevent seed formation, and stimulate the development of new flowers.

Deciduous. Describes a tree, shrub, or vine that drops all its leaves in winter.

Division

Division. Propagation of a plant by separating it into two or more pieces, each piece possessing at least one bud and some roots. Plants commonly divided include perennials, bulbs, grasses, and ferns.

Drainage. Movement of water through soil. If water poured into a foot-deep hole drains completely in a few hours, the drainage is good.

Drip line. The circle of soil beneath a tree mirroring the circumference of the tree's canopy. This area benefits from direct rainfall and "drip" from leaves. Because many of the tree's feeder roots are found along the drip line and beyond, this area is the best for fertilizing and watering.

Dry-laid. Describes a masonry path or wall that is installed without mortar.

Edging. A barrier that serves as the border between lawn and a planting bed. Edgings may be shallow trenches or barriers of plastic, brick, or boards.

Exposure. The characterization of a site according to the sun, wind, and temperature acting upon it.

Formal. Describes a style of landscaping that features symmetrical layouts, with beds and walks related to adjacent buildings, and often with plants sheared to geometric or other shapes.

Foundation planting. Traditionally, a narrow border of evergreen shrubs planted around the foundation of a house. Contemporary foundation plantings often include deciduous shrubs, grasses, perennials, and other plants as well.

Frost heaving. A disturbance or uplifting of soil, pavement, or plants caused when moisture in the soil freezes and expands.

Full shade. Describes a site that receives no direct sun during the growing season.

Full sun. Describes a site that receives at least eight hours of direct sun each day during the growing season.

Garden soil. Soil specially prepared for planting to make it loose enough for roots and water to penetrate easily. Usually requires digging or tilling and the addition of some organic matter.

Grade. The angle and direction of the ground's slope in a given area.

Ground cover. A plant providing continuous cover for an area of soil. Commonly a low, spreading foliage plant such as candytuft, vinca, or ajuga.

Habit. The characteristic shape of a plant, such as upright, mounded, columnar, or vase-shaped.

Hardiness. A plant's ability to survive the winter temperatures in a given region without protection.

Hardscape. Parts of a landscape constructed from materials other than plants, such as walks, walls, and trellises made of wood, stone, or other materials.

Herbicide. A chemical used to kill plants. Preemergent herbicides are used to kill weed seeds as they sprout, and thus to prevent weed growth. Postemergent herbicides kill plants that are already growing.

Hybrid. A plant with two parents that belong to different varieties, species, or genera.

Interplant. To use plants with different bloom times or growth habits in the same bed to increase the variety and appeal of the planting.

Invasive. Describes a plant that spreads quickly, usually by runners, and mixes with or dominates adjacent plantings.

Landscape fabric. A synthetic fabric, sometimes water-permeable, spread under paths or mulch to serve as a weed barrier.

Lime, limestone. Mineral compounds applied to soil to lower its pH, rendering it less acid and thereby allowing plants to absorb nutrients better. Limestone also supplies calcium that plants need.

Loam. Soil rich in organic matter and with mineral particles in a range of sizes. Excellent for many garden plants.

Microclimate. A small-scale "system" of factors affecting plant growth on a particular site, including shade, temperature, rainfall, and so on.

Brick mowing strip

Mowing strip. A row of bricks or paving stones set flush with the soil around the edge of a bed, and wide enough to support one wheel of the lawn mower.

Mulch. A layer of organic or other materials spread several inches thick around the base of plants and over open soil in a bed. Mulch conserves soil moisture, smothers weeds, and moderates soil temperatures. Where winters are cold, mulches help protect plants from freezing. Common mulches include compost, shredded leaves, straw, lawn clippings, gravel, newspaper, and landscape fabric.

Native. Describes a plant that is or once was found in the wild in a particular region and was not imported from another area.

Nutrients. Elements needed by plants. Found in the soil and supplied by fertilizers, nutrients include nitrogen, phosphorus, potassium, calcium, magnesium, sulfur, iron, and other elements, in various forms and compounds.

Organic matter. Partially or fully decomposed plant and animal matter. Includes leaves, trimmings, and manure.

Peat moss. Partially decomposed mosses and sedges. Dug from boggy areas, peat moss is often used as an organic amendment for garden soil.

Perennial. A plant with a life span of more than one year. Woody plants such as trees and shrubs are perennials, in addition to the "herbaceous perennials" more commonly cited, which have no woody tissue that persists from year to year.

Pressure-treated lumber. Softwood lumber treated with chemicals that protect it from decay.

Propagate. To produce new plants from seeds or by vegetative means such as dividing plant parts, taking root cuttings, and grafting stems onto other plants.

Retaining wall. A wall built to stabilize a slope and keep soil from sliding or eroding downhill.

Rhizome. A horizontal underground stem from which roots and shoots emerge. Some swell to store food. Branched rhizomes (those of iris, for instance) can be divided to produce new plants.

Root ball. The mass of soil and roots dug with a plant when it is removed from the ground; the soil and roots of a plant grown in a container.

Rosette. A low, flat cluster or crown of overlapping leaves.

Selective pruning

Severe pruning

Selective pruning. Using pruning shears to remove or cut back individual shoots in order to refine the shape of a shrub, maintain its vigor, or limit its size.

Severe pruning. Using pruning shears or loppers to cut away most of a shrub's top growth, leaving just short stubs or a gnarly trunk.

Shearing. Using hedge shears or an electric hedge trimmer to shape the surface of a shrub, hedge, or tree and produce a smooth, solid mass of greenery.

Specimen plant. A plant placed for individual display.

Spike. An elongated flower cluster on which individual flowers are attached directly to the main stem or are on very short stalks attached to the main stem.

Tender. Describes a plant that is damaged by cold weather in a particular region.

Underplanting. Growing short plants, such as ground covers, under a taller plant, such as a shrub.

Variegated. Describes foliage with color patterns in stripes, specks, or blotches that occur naturally or result from breeding.

Photo Credits

Note: Photographs are keyed by letters corresponding to positions on the page beginning at the upper right corner of the page and proceeding clockwise.

Rita Buchanan: 31 A, B; 38 F; 42 A, B; 67 A; 78 E; 86 B; 107 B; 178; 180 A; 192

Cole Burrell: 47 B; 62 E; 86 A, C

Karen Bussolini: 47 D, F; 50 F; 71 F; 75 E; 78 D; 99 D, E; 185 B; 193 A

Ruth Rogers Clausen: 55 C; 111 A

Michael Dirr: 58 C; 62 C; 78 B; 102 C; 111 C, E; 189 A

John Elsley: 27 C; 189 B

Galen Gates: 22 A; 27 E; 31 E; 35 C; 38 A; 42 C; 50 B; 62 B; 67 F; 71 B; 75 A; 83 F; 86 D; 88 C; 90 A, D, E, F; 94 A; 99 B, C; 107 A; 111 F; 176 A; 177 B; 182 B; 185 A; 191; 193 B

Saxon Holt: 27 B, D; 31 D; 42 D, F; 50 E; 71 D; 75 B, D; 86 F; 94 F; 99 F; 107 D; 108 B; 111 B; 174; 177 A

Dency Kane: 58 F; 94 B

Charles Mann: 22 E, F; 35 B, D, F, G; 38 B, D; 42 E; 47 A, C, E; 55 A, B, D, E; 62 D; 67 B, D, E; 71 E; 75 F; 83 B; 102 A; 107 C, F, G; 175; 179; 181; 183 B; 184 A, B; 188; 195 A, B

Rick Mastelli: 7; 22 D; 187 B

David McDonald: 55 G

Carole Ottesen: 50 D; 58 E; 71 A, C; 78 A; 83 A; 99 A; 102 E

Jerry Pavia: 22 B, C; 27 A; 31 C, F; 35 A, E; 38 B, E; 50 A, C; 58 A, B; 62 A; 67 G; 75 C; 78 C; 83 D, E; 86 E; 90 B; 94 C, D, E; 102 B, D; 176 B; 182 A; 183 A; 186; 196; 197

Cheryl Richter: 107 E

Lauren Springer: 55 F; 58 D; 67 C; 90 C; 111 D; 187 A

Index

Note: Page numbers in *bold italic* refer to illustrations.

Have a home gardening, decorating, or improvement project? Look for these and other fine **Creative Homeowner books** wherever books are sold.

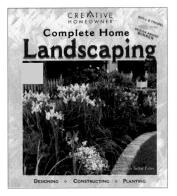

An impressive guide to garden design and plant selection. More than 600 color photos. 320 pp.; 9"×10"
BOOK #: 274615

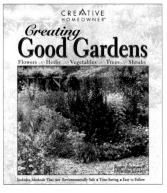

How to prepare, cultivate, and harvest a successful garden. Over 400 color photos. 176 pp.; 9"×10"
BOOK #: 274244

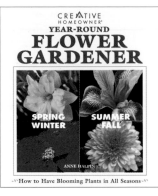

A four-season step-by-step guide to growing flowers. Over 500 photos & illustrations. 224 pp.; 9"×10"
BOOK #: 274791

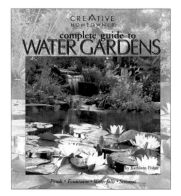

A comprehensive tool for the aspiring water gardener. Over 400 color photos. 208 pp.; 9"×10"
BOOK #: 274452

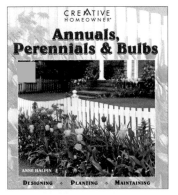

Essential planting tasks shown in over 600 color photographs and 50 watercolors. 208pp.; 9"×10"
BOOK #: 274032

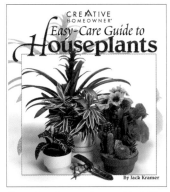

Complete houseplant guide 200 readily available plants; more than 400 photos. 192pp.; 9"×10"
BOOK #: 275243

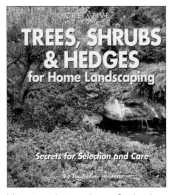

How to select and care for landscaping plants. Over 500 illustrations. 208 pp.; 9"×10"
BOOK #: 274238

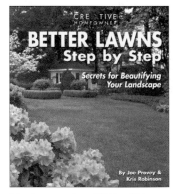

Create more beautiful, healthier, lower-maintenance lawns. Over 300 illustrations. 160 pp.; 9"×10"
BOOK #: 274359

New, updated edition of best-selling house wiring manual. Over 700 color photos. 256 pp.; 8½"×10⅞"
BOOK #: 277049

Take the guesswork out of plumbing repair. More than 550 illustrations. 176 pp.; 8½"×10⅞"
BOOK #: 277620

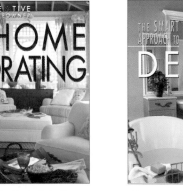

How to create kitchen style like a pro. Over 150 color photographs. 176 pp.; 9"×10"
BOOK #: 279935

All you need to know about designing a bath. Over 150 color photos. 176 pp.; 9"×10"
BOOK #: 287225